International and Regional Perspectives on Cross-Cultural Mediation

STUDIEN ZUR INTERKULTURELLEN MEDIATION

Herausgegeben von Hartmut Schröder und Dominic Busch

Band 5

PETER LANG

Frankfurt am Main · Berlin · Bern · Bruxelles · New York · Oxford · Wien

Dominic Busch / Claude-Hélène Mayer / Christian Martin Boness
(eds.)

INTERNATIONAL AND REGIONAL PERSPECTIVES ON CROSS-CULTURAL MEDIATION

PETER LANG
Internationaler Verlag der Wissenschaften

Bibliographic Information published by the Deutsche Nationalbibliothek
The Deutsche Nationalbibliothek lists this publication in the Deutsche Nationalbibliografie; detailed bibliographic data is available in the internet at http://dnb.d-nb.de.

ISSN 1611-5902
ISBN 978-3-631-59644-9

www.peterlang.de

Contents

Preface

Dominic Busch

Intercultural and cross-cultural mediation in the Western world has emerged as an object of research that has attracted a growing attention over the past thirty years. This growing attention may be motivated by societies' notion that culture contact in whatever form may generate problems that should be dealt with in an active way. In other words, a majority of people from Western societies seem to agree that it would be good to have an instrument or a tool that people may apply whenever they feel they have to solve problems arising from culture contact.

This hypothesis comes to mind when approaching the field of intercultural communication from a highly constructivist perspective. Here, intercultural communication is revealed as a socially constructed category that is used to frame a number of social problems that a society designates as caused by cultures. Regarding this collection of social problems from the perspective of alternative paradigms to that of intercultural communication may reveal the arbitrariness of the boundaries of intercultural communication as a closed topic.

One primary characteristic of intercultural communication as a topic or as a perspective seems to be its problem orientation: To be considered as an aspect of intercultural communication, a field of study will have to be framed as a problem, first. From this perspective, it almost goes without saying that intercultural communication as a subject does not come along with a build-in device to solve its problems. To come to constructive and positive ends with issues and research results on intercultural communication, researchers will thus have to take a creative look to neighboring disciplines that may have adequate tools on offer. Conflict research as well as research on conflict management within the social sciences may be such a neighboring discipline that has even specialized on the development of tools for problem-solving, especially of solving conflicts that are seen as problems. Conflict mediation may be seen as one of these tools, and people interested in intercultural issues are trying to adopt the tool to the management of problems arising from culture contact.

Cross-cultural and intercultural mediation today is being approached by scholars from very different disciplines following very different research goals and looking at very different problem zones in society. Generally, mediation in the large variety of fields of culture contact are of interest for mediation practitioners, for conflict researchers, for cultural anthropologists as well as for researchers on intercultural communication.

International and Regional Perspectives on Cross-Cultural Mediation is a volume that intends to address research questions that arise from the state of the art of at least one or several of these disciplines mentioned. Contributing volume no. 5 to *Studien zur interkulturellen Mediation (Studies on Intercultural Mediation)* series, this book comes as the first contribution to the series that is written in English language. Whereas volumes no. 2 and 3, being anthologies as well, contain several contributions in English language, volume no. 5 is the first one addressing an international audience of the mentioned field at first place.

Beyond this, the volume focuses on an innovative question of research that on the one hand more or less automatically emerges from the current state of research and that on the other hand has rather been neglected to far. The authors of this volume are trying to contribute answers to the question of whether societies are holding notions of how to deal with conflicts that they are engaged in with people from other cultures—or with conflicts that at least they consider as caused from culture contact. Basing on this, it may also be asked whether there are culture-specific or (culturally) different ways of dealing with these specific forms of conflict.

The authors contributing to this volume are presenting approaches from different disciplines answering different aspects of the main research question and applying a variety of methods. This multitude of approaches again my help to give insights into the complexity of the basic issue under research, and it may thus open the field for new emerging questions of research.

Introduction: International and Regional Perspectives on Cross-Cultural Mediation

Dominic Busch, Claude-Hélène Mayer and Christian Martin Boness

Mediation as a conflict resolution practice is deeply rooted in the many diverse cultures that can be found globally. Many of these cultures look back at a long tradition of mediation and conflict resolution practices through third party intervention. At the same time, mediation practices have recently been highly influenced through international and cross-cultural exchanges and global fluxes. This trend has resulted in an increase and contextualisation of mediation and its cross-cultural practices. Many different aspects of mediation have been incorporated into culture-specific practices of mediation within different cultures and countries.

The volume at hand aims to advance international research, practice and development of cross-cultural mediation. The purpose of this volume is to give a deeper insight into theories, practices, methods, techniques and developments of cross-cultural mediation across selected cultures, countries and regions and to contribute to cross-cultural competence building and understanding in the field of conflict resolution processes in cross-cultural settings.

Dominic Busch presents an overview that aims to be adequate to the growing variety of notions, approaches and methods concerned with intercultural and cross-cultural mediation. Comparing approaches from social research on conflict management, cultural anthropological works on the role of conflict in different societies, as well as from research on intercultural communication, Busch comes to the conclusion that the notion of culture may be taken as one of the few core concepts that authors from all fields mentioned refer to. However, while most of the authors on intercultural and cross-cultural mediation extensively discuss what conflict mediation is supposed to be, discussions on the role of culture rather tend to be neglected. The field of research on intercultural communication in particular has undergone considerable debates on what culture is supposed to be and how its influence on social interaction is supposed to be seen. Accesing the field of mediation research, authors from different disciplines at best try to claim that their notion of culture may help to bring approaches from competing disciplines forward even better. Beyond this competition however, comparisons are scarce. Busch analyses publications that may be taken as central to the field of intercultural mediation research from mediation practitioners, cultural anthropologists as well as from researchers on intercultural communication. In his contribution he presents an overview giving valuable insights into the very different and diverging notions of culture that all may be found in any of the disciplines concerned. His overview may show that research results, and even basic notions of the objects under research, may vary significantly depending on their underlying notion of culture. As a result, Busch pleads for a growing consideration and debate on the framings of culture used for research. These debates may be expected to significantly enhance and advance future research on intercultural and cross-cultural mediation.

Claude-Hélène Mayer, Christian Martin Boness, Samuel Togolai Kussaga present qualitative study on emic concepts of conflict and mediation carried out in Tanzania. Basing on the assumption that these concepts will not only vary across cultures but – from a constructivist perspective – between any individuals, the authors have conducted narrative interviews with a large group of interviewees from Tanzania having them relate to example conflicts and mediations. The authors paint a clear picture of the complexity arising from attempts to do research on Western concepts like conflict and mediation in Non-Western cultures: Even the translation of the terms under research results in very different classifications, depending on the contexts of the subjects under research. Mayer, Boness and Kussaga carried out their interviews with people from the educational, the administrative, the ecclesiastical as well as the entrepreneurial sector, and they manage to reconstruct completely different pictures of conflict and mediation for all sectors. Beyond this, all sectors are influenced by Western (here in most cases: Danish) forms of conflict mediation that have been attempted to adopt. Concerning this volume's focus on the management of cross-cultural mediation, the authors manage to reconstruct an emic picture as well. Here, too, concepts of how to deal with conflicts that interactants interpret as caused from intercultural issues may vary significantly, and they can be reconstructed by in-depth qualitative research. From these results, the authors conclude that cultural particularities can neither be dealt with on a national nor even on an intergroup level. Instead, qualitative research on mediation concepts will need to focus on a micro-level of subject orientations on selected and specific contexts.

Stella Ting-Toomey contrasts the previous chapter presenting an etic approach to concepts of intercultural mediation. The conflict face-negotiation theory framework provides a basis that allows inferences on what individuals will expect from a competent mediator. These expectations will vary significantly depending on combinations of different sets of cultural values. Taking mediation cases between people from the Western world and from East Asia as an example, Ting-Toomey discusses the complexity of issues a competent mediator will have to manage. On this basis, Ting-Toomey derives several guidelines for intercultural mediators. Finally, intercultural conflicts may face mediators with enormous challenges that will require them to gradually find their ways to a good mediation practice. To describe this, Ting-Toomey refers to the concept of mindfulness that may also help mediators to transcend ethnocentric viewpoints and to carefully establish spaces of third cultures.

Claudio Baraldi raises the question of what conditions would have to be met at all to speak of intercultural mediation as a distinguishable technique that may be described by empirical research. On the basis of literature reviews, Baraldi sums up that strategies of intercultural mediation will differ from conventional conflict mediation in a number of aspects. For example, mediators in intercultural contexts in most cases will not have to solve escalated disputes. Instead, they will have to prevent and to constructively manage subtle communicative misunderstandings in intercultural interaction. Furthermore, in critical situations, interactants will need to be encouraged to continue their conversation at all. Baraldi thus concludes that the promotion of active participation should be seen as one of the primary goals of intercultural mediation. Baraldi pleads to establish dialogic situations, and to this aim, he presents a framework of dialogic mediation. Having developed a strong theoretical framework, Baraldi enters empirical research: At the example of mediative conversations from medical and educational settings, Baraldi uses conversation analysis to extrapolate several conversational techniques that may be isolated and termed as techniques of intercultural mediation.

Mark Davidheiser has conducted profound empirical research on conflict mediation practices among several different ethnic groups in The Gambia. Using several empirical methods like focus groups, panel discussions as well as interviews, Davidheiser paints a highly complex picture of cultural patterns to mediation in the chosen region. His quantitative analysis may show that mediation styles differ among the ethnic groups. So there are different preferences for strategies like shuttle mediation, judging and blaming, as well as negotiation phases. These preferences seem to correspond with or to reflect more general social and cultural patterns that may be found within the ethnic groups. Thus, this may show that in most cases, mediation styles adapt to local cultural preferences. On a more qualitative level however, Davidheiser reveals strong variations in mediation style even within the ethnic groups. In fact, each mediator has his own style, and mediation processes develop in very singular and particular ways depending on the situational context and depending on the parties involved. Davidheiser thus confirms current pleas from cultural anthropology claiming that cultural analysis will produce reasonable outcomes, but that the level of analysis should not be restrained to the generalized description of whole groups. Instead, individuals should form the level of analysis since every actor will interpret culture and contribute to its production in a distinct and particular way.

Michelle LeBaron and Nadja Alexander remind us of the fact that regional mediation styles in most cases are inspired, created and transformed by forms of cultural transfer: Conflict mediation all over the world on the one hand may be adapted to regional patterns and needs, but on the other hand, global transfers of best practice knowledge and of conflict mediation training cannot be ignored. At the same time, this means that mediation training and education very often will be an intercultural challenge and issue. Beyond this, a training's success or trainees' undertanding of what they have learned will form the success of mediation practice in a given region in a considerable way. Since role plays in mediation trainings are one of the most common training tools, LeBaron and Alexander critically analyse their use for mediation trainings in intra- and in intercultural settings. They point out several pitfalls as well as misunderstandings that even trainers may have about the overall usefulness of role plays. In intercultural settings, pitfalls resulting from mindless uses of role plays may produce outcomes in group dynamics as well as in trainees' learning performance that are even worse. To restore the use of the positive sides of role plays, LeBaron and Alexander present a toolbox for the design of effective role plays. Particularly, they recommend trainers to make more frequent use of experience-based adventure tasks, but references to arts and dama will positively inspire and activate trainees as well. LeBaron and Alexander thus would like to encourage mediation trainers to constructively design training models for a transmission of the ideas of mediation across cultural boundaries.

Claude-Hélène Mayer shows that mediation processes may even profit from the need of spontaneous re-construction arising from a given intercultural setting. To do so, Mayer presents a "Culture-Synergetic Model of Cross-cultural Mediation" (CSTM) that helps to reconstruct how mediators and conflict parties re-build mediation processes that benefit from and that serve to all cultural backgrounds concerned. This synergetic process, if successfully carried through, almost automatically promotes an appreciation of different (cultural) identities of the participants to a mediation. Even more, this focus on the diversity of identities may also be taken as one of the key issues to success in this form of intercultural mediation practice. Managerial and business mediation on the one hand can be seen as a field of mediation in which international participants are more and more common. On the other hand, managerial and business conflicts until today are primarily seen as negotiable issues that can and should be dealt with at an objective and neutral level. Against this, Mayer promotes that an appreciation of different identities in international managerial contexts may hide a huge potential for mediation outcomes that has largely been ignored so far. To systematically consider issues of identity in managerial conflict settings, Mayer thus presents a model of "Identity-based managerial mediation (IMM)" comprising the wide variety of aspects that may play a role when focusing on managerial identity in conflict situations. Relating to the overall topic of the volume at hand, Mayer shows that it may even be helpful and constructive to mediation outcomes to re-culturalize conflict situations that have been tried to de-culturalize in the field of management practice before.

Federico Farini and Viola Barbieri present a case study of professional intercultural mediators in Italian healthcare settings. Here, interpreters are employed to facilitate communication between Italian physicians and migrant patients, primarily working as translators. At the example of conversation analyses of triadic interactions between physicians, interpreters and Arab migrant patients, Farini and Barbieri show that the interpreters in fact may work as intercultural mediators. They may function as a precondition for dialogic understanding and as a cultural bridge. However, interpreters may choose among a wide scope of potential actions, and thus, Farini and Barbieri present examples that may be graded on a scale of growing constructiveness. Interpreters frequently even cut off dialogic interaction by just supporting the physician's position. However, they may also encourage migrant patients to engage in the interactions by different communicative strategies. As a particular finding, Farini and Barbieri state that in fact, these intercultural mediators fulfil an especially vital function in transmitting emotional messages from the patients to the physicians: Translating what and how the patients feel can give physicians a crucial access to dialogic interaction as well as to an adequate anamnesis that would not have remained closed in a dyadic situation.

Angela Mickley reports on a capacity-building project that has been installed by German partners in Namibia from 2003 to 2007. Conflict mediation was one of the central instruments the German partners had at hand to enforce sustainable peace and social structures in Namibia: Mediation processes had been accomplished, and mediation training had been provided to leading social figures like ombudsmen and others. Reyling on these experiences, Mickley stresses the central role of identity work in cross-cultural mediation settings. Here, the case of Namibia may even serve as an exemplary lesson for the constructivist character of identity and for its resulting paradoxes: On the one hand different groups in the multi-ethnic state pronounce the need to maintain their particular identity, which requires a lot of balancing work by the mediators to avoid power imbalances. On the other hand, unity on a larger social level, like the level of state, was one of the core aims of the aid project. Here, mediation may serve as a highly flexible tool that helps mediators to adjust to different legal, moral and social needs and expectations at the same time to work out solutions within a newly created third space.

How Does Culture Affect Conflict Mediation? Disentangling Concepts from Theory and Practice

Dominic Busch

Introduction

Are there any cultural differences in the ways people react to conflicts with people from other cultures? Are there any cultural differences in the ways conflict mediation is used to manage cross-cultural conflicts? These questions were some of the central ideas the editors had in mind when compiling the contributions to the book at hand. Questions like these emerge from tracing the present development of research on mediation and culture, and from trying to consistently think ahead and beyond current notions of the object of research. Numerous authors so far have traced the development of perspective perspectives on interplays between culture and conflict mediation (Merry, 1987a, Avruch, 1998, Avruch and Black, 1991, Goldstein, 1986), and this introduction will therefore sketch the most noteworthy steps in research discourse.[1]

Assuming that in the beginning, cultural influences did not have any relevance to mediation research at all, practitioners could easily observe that more and more often, the conflict parties in mediation processes came from different cultural backgrounds. From this perspective, practitioners wanted to know how to adapt or modify their mediation practices to best deal with cultural differences and to make sure that the conflict parties are served according to their interests. Later on, practitioners learned from (anthropological) researchers that forms of conflict mediation can be found in many cultures but that they may differ significantly in many respects. This diversity began to be explored to potentially learn from the multitude of mediation practices at hand.

A growing awareness of the relevance of culture to research objects does not seem to be peculiar to the field of mediation. Instead, Min-Sun Kim (2007) has traced similar tendencies on the perception of the influence of culture for the field of research on speech communication. Here, cross-cultural research seems to have passed through several stages, changing purposes over time. Early scholars took the standpoint of a "'pre-encounter' research culture: 'I'm not interested'" (Kim, 2007:

---

1 For a short and concise diachronic introduction to the tendencies of trends in research on the field of conflict mediation and culture cf. Avruch (2003).

280). This today may also be termed a universalist perspective, assuming that scientific results on any research question will produce the same results in all cultures. Kim then identifies an "'initial encounter' research culture" of scholars who assumed that "culture is a nuisance" that has to be dealt with as a cumbersome hindrance from insights (Kim, 2007: 281). According to Kim, most current research may be classified as carried out from the "'Captain Cook' research culture" of scholars proposing a "Let's explore and compare" mindset (Kim, 2007: 282). To effectively gain cross-cultural insights, Kim however pleads for a "'paradigm shift' in research culture moving 'beyond ethnocentric paradigms'" (Kim, 2007: 282).

The questions raised in this volume follow a similar impetus. For mediation research, moving beyond ethnocentric paradigms will mean abandoning Western forms of institutionalized conflict mediation as our central object of research, from which even cross-cultural perspectives are normally derived. Instead, we will have to question the object of our research. And even here, we will soon find ourselves limited by our own ethnocentric linguistic world. Assuming we are doing research on cultural forms of conflict management, we would first have to free ourselves from ethnocentric notions of what conflict is.

Cross-cultural, intercultural and transcultural research

Distinguishing between the terms 'cross-cultural', 'intercultural' and 'transcultural', which are all used in research on conflict and mediation may, according to Avruch and Black (1991), help to shed some light onto different foci of research. The article at hand will thus follow their use of terminology: Cross-cultural research in their view refers to studies on aspects of conflict management that are particular to one specific culture. This approach is termed "ethnoconflict" research, and the culture-specific conflict management styles they termed "ethnopraxes" (Avruch and Black, 1991: 22). Although Avruch and Black seem to strongly favour this approach (cf. their collection of respective approaches to quite a number of different cultures in: Avruch et al., 1991), they also hint at its limitations: The descriptions delivered in these approaches will still be carried out from an observer's ethnocentric viewpoint, and the implications of this perspectivation in most cases cannot be revealed in full (Avruch and Black, 1991: 39).

In contrast, intercultural research, according to Avruch and Black, relates to studies looking at conflicts between individuals or groups from at least two different cultures. Avruch and Black state that this approach so far has largely been neglected:

> "For all this apparent activity, we nevertheless feel that the intercultural perspective is quite underdeveloped. Many of the criticisms we noted earlier,

relating to thin or misconceived construals of culture, are germane here" (Avruch and Black, 1991: 38).

Finally, transcultural research refers to attempts to reveal universal rules for constructive conflict resolution. Avruch and Black argue that a combination of cross-cultural and intercultural approaches should provide the best way to come to such results (Avruch and Black, 1991: 38) conclusions The volume at hand will follow these directions, placing special emphasis on culture-specific ways of managing intercultural conflicts. Before these ideas can be framed as an object of research, some preliminary reflections should be considered:

A discourse approach to culture

Following a discourse approach to the notion of culture, it may be assumed that people normally do not experience situations of cross-cultural contact as something completely new and unforeseen. Of course, we may agree with Gudykunst that people will experience cross-cultural contact as situations for which they will need to develop new forms of interaction—what Gudykunst terms as uncertainty reduction (Gudykunst, 1985). However, we should also keep in mind that people perceive socially acknowledged forms of cross-cultural interaction from their participation in inner-societal discourse. Similar to Judith Butler's understanding of the social construction of gender roles (Butler, 1993), it may be concluded that people internalize modes of intercultural interaction from their own social surroundings (Busch, 2009).

This perspective may also be applied to the particular case of research on conflict and mediation. It may then be assumed that if people encounter situations of conflict with people they assign to other cultures or groups, they will always be able to refer to norms from social discourse to decide what to do in their current situations.

The present state of mediation research and research on cross-cultural mediation in particular provides us with a vast range of different approaches to the object of research. A cautious review of these approaches may promise to deliver quite a number of insights helping to answer our question of international and regional perspectives on cross-cultural mediation. This variety may then run the risk of blurring its own objects of research: What is intercultural mediation supposed to be, and what aims should it serve?

This vagueness may result from the insight that more than one of the issue's basic notions needs some clarification. On the one hand, the position of mediation as a concept has to be defined: Is it a Western-based tool or is it completely flexible? To what extent does the Western tool display influences from a variety of cultural backgrounds? On the other hand, the role of culture in communication, especially in conflict interaction, has to be defined: How is culture supposed to be manifested in communication? How does it influence conflict behavior? And what form of conflict management and outcome may be seen as preferable or desirable—from a cross-cultural perspective? These questions seem to become even more relevant and complex if conflict mediation is supposed to be practiced in multicultural contexts.

The article at hand will attempt to shed some light upon the divergent constructions of culture underlying studies on cross-cultural mediation. While mediation techniques as well as the general assumption of existing cultural differences are paid considerable attention to, different notions of culture frequently continue to go unnoticed. As the author has recently shown using the example of linguistic research on intercultural communication, diverging underlying notions of culture will lead to diverging evaluations of people's actual behavior as well as their potential options for action. In other words, what we may expect from people as forms of intercultural competent behavior will be determined significantly by the theoretical understanding of the role of culture itself (Busch, 2009).

Research paradigms on culture

It may be claimed that culture as a paradigm has always been acknowledged by academic research. Currently, however, social scientists term the predominant position of culture in research as the so-called cultural turn (Chaney, 1994, de la Fuente, 2007), and of course, they consequently center their debate around how to transcend this paradigm blurring their view onto reality (Bonnell et al., 1999, Brantlinger, 2002). This tradition may be traced back to the Swiss linguist Ferdinand de Saussure ([2001] 1916). De Saussure renewed linguistic views of language when he introduced structuralist ideas to explain the process of interpersonal understanding. The distinction between *signifier* and *signified* was then adopted by what has later been termed cultural philosophy (Cassirer, 1992 [1947]). While the structuralist paradigm, drawing from semiotic ideas, originally helped to integrate culture into social theory, it hampered linguistics from developing more advanced notions of culture at a later stage. As early as the 1960's, cultural psychologists Kluckhohn and Strodtbeck (1961: 3) argued that for many theories in social research, culture had turned into a feasible linkage to explain interrelations between a social macro-level and the micro-level of individuals' action. The following paragraphs will introduce some of the most widely used distinctions for the classification of academic approaches to culture.

Authors on intercultural communication frequently center their debates on essentialist vs. constructivist notions of culture. US-American anthropologist Arjun Appadurai may be mentioned as one of the most prominent contemporary scholars discussing this distinction in theory (Appadurai, 1996: 14). Appadurai replaces the notion of essentialist with primordialist approaches. From this perspective, culture and the quality of its influences on individuals are taken as givens that existed even before the interaction under research took place. Consequently, culture as such will not be changed by one single interaction. Avruch and Black confirm a similar differentiation for the field of anthropological research on conflict, where they identified essentialist vs. mentalist approaches (Avruch and Black, 1991: 27).

Primordialist conceptions of culture

Taking culture from a primordialist point of view helps researchers to anticipate and to explain the ways people react to cultural influences on their action, although theories will deliver different explanations (Chick, 2001). However, primordialist approaches frequently assume that the interactants under research will not themselves be able to adequately identify, analyse or interpret cultural influences. Instead, at best, researchers will be able to note that interactants feel in some way irritated (Spencer-Oatey, 2002). From this, researchers may then infer that communicative misunderstandings caused by cultural influences may have occurred (Goodenough, 1957, Gudykunst, 1985, Gumperz, 1982, House, 2000).

The kind of influence culture effects will be prescribed by the underlying theory of the approach. Early analytic approaches from social psychology as well as from cultural anthropology specified cultural differences as differences in people's value orientations that would affect their action. In these respects, Kluckhohn and Strodtbeck (1961) refer to „value orientations", and later Geert Hofstede (1980) built his study on the comparison of „work-related values". Interpretive approaches instead assume that cultures differ in their systems of meaning that are communicated via semiotic codes (Triandis, 2002: 16).

In sum, primordialist conceptions of cultural influences on individuals' action assume that individuals from different cultural backgrounds will communicate in different ways. Individual's perceived irritation in intercultural contact, from this perspective, will be caused by communicative misunderstandings that are going unnoticed. To avoid these misunderstandings, experts on intercultural communication may then derive clear guidelines for interculturally competent behavior. Individuals will be required to take in the perspectives of others and to understand foreign points of view (Harden and Witte, 2000). To describe these processes, social theory may contribute approaches from the fields of hermeneutics (Mall, 2000) as well as phenomenology (Knoblauch, 2001).

Constructivist conceptions of culture

While studies from a primordialist perspective scan empirical data for indirect indications of cultural influences like irritations, constructivist approaches concede more extensive degrees of cultural awareness to their subjects under research. Basically, constructivist conceptions of culture mostly lead to the assumption that individuals will at least be able to perceive each other as being different in some way. On this basis, authors with a constructivist perspective on the influence of culture will then describe how interactants produce culture in a given situation.

Empiricists from this stance will scan their data for indications of people treating partners who are seen as having different cultural backgrounds in distinctive ways, i.e. for subtle forms of discrimination along cultural lines. In theory, these forms of distinctive treatments of others may be traced back to Lippmann's (1922) early works on stereotyping that were later elaborated on the particular field of intercultural communication (Dahl, 1999, Katz and Braly, 1933, Lehtonen, 1994). In the field of cultural anthropology, Fredrick Barth (1969) had declared the basically constructivist character of cultural differences and boundaries.

To cross-cultural research, Harry Triandis introduced the notion of „subjective culture" (Triandis, 1972: 4) and epitomized the perspective and constructivist character of cultural affiliation. In the field of student exchange research, ennett (1986) and Hammer (1999) presented their Developmental Model of Intercultural Sensitivity (DMIS), which sees an individual's perception of culture and cultural differences as a process passing several stages of awareness and competence. Since culture in these debates has become more and more disguised as a social construction, some authors complained that the notion would no longer be able to serve academic purposes. Therefore, they recommended starting to ignore the notion of culture in research (Tajfel, 1981) or even to write against its impact (Abu-Lughod, 1991). In cultural anthropology, the notion of culture and its constructivist character underwent considerable debate in the 1990's (Stolcke, 1995) but in the end, culture turned back into research (Brumann, 1999, Fox, 1999) and experienced further theoretical operationalization. In the veins of constructivist thinking, Appadurai claims that the notion of culture should be taken as a result of social discourse:

> "Culture is a pervasive dimension of human discourse that exploits difference to generate diverse conceptions of group identity. [...] I propose however that we restrict the term culture as a marked term to the subset of these differences that has been mobilized to articulate the boundary of difference" (Appadurai, 1996: 13).

Intercultural competence from a constructivist perspective on culture will be defined differently than from a primordialist perspective. While primordialist approaches to culture will require individuals to understand foreign perspectives, constructivist approaches will challenge individuals to find common perspectives on what culture means to them. Theorists have described this process as entering a third space (Bhabha, 1994), as building a third culture (Casmir, 1993) or a discursive interculture (Koole and ten Thije, 1994).

Culture as knowlege vs. culture as values

Another crucial distinction influencing the conception of cultural influences may be seen in the equation of culture either with knowledge, or with values or beliefs. In the first case, approaches see culture as a form of specific knowledge either of particular interaction contexts or of particular communicative rules or conventions. Members of a given cultural group are said to share this knowledge as their characteristic feature. Some approaches further specify this culture-specific knowledge as needed to deal with problems of social life that are universally given in all cultures. To enter a new group or to get acquainted with a group's culture, outsiders will need to learn and internalize this knowledge.

Theories conceiving culture as beliefs or values underlying people's interaction, instead see culture as a preferential system. According to this approach, members of a specific culture will prefer certain forms of action at the expense of other forms. Consequently, it may be assumed that on the one hand individuals of one culture indeed will prefer some forms of action, but that on the other hand they will always be able to act in alternative ways (Auernheimer, 2002). Considering this last point, both conceptions significantly shape individuals' assumed scope of action.

Beyond this distinction, some anthropologists like Swidler (1986, 2001) hint at the shortcomings resulting from a separation of these two approaches to understanding cultural influences on action. Swidler instead proposes combining both approaches, arguing that culture may be conceived as a repertoire of knowledge people may, but do not necessarily have to, make use of. Drawing on this perspective, individuals then will decide how to interact—and theory may then take this interaction as influenced by culture. In this paper however, works using this approach will be put into the category of constructivist approaches.

Emic vs. etic approaches to culture

Another classification of approaches may be seen in the distinction between etic and emic research methods (Berry, 1969). In etic approaches, researchers look at cultures from an external point of view. They formulate universal categories and dimensions helping to classify and to compare different cultures. In contrast, authors of emic studies try to take in the perspective of their subjects of research. While both approaches may contribute significant insights into intercultural communication, the distinction mentioned neither fixes nor specifies the way culture is supposed to influence interaction.

Normative orientations from cultural politics

Beyond these distinctions claiming purely academic categorizations, it should be noted that research on intercultural communication in most cases is significantly motivated and controlled by implicit normative expectations from cultural politics. This means that descriptive research is only done to check whether pre-selected critical aspects of people dealing with cultural influences match with respective normative ideals or not. If people meet these criteria, they may pass as interculturally competent. If not, they may require appropriate education and training. However, these normative beliefs may differ significantly depending on the context. Moosmüller (2004: 63) for example points at the two opposing fields of research on international business management versus migration research. In general, management research may here be termed as dominated by primordial notions of culture, whereas scholars of migration research tend to favour constructivist perspectives. Both approaches prove to be quite functional in their respective contexts, which are governed by diverging goals. Scholars in management research frequently assume that cultural differences do exists and that business people will normally cope best when overcoming these differences for a short period in time. Migration research instead takes cultural differences as people's products that at best should be valued and preserved. As an alternative to Moosmüller's distinction, Hannerz refers to an even more differentiated choice of contexts with diverging underlying aims like communities open to the world, translocalities, border studies, migration, diasporas, transnational corporations and occupations, tourism, cyberspace, media as well as commodities (1998: 237-246).

Disciplinary perspectives on mediation research

Similar to the various interests from cultural politics on research on intercultural communication, mediation research and research on intercultural mediation in particular, has been carried out by scholars from different disciplines and with different motivations. As a rough classification, this article will distinguish between three groups contributing to and challenging research on interplays between mediation and culture, namely mediation practitioners, anthropologists and researchers from the field of intercultural communication. It is very obvious that these three categories do not form homogeneous groups in any respect. Instead, all three groups include wide varieties of theoretical and practical approaches favoured by their scholars. However, from the standpoint of this article, it may be useful to take in at least a few different perspectives on the interplay between mediation and culture.

Practitioners and conflict researchers, according to Avruch and Black (1996: 50), originally became interested in anthropological research when they got the idea that tribal modes of conflict resolution might hint at ways to improve Western institutionalized ways of conflict management. Beyond this, many of them found themselves faced with mediation cases they interpreted as intercultural by themselves. Here, they were interested in finding appropriate solutions.

Anthropologists, according to Avruch and Black (1991), first became interested in cross-cultural research on conflict management since they hoped to find out more about a given society's ideas of human and social life in general. Definitions of conflict and its management here had to be placed into wider social contexts. In return, this analysis in context could serve to better understand and to explain culture-specific conflict behavior.

Intercultural communication as a research field steered its scholars towards the analysis of conflict as well. Intercultural communication for a long time has widely been framed as a problem situation that has to be alleviated by strategies that should be found by research. Intercultural communication primarily had been characterized as a situation prone to misunderstandings that ran the risk of laying the ground for subsequent conflict (Knapp, 1998). From this perspective, intercultural competence in conflict management emerged as one important field of research.

Who is helping whom?

In several contexts, authors from any one of the three mentioned fields of practitioners, anthropologists and interculturalists tend to claim a hegemonic role for their branch on the issue. So everybody claims that people from the other branches may and should learn from his or her own original research.

Mediators can help anthropologists

Avruch confirms and complains that conflict theory frequently does not keep track with the practice of conflict management:

> „The practice of conflict management seems far better developed than theories of conflict management; indeed, seasoned practitioners are sometimes proudly antitheory—a reflection, I suspect, of many practitioners' anti-academism." (Avruch, 1994: 424).

For the case of conflict resolution research, Avruch (1991: 4) pleads for theory-building on the basis of practical experience—since experience will be culture-specific.

Moore and Sanders (1996: 132) state that conflict management practice to some extend even determines directions of anthropological research. Conflict management practice puts forward mediation by singular third party individuals as one of the most promising ways of settling conflicts. What they need is strong internal social networks as well as knowledge of existing norms and values that may cause conflicts when contradicting one another. In the case of anthropologically driven conflict research on Northern Ireland, the authors state that this may be the reason for political anthropologists having concentrated on the analysis of networks as well as values.

Some conflict researchers even claim that looking at conflict behavior may be an especially fruitful entry point into general anthropological research on a given society. However, it should be noted that this logic is limited to certain assumptions on what culture is supposed to be. The management of conflicts may provide a helpful entry point into anthropological research, if, and only if, culture is defined as a set of particular norms that generally go unnoticed by members of a culture in everyday life.

If this condition is met—or if researchers decide to agree upon these preconditions—conflict research may provide one additional advantage to anthropologists' methodological work. Mediation settings may be an ideal place to identify underlying social norms, which may be made explicit here while otherwise going unnoticed. This would mean that mediation settings could provide immediate access to insights of anthropological interest. These conditions and assumptions are purported by Gulliver (1979), for example:

> "What can be said, briefly, is that first, virtually all negotiations involve the consideration of norms. Most disputes originate in the claim by one or both parties that rights have been infringed or denied; and rights logically imply norms, even though the parties may disagree as to the relevance, content, and applicability of the norms they cite. [...] Third, some norms are so intrinsic to the culture that they are scarcely articulated. They are taken for granted in tacit agreement, yet they considerably affect both the process and the content of joint decision making" (Gulliver, 1979: 10).

Anthropologists can help mediators

Anthropologists generally do not feel comfortable with these obtrusive motivations from the side of conflict researchers and practitioners. Indeed, anthropologists in the 1990's frequently felt that authors from outside their own discipline more and more often attempted to impose their notion of culture on anthropologists. The latter in contrast felt that culture was their central object of research, and should be defined by them. Anthropologists thus initiated discussions quite central to scholars of the subject on how to regain their autonomy in the definition of culture (Fox, 1991, Borofsky et al., 2001)

In return, Fry and Björkqvist (1997b: 5) moderate the impact of anthropological research on mediation practice. Anthropological looks at other cultures' conflict management strategies may broaden our perspectives on potential strategies available. However, it has to be taken into account that not all tools detected will automatically be suited for mediation practice in any setting in the Western world.

With reference to mediation research that had started from rather universalist premises in the 1970's, Gulliver (1979: xiv) states that cross-cultural anthropological research may help to contest these universalist assumptions in favour of cultural sensitivity and relativism.

Anthropologists can help interculturalists

Anthropologists today frequently complain that scholars interested in intercultural research no longer participate in debates on culture as their central term on a theoretical basis. Instead, anthropologists accuse interculturalists of following outdated, essentialist understandings of culture, applying categories that are much too broad to be adequate. Anthropologists thus claim to be able to bring adequate notions of culture back to intercultural research as new and fruitful paradigms (Breidenbach and Nyírí, 2001, Dahlén, 1997, Hüsken, 2003).

Interculturalists can help anthropologists

In return, interculturalists, though less frequently, may claim that they can give something back to anthropologists as well. Anthropologists traditionally looked at people they attributed to foreign cultures, and they preferred to focus on underprivileged and disadvantaged social groups. Interculturalists instead looked at privileged executive positions within Western societies (Moosmüller, 2004: 46). Interculturalists might thus have helped anthropologists to slowly turn to social groups that had not been their primary focus of research, so far.

Mediators can help interculturalists

Interculturalists have uncovered a wide range of problems that potentially may arise in situations of intercultural contact. However, they cannot really come up with tools to actively prevent or constructively deal with these issues. Instead, interculturalists sometimes feel constrained to recommend that people observe their surroundings in a more sensitive way. Raising awareness frequently seems to be the only thing that can be done. Practitioners in conflict mediation here may bring some help. They can provide a ready-made tool that has proved useful in the constructive management of difficult situations. However, the tool may not always be suited to manage the problems identified in intercultural communication, and sometimes the tool may even hinder interactants from seeing the full range of problems present in an intercultural situation. Thus, the applicability of mediation as a tool to resolve intercultural problems should be assessed in a very cautious way (Busch, 2005).

Interculturalists can help mediators

Since interculturalists have specialized in potential influences of culture in intercultural situations, they may help mediators to gain an overview of the potential array of interferences, and they may raise mediators' awareness of these issues. Some interculturalists even plead for a concept of intercultural mediation that is primarily based upon insights from intercultural research, e.g. matters of cultural translation (Müller-Jacquier and ten Thije, 2000).

Categories on culture in intercultural research

The previous sections have outlined some of the central paradigms in research on culture. Furthermore, some of the central concerns and points of departure in research on culture and conflict mediation have been identified. The following passages will review some of the central publications in the field in question.

The implementation of culture in approaches from the perspective of practitioners and conflict researchers

Primordialist approaches to culture

Folberg and Taylor (1984) presented a monograph on mediation that for a long time has been considered seminal in the Western world. They provide a full manual on how to mediate in a wide range of conflict situations. Although they introduce mediation as a tool that has its origins in non-Western cultures (Folberg and Taylor, 1984: 1-7), in the end they present a rather ethnocentric approach to culture and mediation. Mostly based on results from primordialist cultural research like the works of Hall (1959, 1976), they assume that people from different cultures will prefer different mediation styles according to the character of their national cultures. Beyond this, some of them will tend to even disprefer mediation as a tool. In these cases, (Western) mediators are advised to carefully convince these skeptics of the advantages of mediation (Folberg and Taylor, 1984: 321). In general, cultural variation in conflict mediation here is seen as one potential special case of limited range and relevance. Folberg and Taylor narrow narrowly deal with this issue in their chapter on „ethnic and sociocultural perspectives" (Folberg and Taylor, 1984: 318) which is a subsection of what they delimit as „dealing with special concerns" (318) including cases of depression and suicide. Folberg and Taylor thus conceive culture as an *a priori* existing factor in mediation that may emerge in terms of preferences based on participants' values. Conflict mediation, however, is seen as a universal tool that may be appreciated by people from any culture, once they are convinced.

In this vein, Goldstein (1986) presents an early literature review outlining and defining „cultural issues in mediation". Goldstein here gives a telling example of a so-called additive approach to intercultural mediation (Busch, 2005: 317) that can frequently be found in early literature on culture and mediation. Initially, intercultural communication and conflict mediation here are taken as two separate problems. A combination of both roughly will mean that intercultural mediation may be taken as a form of conflict mediation that is just more difficult than intracultural mediation, since participants will additionally have to tackle problems of intercultural communication. Taking Goldstein's approach as an example, the author refers to a heightened level of anxiety as well as a higher number of communicative errors and misunderstandings. Besides that, Goldstein also elaborates culturally different notions of conflict behavior and mediation practices.

Kressel and Pruitt (1989b) present a voluminous anthology on mediation research. While the contributions included are compiled in a way that seems to attempt to ensure a complete coverage of any issue relevant to mediation practice, culture tends to play a minor role. Even the two authors who consider international differences (Merry, 1989, Bercovitch, 1989) take Western conflict mediation as a starting point. The editors themselves (1985, 1989a) do not mention cultural variation as an object relevant to future research.

In a similar way, Rahim (1989) presents an interdisciplinary volume on conflict management in which mostly practitioners publish their reports. Here, the only author taking culture into consideration is Kumar (1989). He speaks of cultural differences in negotiation behavior between North Americans and Japanese. These different behaviors may lead to negative attributions and thus to an enforcement of conflicts (Kumar, 1989: 188).

Early approaches to culture and mediation frequently tend to favor universalist standpoints of conflict behavior—which in the end help the authors to legitimize Western forms of mediation as a tool that may be used in universal contexts. For example, Augsburger (1992) presents a handbook explicitly centering on issues of cross-cultural mediation. The author departs from a primordialist notion of culture and takes a rather universalist perspective on conflict behavior. According to him, there may be cultural differences in people's disputing behavior. Besides that,

Augsburger claims that there are universal basics of conflict behavior that may lay sufficient ground for universal ways of constructive conflict management—and these ways may even be termed as mediation. For example, Augsburger claims that people in any culture conceive conflict as a triadic constellation. Parties in conflict will always try to form coalitions with third parties to bolster their own position. Following Augsburger, third parties may always make use of this tendency to triangulation and transform it into a triad in which a more or less Western-based form of discursive and equal conflict management may be developed (Augsburger, 1992: 152-163).

Relativist approaches from practitioners' standpoints instead are frequently brought across in terms of contrastive case studies. As an example, Abu-Nimer (1996) compares two mediation processes in two different cultural contexts that he describes as intercultural. Here, one major issue with contrastive approaches comes to light. Normally, the authors themselves select and decide which processes observed in non-Western cultural settings should be taken to be contrasted with Western forms of conflict mediation. This approach strongly contributes to misleading authors towards ethnocentric standpoints when they define what needs to be fulfilled for a conflict to be solved in a constructive way. Kuhn and Poole (2000) warn that here, many authors fall prey to the assumption that integrative communication instead of avoidance has to be taken as the only possible route to constructive conflict resolution. This assumption is then claimed as culturally universal.

But the universality of mediation's constructive effects is not the only thing that has to be questioned. Even more, according to Brigg (2003), Western forms of conflict mediation applied to non-Western conflict parties must be seen as an instrument of exerting power upon them. Western forms of mediation take conflict as something that should be eliminated in favour of a harmonious state. To reach this state, parties should explicitly talk about their conflict, and Brigg calls this a form of confession that more or less automatically leads parties to a somewhat weak point at which they are ready to give up their original positions. According to Brigg, none of these assumptions may be expected to be shared by members of other cultures. Conflicts do not necessarily have to be seen as something to be solved as soon as possible, nor do conflict parties experience confession and open telling as a relief. Instead, Brigg concludes that non-Western parties are forced into a conflict resolution process that brings advantages to Western parties and that will not be able to serve the needs of non-Western parties.

While the approaches mentioned so far take culture as primordially given forms of differing knowledge, Carnevale and Pruitt (1992) assume that culture interferes in forms of differing value orientations. Based on Hofstede's (1980) dimensions for the categorization of value orientations, Carnevale and Pruitt's discussion centers around Triandis' (2000)(2000) assumption about different conflict styles in individualist vs. collectivist societies. In practice, the conception of culture as different value orientations helps Carnevale and Choi (2000) to give recommendations for conflict mediation. In international mediations, they assume that neutral mediators will be hard to find. To serve conflict parties' different value orientations, they recommend engaging two mediators, each one biased towards one of the cultures concerned. In this way, participants' value orientations should be acknowledged in a way sufficient for an implementation of mediation as a universal tool.

Constructivist approaches to culture

Lederach (1995, 1997) has promoted didactic concepts for constructive conflict management in intercultural settings, which are based on his own practical training experience. Theoretically, Lederach departs from a social constructivist perspective referring to Schütz' phenomenology. Here, conflict is seen as a social construction, and it is thus cultural in itself (Lederach, 1995: 7-10). Within this framework, however, Lederach accepts the a priori existence of cultures. On the other hand, its constructivist character holds an opportunity for cultural change and transformation. Starting from a Western approach to intercultural training as well as conflict resolution training, Lederach develops an emic approach by which people in non-Western cultures can be empowered and enabled to develop their own culture-specific tool for conflict resolution. Although re-locating his approach in social theory, Lederach emphasizes that his approach is primarily of an inductive and experience-based nature (Lederach, 1997: xvi). While LeBaron (1998) recommends relying upon Western forms of mediation training and keeping it open to as much variation as possible, Lederach, from a constructivist viewpoint, goes one step further. Taking a relativist perspective, he recognizes conflict management concepts from other cultures as equal to Western concepts. According to him, these concepts may even serve as a genuine basis for the development of (culture-specific) conflict management tools.

In a similar vein, Abu-Nimer (2001) promotes a model for intercultural conflict training that is based on observations interpreted by means of the Developmental Model of Intercultural Sensitivity (DMIS) by Bennett (1986) and Hammer (1999). The model assumes that individuals subjectively construct perceptions of cultural differences as well as their salience. Studies on the basis of this tool may allow practitioners to foresee to what degree individuals will be ready to make concessions if cultural issues are to be negotiated. The management of cultural differences from this perspective turns out to be an issue that may be transformed by re-constructing cultural issues.

Instead of universal training experiences, Comaroff and Comaroff (2003) base their arguments on practical observations on conflict management in South Africa. Here, the post-apartheid era has brought along a legal constitution that in social practice still has to compete with traditional understandings of law from the apartheid era. The authors take this as an example for people constructing culture-specific assumptions on ideal ways for conflict management that may conflict in themselves in social practice. Postcolonial implications of the conception of law had even earlier been central issues of academic debate (Merry, 1992: 363).

Taking a constructivist stance and considering cultures as values, Mayer (2005) develops a culture-synergetic model of intercultural mediation resulting from practical observations in South Africa. Here, Western forms of mediation, as well as local forms of conflict management are recommended to be combined in their most constructive way.

Seeing culture as a preferential system building on underlying values is particularly suitable for the description of social changes in conflict management preferences. These changes themselves may emerge in terms of conflict. Grose (1995) for example discusses the challenges of integrating Aboriginal groups in Australia into a fair system of law and justice, especially mediation. According to Grose, Aboriginal culture has to be taken as a product of permanent change and growth. Traditional culture constantly changes and transforms by contact and exchange with the majority Australian culture. Beyond this, it has to be acknowledged that Aboriginal subgroups differ significantly in their degree of adaptation to the majoritarian culture. To serve the needs resulting from this transitional context, Grose pleads for a consideration of the concept of *cultural analogue* (Grose, 1995: 336) according to Tafoya (Tribal Community Boards Project, 1986: 3) in mediation practice.

The implementation of culture in approaches from the perspective of cultural anthropologists

Cultural anthropologists today provide a vast range of reports on single case studies on conflict management from a wide variety of cultural settings. Many of them have been compiled in anthologies, e.g. on culture-specific assumptions on the role of law (Nader, 1997), on ethnopraxes of conflict management (Avruch et al., 1991), on selected cases analyzed with a narrowed academic approach (e.g. for approaches from linguistic anthropology cf. Fry and Björkqvist, 1997a) or on a narrowed geographical region (e.g. for the Pacific region cf. Watson-Gegeo and White, 1990). Avruch and Black (1991) argue that this form of research by case studies on the one hand avoids the pitfalls of ethnocentric comparisons and on the other hand remains open for the observation of intercultural contexts in mediation.

While conflict researchers tend to run the risk of unnoticed ethnocentrism, cultural anthropologists conducting their research around one central topic, e.g. conflict and mediation, seem to tend to feel a strong need not only to describe what they see but also to give evaluations (for a discussion of this issue on a general level cf. Zurn, 2000). Even studies in intracultural settings strongly challenge issues of mediator ethics, especially the transparent management of mediator neutrality (Jacobs, 2002) and mediator power (Silbey and Merry, 1986).

Critical assessments are quite common when intercultural issues are to be considered, too. Augusti-Panareda (2006) for example describes the practice of intercultural mediators employed by the city of Barcelona, Spain, in the field of social work. Formally, these mediators are supposed to bridge the cultural gap between immigrants and local norms and customs to help them to work in Catalonia without getting into conflict with the local law. The author however argues that these mediators actually will always support the local system with their work. In the end, immigrant groups are gently pushed into assimilation.

Similarly, Brigg (2007) addresses local governments' uses of mediation in intercultural issues. Although mediation in these premises may be abused as a tool to implicitly exert power over minorities, Brigg argues that this does not necessarily have to be the case. Instead, Brigg refers to a model by Levinas that helps to delineate how relationships between local majorities and minorities may constructively be transformed by means of mediation.

Ethnocentrism in research on conflict resolution is targeted by Bonta's (1996) criticism, too. The author compares conflict resolution strategies of 24 peaceful societies with Western ideas of conflict resolution and mediation. Bonta comes to the conclusion that peaceful relations can be established in many different ways beyond Western ideals.

Primordialist approaches to culture

Conceptions of culture as special forms of knowledge may centrally be found in the contributions in (Avruch et al., 1991). In their introduction, the editors show that understandings of what conflict is, and how it can be solved are deeply rooted in culture-specific assumptions and knowledge of humankind and on social interaction in general (Avruch, 1991: 4-7). Merry additionally pointed out that these forms of cultural knowledge normally are unconscious to interactants in a given situation (Merry, 1987a: 1, Handwerker, 2002: 107).

The US-American strand of *Alternative Dispute Resolution (ADR),* however, does not see conflict behavior in its cultural context. LeBaron (1998) points out that this cultural ignorance of ADR is rather surprising since Western forms of mediation mostly rely upon encouraging conflict parties to create narrative framings of their conflict perspectives. Contextualizing perspectives by narration, and thus mediation as well may actually be seen as a genuine form of cultural (and culture-specific) production (Rifkin et al., 1991).[2]

Since these thoughts however have been neglected by approaches from ADR, Avruch (1991: 6ff) and Merry (1987b: 2064) warn that conflict management practices which in the Western world had been considered innovative and conducive to social sustainability centrally ignore potential cultural variation. Avruch and Merry thus plead for more anthropological analyses of people's conflict behavior and conflict management styles.

Primordialist approaches to culture as values seem to be much more prevalent in anthropological research on the issue. Here, a very early and seminal study was presented by Gulliver (1979), reporting on conflict negotiation processes in two East African societies, the Arusha and the Ndendeuli (Gulliver, 1979: xv). Gulliver conceives cultural influences as matters of specific norms (Gulliver, 1979: 10), although he assumes that they will play a minor role compared to far-reaching similarities between all cultures. To describe these universals, Gulliver is confident of finding a small number of categories that can be found in any context:

> "In all societies, regardless of their location in time and space, there is a wide variety of modes by which disputes are handled and resolution sought. In general terms, the range of these procedures and their variation can be comprehended in a few broad categories" (Gulliver, 1979: 1).

Finally, Gulliver comes to the conclusion that negotiations in any society pass through similar stages and processes.

Beyond the search for universals, anthropologists in this field have attempted to link culture-specific conflict behavior to other, more general cultural characteristics. Here, Merry (1987b) for example relies upon the assumption that conflict behavior is related to a context's social complexity:

> „In general, anthropological studies indicate that when disputants are bound together by multi-stranded social relationships, they will seek to compromise their differences, but when they have only single-stranded social ties, they will seek victory in adversarial contests rather than attempt to reach compromise" (Merry, 1987b: 2061).

Merry (1989) confirms this assumption by contrasting mediation procedures from four nonindustrial societies (i.e. Sudan, the Philippines, Afghanistan and Mexico) with North American mediation standards. Merry comes to the conclusion

2 Other authors take narrative elements in mediation as a potential element of Western mediation without referring to intercultural adoptions (Rifkin et al., 1991).

that—despite numerous structural differences—mediation is seen as more attractive when people are tied in complex social networks.

A great deal of comparative literature on this issue is provided by works based on psychological assumptions. Many of them have in common that they do not directly focus on how people from given societies deal with intercultural conflict. However, they are interested in identifying heuristic and generalizable rules. To do so, they try to extrapolate from data on neighboring fields to patterns of intercultural conflict.

One prominent example may be seen in attempts of inferring from culture-specific patterns of child-rearing to people's later preferences in conflict behavior. In this vein, Avruch (1994: 426) quotes Ross (1993) in his claims that „harshness of childrearing practices, absence of warmth and affection in socialization and the presence of male gender-identity conflicts" (Avruch, 1994: 426) will result in so-called high conflict societies. This assumption is even more prominent in (Roberts Callister and Wall, 2004) who compare Thai and American mediators.

Ember and Ember (Ember and Ember, 1994) instead argue, on the basis of quantitative data, that children's early education towards aggressiveness does not lead to a higher probability of war. However, frequent occurrences of war encourage members of a society to educate their children to be aggressive. This again may lead to a continuation of war.

Kagan et al. (Kagan et al., 1982) compare conflict style preferences between Mexican and US-American children. According to them, cultural differences diminish with age.

The anthropological debate on primordialist vs. constructivist approaches to culture was sketched earlier in this article. Countering constructivist critique, anthropologists in the field of mediation research frequently argue that cultural differences cannot be captured by means of broad categories as was attempted by earlier scholars. Instead, cultural differences have to be identified from contexts that tend to be singular and highly complex (Handwerker, 2002, LeBaron, 1998, Davidheiser, 2005). Adequate empirical analyses will thus require very detailed and differentiating looks to avoid overgeneralizations.

The German literary critic Bachmann-Medick takes a constructivist standpoint on culture referring to Bhabha (1994). Taking Bhabha's anti-essentialist grounds seriously (Bhabha, 1994: 83), Bachmann-Medick concludes that conversely, anti-essentialist claims cannot be maintained but until researchers have not managed to aptly describe a culture's essence (Bachmann-Medick, 2008: 148).

Constructivist approaches to culture

In their volume on conflict management strategies in Pacific societies, Watson-Gegeo and White (1990) assemble contributions from linguistic and psychological anthropology. According to them, culture is strongly tied to language, and it emerges in a given situation by the interactants' construction. Culture here may thus be taken as implicit knowledge on how to negotiate cultural belongings. This knowledge may be situationally activated.

Conceiving cultural constructions in terms of values and norms, Nader (1997) in a similar vein presents an anthology on construction processes of understandings of law in different societies. According to Nader, local law thus emerges as a process from social discourse.

While Nader tries to emphasize the culture-dependent and flexible nature of law, Silbey (1992) using similar theoretical assumptions takes the opposite stance. According to her, law contributes to the discursive construction and maintenance of power relations. Basing her theory on Foucault, Silbey pleads for discourse analyses that may reveal how power is constructed through legal discourse. In terms of theory, Silbey argues that culture should be used as a notion to overcome the dichotomy between agency and structure (Silbey, 1992: 41).

The implementation of culture in approaches from the perspective of intercultural research

Researchers interested in intercultural communication did not center their approaches on aspects of conflict communication. In this field of research, conflict instead was rather considered as a potential consequence of intercultural communication, the probability of which depended on the underlying theory. Taking a short look at the emergence of intercultural communication as a field of research, it should always be kept in mind that collecting publications centering on the term of culture will necessarily paint a picture of inner-societal constructions of discourses in the Western world instead of opening a category for global insights. Instead of tracing back a research tradition on intercultural communication, such an attempt will necessarily trace back the social construction of self-identifications in the Western world.

Philosophers in France and England had used culture as a term referring to individuals' intellectual capacities until the 17th century. In the period of the enlightenment, German philosophers then started to take culture as consisting of social relationships, abilities and virtues (cf. Pufendorf, 1684). Herder (1974 [1784-1791]) then takes culture as the historical emergence of different peoples' ways of life. Taking this stance, several different cultures could now be separated and compared (Welsch, 2000: 329). In the 20th century, the social anthropologist Malinowski (1922) introduced a functional view stating that culture helped people to satisfy (culturally) universal needs. In the U.S. cultural anthropologists developed the *Culture and Personality School* in the 1930s trying to capture selected cultures as a whole. Here, scholars assumed that every culture had its own particular style that would shape its members' personalities (Benedict, 1934).

Aside from this, European thinkers steered towards an interpretive paradigm. Still, Humboldt (1995 [1836]) had claimed that languages shape human thought, and this was later confirmed by Sapir and Whorf (1936 [1956]) as linguistic relativity. As described in the introduction of this chapter, de Saussure instead claimed that human communication is mediated by symbols. The relatedness of these symbols to the extralinguistic world had to be seen as arbitrary, and people were constantly challenged to re-interpret this relationship. On this basis, French structuralist Lévi-Strauss (1987 [1952]) detached the notion of culture from individual personality traits. Instead, he defined culture as a system of symbolic rules that had to be interpreted by its users.

However, when intercultural research became known as a tool to practically improve international contacts and interaction, approaches on the basis of the *Culture and Personality School* turned out to be much easier to grasp for practitioners than the interpretive approach did. In the 1950's American ethnographer Hall (1959, 1976) published his seminal works distinguishing cultures according their understandings of time and space. Even today, management researchers are particularly interested in the identification of cultural characteristics that help to distinguish and to compare cultures in the fields of international delegations of business managers (Hofstede, 1980, Trompenaars, 1993, House et al., 2004). In intercultural settings, conflicts caused by culture may then arise from communicative misunderstandings as well as conflicting cultural goals and preferences.

No later than the 1960's, anthropologists and interculturalists[3] began a paradigm breach, and anthropologists turned towards interpretive as well as constructivist approaches that were no longer followed by interculturalists (Moosmüller, 2004: 46f, 2007: 19). However, especially in the field of linguistic research on intercultural communication, authors strived to follow constructivist approaches and debates. Gumperz (1982, 2001) emphasized the role of context in communica-

3 The term interculturalist here is used with reference to Dahlén (1997: 9). Dahlén stated that practitioners working in this field themselves used this term. According to Dahlén, the term does not only refer to those maintaining a "culture shock prevention industry" but to all "institutionalized forms for preparing people to cope with other cultures than their own (Hannerz, 1992: 251).

tive understanding and interpretation. Later on, sociolinguists and ethnographers of communication assumed that culture would always be generated and activated by interactants in their singular and respective situation (Auer and di Luzio, 1992). In intercultural situations, conflicts caused by culture may arise from people's unwillingness to cooperate and their need to build social boundaries and differentiations.

Against the background of this general introduction, the following sections will confine their assessment only to those works from the intercultural field that explicitly center around aspects of intercultural conflict.

Primordial approaches to culture

Taking culture as forms of existing knowledge, Ting-Toomey introduces the notion of face and facework (Goffman, 1955) to grasp aspects that seem to be salient to people in conflict in a universal way. Cultures here may differ in their preferences and in their ways of saving a person's own vs. his or her partner's positive and negative face (Ting-Toomey, 1985, Ting-Toomey, 1988, Oetzel and Ting-Toomey, 2003). In mediation research, Ogawa (1999) explores the role of facework in differing cultural settings.

Intercultural management researcher Trompenaars (1996: 54) promotes a functional approach to culture, still taking culture as pre-existing knowledge. Accordingly, cultures are seen as different ways to solve the same universal everyday problems. Trompenaars follows an approach similar to Hofstede's, categorizing cultures along a number of dimensions. The more cultures differ within these dimensions, the more likely conflicts are assumed to occur in intercultural contact. To successfully manage or avoid these conflicts, Trompenaars recommends dialectically integrating values of one culture into those of another one instead of finding a balance in between them. A similar approach is also proposed by Buller et al. (1997), though they take cultures as pre-existing values causing ethical conflict.

In a similar vein, Triandis (2000) presents a systematics allowing researchers to categorize cultures according to their styles of dealing with conflict with foreign cultures. According to Triandis, cultures differ in the amount of violence occurring internally. The more violence can be found within a culture, Triandis concludes, the more likely people from that culture will establish violent relationships towards other cultures (Triandis, 2000: 146). Besides that, Triandis assumes that if certain cultural attributes are combined, this will lead to more aggressive behavior towards other cultures:

> „Thus, when a particular combination of cultural syndromes is found, namely active, universalistic, diffuse, instrumental, vertical collectivism, inhuman treatment of out-groups is likely to occur." (Triandis, 2000: 151).

So Triandis comes to the general assumption that democratic nations have never and will never enter into violent warfare with each other (Triandis, 2000: 146). Furthermore, Triandis states that collectivist cultures, because of their strong homogeneous self-image, are more likely to produce aggression towards outgroups than individualist cultures (Triandis, 2000: 150). However plausible this line of arguments might seem, it runs the risks of being described as ethnocentric. So it does not come as a surprise that authors from Western cultures come to the conclusion that their own culture seems more acceptable, here more peaceful, than other cultures.

Cai et al (2000) confirm the influence of individualist vs. collectivist attitudes and behavior on negotiation outcomes, tested in dyadic settings. Accordingly, collectivist attitudes, especially from the side of a seller towards a buyer, tend to produce faster and more satisfying outcomes.

Gabrielidis et al. (1997) make use of the dual-concern model of interpersonal conflict styles. According to the model, interactants have to take care of the concerns of others and of themselves. As it may be expected, collectivist cultures to a higher degree tend to consider the interests of others.

Constructivist approaches to culture

Focusing on situations of intercultural contact, constructivist perspectives on culture frequently describe how (cultural) knowledge is used to construct social boundaries and distinctions. In social research, these strands in many cases refer to notions from phenomenology and sociology of knowledge (Schutz, 1967, Schutz and Luckmann, 1973). Cultural boundaries normally serve to maintain a person's social group, its status as well as advantageous power relations in general. From a linguistic perspective, Day (1994) has shown how individuals activate ethnic categorizations in their conversation to establish group boundaries. Using narrative research, Pütz (2004) shows how owners of small enterprises in migrant contexts establish and constructively deal with limitations from ethnic boundaries on their business.

Constructivist approaches seeing cultures as values frequently are based on discourse theory. A society's majorities shape a hegemonic discourse on inclusion and exclusion based upon cultural differentiations. This practice may also be termed as racism.(van Dijk, 1987, Koole and ten Thije, 1994). Constructivist approaches to conflict in intercultural research, in most cases confine themselves to avoidance as the only quality of conflict behavior.

Approaches to culture	Practitioners	Cultural Anthropologists	Interculturalists
primordialist approaches to culture as knowledge	(Goldstein, 1986) (Merry, 1989) (Bercovitch, 1989) (Kumar, 1989) (Rahim, 1989) (Abu-Nimer, 1996)	(Augusti-Panareda, 2006) (Brigg, 2003) (Bonta, 1996) (Avruch et al., 1991) (Merry, 1987a) (Handwerker, 2002) (LeBaron, 1998) (Davidheiser, 2005)	(Ting-Toomey, 1985) (Ting-Toomey, 1988) (Oetzel and Ting-Toomey, 2003) (Trompenaars, 1993)
primordialist approaches to cultures as values	(Folberg and Taylor, 1984) (Augsburger, 1992)	(Gulliver, 1979) (Merry, 1987b) (Merry, 1989) (Avruch, 1994) (Ross, 1993) (Roberts Callister and Wall, 2004) (Ember and Ember, 1994) (Kagan et al., 1982)	(Buller et al., 1997) (Triandis, 2000) (Gabrielidis et al., 1997) (Cai et al., 2000)
constructivist approaches to culture as knowledge	(Lederach, 1995, 1997) (Abu-Nimer, 2001) (Comaroff and Comaroff, 2003)	(Watson-Gegeo and White, 1990)	(Day, 1994) (Day, 2006) (Pütz, 2004)
constructivist approaches to culture as values	(Grose, 1995) (Mayer, 2005)	(Nader, 1997) (Silbey, 1992)	(van Dijk, 1987) (Koole and ten Thije, 1994)

Table 1: Overview on theoretical conceptions on culture's role in conflict mediation.

Discussion: Consequences from the diversity of concepts of culture

Although the preceding section may paint a detailed picture of the different uses of the term of culture in different strands of research on mediation, of course, it can only be taken as a small selection of exemplary concepts. Beyond this, the research literature will hold an even wider variety of concepts, and even the categories proposed in this article are in no way homogeneous containers. The different categorizations of selected approaches may in some cases even look surprising. In the end, it should be kept in mind that according to this survey, studies on culture and mediation conceive their objects of research in very different ways, which will also mean that they will come to very different conclusions on how to practically deal with culture in mediation. Avruch (1992) earlier pointed out this problem, and he hints at the fact that this diversity of concepts will be hidden in many other constructed terms like tribes, ethnicities and nations, as well.

Considering anthropologists' concerns about being deprived of their rights to define their own objects of research, this survey may reassure and comfort anthropologists. Their approaches to the issue still show the largest advancement of theoretical debate as well as the largest number of publications, covering a great number of aspects of the issue.

Furthermore, it may be concluded that a great number of conceptions of culture can be found in the academic literature that seem to compete in terms of their validity. While a variety of different approaches normally may contribute to the advancement of research in general, culture as a central term in this case takes on a double function and role. Talking about intercultural communication and understanding leads to the fact that in an intercultural sphere, academics and practitioners even cannot be sure how to circumscribe their space of interaction and understanding.

Culture as a matter of social discourse

One last point in case may remain in the insight that culture can be taken as a matter relevant to social discourse. People in the Western world are talking about culture as a factor of influence on their lives, and researchers are challenged to deliver more precise explanations of the role of culture, Intercultural communication may thus be taken as a discursive topic collecting all aspects of a social groups' interaction with individuals and groups from outside.

This line of thinking will consequently lead to the implication that not only researchers but also any member of a society will have his or her subjective notion of what culture is, how it influences a person's action and how best to deal with this influence. These subjective notions will be derived from a person's participation in social discourse transmitting general assumptions of culture.

In contrast to theory-based definitions on culture, these subjective notions tend to be the only concepts that are immediately relevant to people's action. Depending on what individuals see as cultural, they will interpret their interactions in very individual ways and they will make decisions on their future actions accordingly.

Methods for the description on how discourse about culture arises and what this discourse may contain, can be found in concepts from gender studies. A check on whether and to what extent these approaches may be transferred to intercultural communication research may promise valuable insights into individuals' use of discourse on culture. Much more than scholars from intercultural research, those from gender studies have learned to constantly consider the constructionist character of their object of study—and its consequences for research (Hark, 2001: 153). Apart from this different state of reflection, both gender studies and intercultural studies center their focus of research on discursive topics dealing with varying forms of differences and differentiations (Mae, 2003: 195). Judith Butler (1990, 1993) may be taken as one of gender studies' most prominent thinkers. Discussing Foucault's works on discourse theory, Butler concludes that the notion of a person's biological sex is not—as commonly taken—the basis for social constructions of gender. Instead, the idea of the existence of a biological sex itself will have to be taken as part of the social constructions on people's gender (Butler, 1993: 4).

Transferring this notion of a constructed basis from gender studies to intercultural research may lead to the insight, that similar to sex and gender, the notion of an *a priori* existence of culture before producing discourse on it must be taken as part of this discourse itself. Butler discusses the hegemonic dichotomization between males and females in Western societies and wants to break it on a political level. A similar approach may reveal comparable "materializations" (Butler, 1993: 4) in intercultural research. Here, many cultural boundaries turn out to be produced by hegemonic discourse (Ang and St Louis, 2005).

One central advantage of the proposed concept should be seen in its immediate relevance to people's action. Subjective notions of culture and its influence are those notions people really rely upon when deciding what to do next in a given situation. This point so far has largely been neglected in research. Instead, two theory-based traditions had been followed primarily, avoiding the central question of a concept's relevance for action. Schondelmayer (2008) summarizes that current studies in cultural anthropology continue roughly two traditions: Cognitive anthropology, initiated by Goodenough (1957) and today represented by D'Andrade (1995) take culture as a system of mental knowledge that can be described. Researchers in this tradition will concentrate on people's attitudes and interpretations, but they will tend to neglect to check how people act in the end. This may be opposed to what today can be termed as interpretive anthropology (Geertz, 1973). Here, authors assume that individuals produce culture in interaction. Research will thus center around people's practices, and it will tend to neglect people's underlying attitudes and beliefs. Schondelmayer, in her study, points out that there is not only an obvious gap between these two strands, but results from each strand frequently contradict each other, i.e. people do not act according to what they pronounce as their attitudes (Schondelmayer, 2008: 265). Insights into subjective concepts of culture may help to adequately fill the research gap found, thereby circumventing this paradox.

Consequences for mediation research and practice

Considering this alternative notion of culture may lead to respective forms of intercultural mediation research and practice. Researchers would thus be required to uncover implicit and subjective notions of culture from all individuals in a mediation setting. Researchers would need to identify what culture means to their subjects under research in the relevant situation, how they evaluate culture's influences on their situations, and what consequences they would derive for their future interaction. Mediation practitioners as well should then try to reveal these constructions and help their clients verbalize and reflect on them in intercultural settings. Issues of intercultural mediation, as well as the question of how people from different cultures deal with intercultural conflict, then turns out to be a highly subjective issue. However, in contrast to the difficulties connected to this research question that have been outlined in this article above, the issue may now be dealt with in a way meeting academic requirements from social research.

Mediation, similar to the notion of culture, should be taken as an extra-academic topic. Instead of one theory underlying the concept, mediation and culture can rather be taken as themes that may be analyzed by means of empirical methods and interpreted by means of scientific theories. Following the discourse approach outlined above, not only culture but also mediation should be questioned.

In this vein, Baraldi (2006) shows that many theoretical concepts from Western-based intercultural research, like intercultural dialogue, diversity and transcultural communication may even contradict each other. These contradictions may point at the concepts' constructivist nature. Instead of discussing the adequacy of these competing concepts, Baraldi proposes focusing on the existence of many concepts on similar issues that may be culturally different.

Instead of departing from one or from a variety of concepts on mediation (and maybe debating their potential ethnocentric origin), subjects may also possess ideas on how conflict should be dealt with in triadic settings. To analyze this, researchers should free themselves from their notions of mediation and instead openly focus on triadic forms of conflict management in general. Finlay (2008) for example has presented an analysis of the Northern Ireland conflict showing that one of the central issues impeding the region from coming to peace may be seen in the notion of culture that all groups concerned have constructed and that prevails.

In mediation research, more recent approaches have started to look at individual motivations of mediation practitioners and to put them into different categories. Bush and Folger (1994) sum up mediators' motivations as stories. In a similar vein, Harrington and Merry (1988) speak of mediation projects, and so does Breidenbach (1995).

Some scholars have analyzed triadic interaction and informal triadic conflict management. Caplow (1968) from a psychologist's perspective has analyzed people's behavior in situations in which three persons were present. Similar questions have been dealt with by Pike (1975). Both authors come to the conclusion that human beings tend to avoid situations that are genuinely triadic, i.e. situations in which three persons participate equally. The authors explain that human beings try to reduce the relatively high complexity of the triad by transforming it into a dyad. In this dyad, logically there will always be two against one (Caplow, 1968), automatically establishing coalitions and power inequalities. In contrast to this, mediation researcher Augsburger (1992: 143ff) claims that people in all culture will universally tend to manage conflict by means of triangulation. They will try to engage third persons into their conflict, mostly to form a stronger coalition against their enemy. This can be done by confessing one's problems to a friend, but also by appealing to a court.

In conversation analysis, Kerbrat-Orecchioni (2004) has presented ground-laying work in the operationalization of the management of conversation in triadic situation. Here, empirical analysis may show that people are well able to distinguish several different participant and speaker roles in a given situation, and that they are able to communicate in a way that helps them to constructively organize and manage the situation. One early reference to ways of informal mediation was published by Sheppard et al. (1989). Busch (2005) has presented a descriptive model for empirical research on triadic interaction in intercultural situations. This concept may help to see what effects third persons will have on a prior dyad, if any. It may help to assess whether third persons' influences should be evaluated as constructive or as hindering from interpersonal understanding in the previous dyad. If dyadic understanding may be enhanced by third persons, this may be described as spontaneous lay mediation.

References

ABU-LUGHOD, L. (1991) Writing against culture. IN FOX, R. G. (Ed.) *Restructuring Anthropology: Working in the Present.* (137-162), Santa Fe, NM, UVK Verlagsgesellschaft.

ABU-NIMER, M. (1996) Conflict resolution approaches: Western and Middle Eastern lessons and possibilities. *The American Journal of Economics and Sociology,* 55(1), 35-53.

ABU-NIMER, M. (2001) Conflict resolution, culture, and religion: Toward a training model of interreligious peacebuilding. *Journal of Peace Research,* 38(6), 685-704.

ANG, I. & ST LOUIS, B. (2005) Guest editorial: The predicament of difference. *Ethnicities,* 5(3), 291-304.

APPADURAI, A. (1996) *Modernity at Large. Cultural Dimensions of Globalization,* Minneapolis, University of Minnesota Press.

AUER, P. & DI LUZIO, A. (Eds.) (1992) *The Contextualization of Language,* Amsterdam/ Philadelphia, John Benjamins.

AUERNHEIMER, G. (2002) Kultur, Lebenswelt, Diskurs—drei konkurrierende Konzepte. *Tertium Comparationis,* 8(2), 93-103.

AUGSBURGER, D. W. (1992) *Conflict Mediation Across Cultures: Pathways and Patterns,* Louisville, KY, Westminster John Knox Press.

AUGUSTI-PANAREDA, J. (2006) Cross-cultural brokering in the legal, institutional and normative domains: Intercultural mediators managing immigration in Catalonia. *Social & Legal Studies,* 15(3), 409-433.

AVRUCH, K. (1991) Introduction. Culture and conflict resolution. IN AVRUCH, K., BLACK, P. W. & SCIMECCA, J. A. (Eds.) *Conflict Resolution. Cross-Cultural Perspectives.* (1-18), New York/Westport/London, Greenwood.

AVRUCH, K. (1992) Making culture, and its costs. *Ethnic and Racial Studies,* 15(4), 614-626.

AVRUCH, K. (1994) Linking theory and conflict management. *Peace & Change,* 19(4), 424-430.

AVRUCH, K. (1998) *Culture and Conflict Resolution,* Washington, DC, United States Institute of Peace Press.

AVRUCH, K. (2003) Type I and type II errors in culturally sensitive conflict resolution practice. *Conflict Resolution Quarterly,* 20(3), 351-371.

AVRUCH, K. & BLACK, P. W. (1991) The culture question and conflict resolution. *Peace & Change,* 16(1), 22-45.

AVRUCH, K. & BLACK, P. W. (1996) ADR, Palau, and the Contribution of Anthropology. IN WOLFE, A. W. & YANG, H. (Eds.) *Anthropological Contributions to Conflict Resolution.* (47-63), Athens/London, The University of Georgia Press.

AVRUCH, K., BLACK, P. W. & SCIMECCA, J. A. (Eds.) (1991) *Conflict Resolution. Cross-Cultural Perspectives,* New York, Greenwood Press.

BACHMANN-MEDICK, D. (2008) Übersetzung in der Weltgesellschaft. Impulse eines 'translational turn'. IN GIPPER, A. & KLENGEL, S. (Eds.) *Kultur, Übersetzung, Lebenswelten. Beiträge zu aktuellen Paradigmen der Kulturwissenschaften.* (141-160), Würzburg, Königshausen & Neumann.

BARALDI, C. (2006) New forms of intercultural communication in a globalized world. *The International Communication Gazette,* 68(1), 53-69.

BARTH, F. (1969) Introduction. IN BARTH, F. (Ed.) *Ethnic Groups and Boundaries: The Social Organization of Cultural Difference.* Boston, Little Brown.

BENEDICT, R. (1934) *Patterns of Culture,* Boston, Houghton Mifflin.
BENNETT, M. J. (1986) Towards ethnorelativism: A developmental model of intercultural sensitivity. IN PAIGE, M. R. (Ed.) *Cross-cultural Orientation: New Conceptualizations and Applications.* (27-70), Lanham, University Press of America.
BERCOVITCH, J. (1989) International dispute mediation: A comparative empirical analysis. IN KRESSEL, K. & PRUITT, D. G. (Eds.) *Mediation Research: The Process and Effectiveness of Third-Party Intervention.* (284-299), San Francisco, CA, Jossey Bass.
BERRY, J. W. (1969) On cross-cultural comparability. *International Journal of Psychology,* 4, 119-128.
BHABHA, H. K. (1994) *The Location of Culture,* London/New York, Routledge.
BONNELL, V. M., HUNT, L. A. & BIERNACKI, R. (Eds.) (1999) *Beyond the Cultural Turn. New Directions in the Study of Society and Culture. Papers presented at a Conference held Apr. 26-27, 1996, in California,* Berkeley, Calif./ Los Angeles/ London, University of California Press.
BONTA, B. D. (1996) Conflict resolution among peaceful societies: The culture of peacefulness. *Journal of Peace Research,* 33(4), 403-420.
BOROFSKY, R., BARTH, F., SHWEDER, R. A., RODSETH, L. & STOLZENBERG, N. M. (2001) WHEN: A Conversation about Culture. *American Anthropologist,* 103(2), 432-446.
BRANTLINGER, P. (2002) A response to *Beyond the Cultural Turn. The American Historical Review,* 107(5), http://www.historycooperative.org/journals/ahr/107.5/ah0502001500.html [last accessed: 05-07-2009].
BREIDENBACH, J. & NYÍRÍ, P. (2001) Interkulturelle Kompetenz als Business. *OrganisationsEntwicklung,* 4/2001, 70-75.
BREIDENBACH, S. (1995) *Mediation. Struktur, Chancen und Risiken von Vermittlung im Konflikt,* Köln, Schmidt.
BRIGG, M. (2003) Mediation, power, and cultural difference. *Conflict Resolution Quarterly,* 20(3), 287-306.
BRIGG, M. (2007) Governance and susceptibility in conflict resolution: Possibilities beyond control. *Social & Legal Studies,* 16(1), 27-47.
BRUMANN, C. (1999) Writing for culture: Why a successful concept should not be discarded. *Current Anthropology,* 40(S1), S1-S13.
BULLER, P. F., KOHLS, J. J. & ANDERSON, K. S. (1997) A model for addressing cross-cultural ethical conflicts. *Business & Society,* 36(2), 169-193.
BUSCH, D. (2005) *Interkulturelle Mediation. Eine theoretische Grundlegung triadischer Konfliktbearbeitung in interkulturell bedingten Kontexten,* Frankfurt am Main/ Berlin/ Bern/ Bruxelles/ New York/ Oxford/ Wien, Peter Lang.
BUSCH, D. (2009) The notion of culture in linguistic research. *Forum Qualitative Sozialforschung / Forum: Qualitative Social Research,* 10(1), Art. 50, http://nbn-resolving.de/urn:nbn:de:0114-fqs0901508 [last accessed: 01-08-2009].
BUSH, R. A. B. & FOLGER, J. P. (1994) *The Promise of Mediation: Responding to Conflict through Empowerment and Recognition,* San Francisco, Jossey Bass.
BUTLER, J. (1990) *Gender Trouble. Feminism and the Subversion of Identity,* New York/ London, Routledge.
BUTLER, J. (1993) *Bodies That Matter: On the Discursive Limits of "Sex",* New York, Routledge.

CAI, D. A., WILSON, S. R. & DRAKE, L. E. (2000) Culture in the context of intercultural negotiation. individualism-collecitivsm and paths to integrative agreements. *Human Communication Research,* 26(4), 591-619.
CAPLOW, T. (1968) *Two Against One. Coalitions in Triads,* Englewood Cliffs, N.J., Prentice Hall.
CARNEVALE, P. J. & CHOI, D.-W. (2000) Culture in the mediation of international disputes. *International Journal of Psycholoy,* 35(2), 105-110.
CARNEVALE, P. J. & PRUITT, D. G. (1992) Negotiation and Mediation. *Annual Review of Psychology,* 43, 531-582.
CASMIR, F. L. (1993) Third-Culture-Building: A Paradigm-Shift for International and Intercultural Communication. *Communication Yearbook,* 16, 407-428.
CASSIRER, E. (1992 [1947]) *Versuch über den Menschen. Einführung in eine Philosophie der Kultur. Aus d. Engl. von Reinhard Kaiser (zuerst erschienen 1947 als: An essay on man : An introduction to a philosophy of human culture New Haven : Yale University Press),* Frankfurt/Main, Fischer.
CHANEY, D. C. (1994) *The cultural turn: scene-setting essays on contemporary cultural history,* London, New York, Routledge.
CHICK, G. (2001) Culture-bearing units and the units of culture: An introduction. *Cross-Cultural Research,* 35(2), 91-108.
COMAROFF, J. & COMAROFF, J. (2003) Reflections on liberalism, policulturalism, and ID-ology: Citizenship and difference in South Africa. *Social Identities,* 9(4), 445-473.
D'ANDRADE, R. G. (1995) *The Development of Cognitive Anthropology,* Cambridge, Cambridge University Press.
DAHL, O. (1999) The use of stereotypes in intercultural communication. IN KNAPP, K., KAPPEL, B. E., EUBEL-KASPER, K. & SALO-LEE, L. (Eds.) *Meeting the Intercultural Challenge. Effective Approaches in Research, Education, Training and Business.* (453-463), Sternenfels, Verlag Wissenschaft & Praxis.
DAHLÉN, T. (1997) *Among the Interculturalists. An Emergent Profession and its Packaging of Knowledge,* Stockholm, Department of Social Anthropology.
DAVIDHEISER, M. (2005) Mediation and multiculturalism: Domestic and international challenges. *Beyond Intractability,* http://www.beyondintractability.org/essay/mediation_multiculturalism/?nid=1190 [last accessed: 01-08-2009].
DAY, D. (1994) Tang's dilemma and other problems: ethnification processes at some multicultural workplaces. *Pragmatics,* (4:3), 315-336.
DAY, D. (2006) Ethnic and social groups and their linguistic categorization. IN BÜHRIG, K. & TEN THIJE, J. D. (Eds.) *Beyond Misunderstanding. Linguistic Analyses of Intercultural Communication.* (218-244), Amsterdam/ Philadelphia, Benjamins.
DE LA FUENTE, E. (2007) The place of culture in sociology: Romanticism and debates about the `cultural turn'. *Journal of Sociology,* 43(2), 115-130.
EMBER, C. R. & EMBER, M. (1994) War, socialization, and interpersonal violence. A cross-cultural study. *Journal of Conflict Resolution,* 38(4), 620-646.
FINLAY, A. (2008) The persistence of the 'old' idea of culture and the peace process in Ireland. *Critique of Anthropology,* 28(3), 279-296.
FOLBERG, J. & TAYLOR, A. (1984) *Mediation. A Comprehensive Guide to Resolving Conflicts Without Litigation,* San Francisco, Jossey Bass.

FOX, R. G. (Ed.) (1991) *Recapturing Anthropology: Working in the Present,* Santa Fe, NM, School of American Research Press.
FOX, R. G. (1999) Editorial: Culture—A second chance? *Current Anthropology,* 40(S1), Si-Sii.
FRY, D. P. & BJÖRKQVIST, K. (Eds.) (1997a) *Cultural Variation in Conflict Resolution: Alternatives to Violence,* Mahwah, NJ, Lawrence Erlbaum.
FRY, D. P. & BJÖRKQVIST, K. (1997b) Introduction: Conflict resolution themes. IN FRY, D. P. & BJÖRKQVIST, K. (Eds.) *Cultural Variation in Conflict Resolution: Alternatives to Violence.* (3-7), Mahwah, NJ, Lawrence Erlbaum.
GABRIELIDIS, C., STEPHAN, W. G., YBARRA, O., DOS SANTOS PEARSON, V. M. & VILLAREAL, L. (1997) Preferred Styles of Conflict Resolution: Mexico and the United States. *Journal of Cross-Cultural Psychology,* 28(6), 661-677.
GEERTZ, C. J. (1973) *The Interpretation of Cultures,* New York, Basic Books.
GOFFMAN, E. (1955) On facework: an analysis of ritual elements in social interaction. *Psychiatry,* 18, 213-231.
GOLDSTEIN, S. B. (1986) *Cultural Issues in Mediation: A Literature Review,* Manoa, HI, Matsunaga Institute for Peace, University of Hawai'i at Manoa: http://www.peace institute.hawaii.edu/pages/resources/documents/wp_1986_01.pdf [last accessed: 25-09-2008].
GOODENOUGH, W. H. (1957) Cultural anthropology and linguistics. IN GARVIN, P. C. (Ed.) *Report of the Seventh Annual Roundtable Meeting on Linguistics and Language Study.* (167-173), Washington, DC, Georgetown University.
GROSE, P. R. (1995) An indigenous imperative: The rationale for the recognition of aboriginal dispute resolution mechanisms. *Mediation Quarterly,* 12(4), 327-338.
GUDYKUNST, W. B. (1985) A model of uncertainty reduction in intercultural encounters. *Journal of Language and Social Psychology,* 4, 79-98.
GULLIVER, P. H. (1979) *Disputes and Negotiations: A Cross-Cultural Perspective,* New York, Academic Press.
GUMPERZ, J. J. (1982) *Discourse Strategies,* Cambridge, Cambridge University Press.
HALL, E. T. (1959) *The Silent Language,* Garden City, N.Y., Doubleday.
HALL, E. T. (1976) *Beyond Culture,* New York, Random House.
HAMMER, M. R. (1999) A Measure of Intercultural Sensitivity: The Intercultural Development Inventory. IN FOWLER, S. M. & MUMFORD, M. G. (Eds.) *Intercultural Sourcebook: Cross-Cultural Training Methods. Vol. 2.* (61-72), Yarmouth/Maine, Intercultural Press.
HANDWERKER, W. P. (2002) The construct validity of cultures: Cultural diversity, culture theory, and a method for Ethnography. *American Anthropologist,* 104(1), 106-122.
HANNERZ, U. (1992) *Cultural Complexity: Studies in the Social Organization of Meaning,* New York, Columbia University Press.
HANNERZ, U. (1998) Transnational Research. IN BERNARD, H. R. (Ed.) *Handbook of Methods in Cultural Anthropology.* (235-256), Walnut Creek, CA, Altamira Press.
HARDEN, T. & WITTE, A. (Eds.) (2000) *The Notion of Intercultural Understanding in the Context of German as a Foreign Language,* Oxford, Bern, Berlin, Bruxelles, Frankfurt/M., New York, Wien, Lang.
HARK, S. (2001) Feministische Theorie—Diskurs—Dekonstruktion. Produktive Verknüpfungen. IN KELLER, R., HIRSELAND, A., SCHNEIDER, W. & VIEHÖVER, W. (Eds.) *Handbuch Sozialwissenschaftliche Diskursanalyse. Band 1: Theorien und Methoden.* (353-371), Opladen, Leske + Budrich.

HARRINGTON, C. B. & MERRY, S. E. (1988) Ideological production: The making of community mediation. *Law & Social Review,* 22(4), 709-735.

HERDER, J. G. V. (1974 [1784-1791]) *Ideen zur Philosophie der Geschichte der Menschheit,* Stuttgart, Union Dt. Verl.-Ges.

HOFSTEDE, G. (1980) *Culture's Consequences: International Differences in Work-Related Values,* Beverly Hills, CA., Sage.

HOUSE, J. (2000) Understanding Misunderstanding: A Pragmatic-Discourse Approach to Analysing Mismanaged Rapport in Talk Across Cultures. IN SPENCER-OATEY, H. (Ed.) *Culturally Speaking. Managing Rapport through Talk Across Cultures.* (145-164), London/New York, Continuum.

HOUSE, R. J., HANGES, P. J., JAVIDAN, M., DORFMAN, P. W. & GUPTA, V. (Eds.) (2004) *Culture, Leadership, and Organizations. The GLOBE Study of 62 Societies,* Thousand Oaks, London, New Delhi, Sage.

HUMBOLDT, W. V. (1995 [1836]) *Über die Verschiedenheit des menschlichen Sprachbaues und ihren Einfluß auf die geistige Entwickelung des Menschengeschlechts. (Reprint [der Ausg.] Berlin, Dümmler, 1836 und 1852),* London, Routledge/ Thoemmes Press.

JACOBS, S. (2002) Maintaining neutrality in dispute mediation: managing disagreement while managing not to disagree. *Journal of Pragmatics,* 34(10-11), 1403-1426.

KAGAN, S., KNIGHT, G. P. & MARTINEZ-ROMERO, S. (1982) Culture and the development of conflict resolution style. *Journal of Cross-Cultural Psychology,* 13(1), 43-58.

KATZ, D. & BRALY, K. W. (1933) Racial stereotypes of one hundred college students. *Journal of Abnormal and Social Psychology,* 28, 280-290.

KERBRAT-ORECCHIONI, C. (2004) Introducing polylogue. *Journal of Pragmatics,* 36, 1-24.

KIM, M.-S. (2007) The Four Cultures of Cultural Research. *Communication Monographs,* 74(2), 279—285.

KLUCKHOHN, F. R. & STRODTBECK, F. L. (1961) *Variations in Value Orientations,* Evanston, Ill, Row, Peterson and Company.

KNAPP, K. (1998) *Intercultural communication in EESE. EESE strategy paper No. 4,* Erfurt, http://www.uni-erfurt.de/eestudies/eese/strategy/knapp/4_st.html [last accessed: 01.08. 2009].

KNOBLAUCH, H. (2001) Communication, context and culture. A communicative constructivist approach to intercultural communication. IN DI LUZIO, A., GÜNTHNER, S. & ORLETTI, F. (Eds.) *Culture in Communication. Analyses of Intercultural Situations.* (3-33), Amsterdam/ Philadelphia, Benjamins.

KOOLE, A. J. & TEN THIJE, J. D. (1994) *The Construction of Intercultural Discourse. Team Discussions of Educational Advisers,* Amsterdam/Atlanta, Rodopi.

KRESSEL, K. & PRUITT, D. G. (1985) Themes in the mediation of social conflict. *Journal of Social Issues,* 41(2), 179-198.

KRESSEL, K. & PRUITT, D. G. (1989a) Conclusion: A research perspective on the mediation of social conflict. IN KRESSEL, K. & PRUITT, D. G. (Eds.) *Mediation Research: The Process and Effectiveness of Third-Party Intervention.* (394-435), San Francisco, CA, Jossey Bass.

KRESSEL, K. & PRUITT, D. G. (Eds.) (1989b) *Mediation Research: The Process and Effectiveness of Third-Party Intervention,* San Francisco, CA, Jossey Bass.

KUHN, T. & POOLE, M. S. (2000) Do Conflict Management Styles Affect Group Decision Making? Evidence From a Longitudinal Field Study. *Human Communication Research,* 26(4), 558-590.

KUMAR, R. (1989) Affect, cognition, and decision making in negotiation: A conceptual integration. IN RAHIM, A. M. (Ed.) *Managing Conflict: An Interdisciplinary Approach.* (185-194), New York, Praeger.

LEBARON, M. (1998) Mediation and multicultural reality. *Peace and Conflict Studies,* 5(1), http://www.gmu.edu/academic/pcs/lebaron.htm [last accessed 01-08-2009].

LEDERACH, J. (1995) *Preparing for Peace. Conflict Transformation Across Cultures,* Syracuse, Syracuse University Press.

LEDERACH, J. (1997) *Building Peace. Sustainable Reconciliation in Divided Societies,* Washington, United States Institutes of Peace Press.

LEHTONEN, J. (1994) National attitudes as a self-protection strategy. IN MARSH, D. & SALO-LEE, L. (Eds.) *Europe on the Move. Fusion or Fission? Proceedings of the 1994 SIETAR Europa Symposium.* (100-105), Jyväskylä, University of Jyväskylä.

LÉVI-STRAUSS, C. (1987 [1952]) *Race et histoire,* Paris, Gallimard.

LIPPMANN, W. (1922) *Public Opinion,* New York, Macmillan.

MAE, M. (2003) Transkulturalität und interkulturelle Kompetenz. *Erwägen—Wissen—Ethik. Themenheft "Interkulturelle Kompetenz—Grundlagen, Probleme und Konzepte",* Dritte Diskussionseinheit, Heft 1 (2003), 194-196.

MALINOWSKI, B. (1922) *Argonauts of the Western Pacific,* London,, G. Routledge & Sons.

MALL, R. A. (2000) *Intercultural philosophy,* Lanham, Md., Rowman & Littlefield.

MAYER, C.-H. (2005) Interkulturelle Mediation im Spannungsfeld westlicher und afrikanischer Perspektiven. IN BUSCH, D. & SCHRÖDER, H. (Eds.) *Perspektiven interkultureller Mediation. Grundlagentexte zur kommunikationswissenschaftlichen Analyse triadischer Verständigung.* 1. Aufl. ed. (245-266), Frankfurt am Main, Peter Lang.

MERRY, S. E. (1987a) Cultural frameworks of mediation. *PCR Occasional Paper Series: Cultural Aspects of Disputing,* 1987-02, 1-23.

MERRY, S. E. (1987b) Disputing without culture. *Harvard Law Review,* 100, 1057-2073.

MERRY, S. E. (1989) Mediation in nonindustrial societies. IN KRESSEL, K. & PRUITT, D. G. (Eds.) *Mediation Research: The Process and Effectiveness of Third-Party Intervention.* (68-90), San Francisco, CA, Jossey Bass.

MERRY, S. E. (1992) Anthropology, law, and transnational processes. *Annual Review of Anthropology,* 21(1), 357-379.

MOORE, R. & SANDERS, A. (1996) The limits of an anthropology of conflict: Loyalist and republican paramilitary organizations in Northern Ireland. IN WOLFE, A. W. & YANG, H. (Eds.) *Anthropological Contributions to Conflict Resolution.* (131-142), Athens/London, The University of Georgia Press.

MOOSMÜLLER, A. (2004) Das Kulturkonzept in der interkulturellen Kommunikation aus ethnologischer Sicht. IN LÜSEBRINK, H.-J. (Ed.) *Konzepte der Interkulturellen Kommunikation. Theorieansätze und Praxisbezüge in interdisziplinärer Perspektive.* (45-67), St. Ingbert, Röhrig Universitätsverlag.

MÜLLER-JACQUIER, B. & TEN THIJE, J. D. (2000) Interkulturelle Kommunikation: interkulturelles Training und Mediation. IN BECKER-MROTZEK, M., BRÜNNER, G. & CÖLFEN, H. (Eds.) *Linguistische Berufe. Ein Ratgeber zu aktuellen linguistischen Berufsfeldern.* (39-59), Frankfurt am Main, Peter Lang.

NADER, L. (Ed.) (1997) *Law in Culture and Society,* Berkeley, University of California Press.
OETZEL, J. G. & TING-TOOMEY, S. (2003) Face concerns in interpersonal conflict: A cross-cultural empirical test of the face negotiation. *Communication Research,* 30(6), 599-624.
OGAWA, N. (1999) The concept of facework: Its functions in the Hawaii model of mediation. *Mediation Quarterly,* 17(1), 5-20.
PIKE, K. L. (1975) On kinesic triadic relations in turn-taking. *Semiotica,* 13(4), 389-394.
PUFENDORF, S. (1684) *De iure naturae et gentium libri octo,* Frankfurt am Main.
PÜTZ, R. (2004) *Transkulturalität als Praxis. Unternehmer türkischer Herkunft in Berlin,* Bielefeld, transcript.
RAHIM, A. M. (Ed.) (1989) *Managing Conflict. An Interdisciplinary Approach,* Westport, Connecticut/London, Praeger.
RIFKIN, J., MILLEN, J. & COBB, S. (1991) Toward a new discourse for mediation: A critique of neutrality. *Mediation Quarterly,* 9(2), 151-164.
ROBERTS CALLISTER, R. & WALL, J. A. J. (2004) Thai and U.S. community mediation. *Journal of Conflict Resolution,* 48(4), 573-598.
ROSS, M. H. (1993) *The Culture of Conflict,* New Haven, Yale University Press.
SAUSSURE, F. D. ([2001] 1916) *Grundfragen der allgemeinen Sprachwissenschaft. (Cours de linguistique générale). Hrsg. v. Charles Bally und Albert Sechehaye. Übers. von Alfred Lommel,* Berlin/New York, de Gruyter.
SCHONDELMAYER, S. (2008) *Stereotypisierung am Arbeitsplatz. Zur Handlungsrelevanz von Selbst- und Fremdbildern in der deutsch-polnischen Interaktion,* Münster, Waxmann.
SCHÜTZ, A. (1967) *The Phenomenology of the Social World,* [Evanston, Ill.], Northwestern University Press.
SCHÜTZ, A. & LUCKMANN, T. (1973) *The structures of the life-world,* Evanston [Ill.], Northwestern University Press.
SHEPPARD, B. H., BLUMENFELD-JONES, K. & ROTH, J. (1989) Informal thirdpartyship: Studies of everyday conflict intervention. IN KRESSEL, K. & PRUITT, D. G. (Eds.) *Mediation Research: The Process and Effectiveness of Third-Party Intervention.* (166-189), San Francisco, CA, Jossey Bass.
SILBEY, S. S. (1992) Making a place for cultural analyses of law. *Law and Social Inquiry,* 17(1), 39-48.
SILBEY, S. S. & MERRY, S. E. (1986) Mediator settlement strategies. *Law & Policy,* 8(1), 7-32.
SPENCER-OATEY, H. (2002) Managing rapport in talk: Using rapport sensitive incidents to explore the motivational concerns underlying the management of relations. *Journal of Pragmatics,* 34, 529-545.
STOLCKE, V. (1995) Talking culture. New boundaries, new rhetorics of exclusion in Europe. *Current Anthropology,* 36(1), 1-24.
SWIDLER, A. (1986) Culture in action: Symbols and strategies. *American Sociological Review,* 51, 273-286.
SWIDLER, A. (2001) *Talk of Love. How Culture Matters,* Chicago, University of Chicago Press.
TAJFEL, H. (1981) *Human Groups and Social Categories. Studies in Social Psychology,* Cambridge, Cambridge University Press.
TING-TOOMEY, S. (1985) Toward a theory of conflict and culture. IN GUDYKUNST, W., STEWART, L. & TING-TOOMEY, S. (Eds.) *Communication, Culture and Organizational Processes.* (71-86), Beverly Hills, C.A., Sage.

TING-TOOMEY, S. (1988) Intercultural conflict styles: A face-negotiation theory. IN KIM, Y. & GUDYKUNST, W. (Eds.) *Theories in Intercultural Communication.* (213-235), Newbury Park, CA, Sage.

TRIANDIS, H. C. (1972) *The Analysis of Subjective Culture,* New York, London, Sidney, Toronto, Wiley-Interscience.

TRIANDIS, H. C. (2000) Culture and conflict. *International Journal of Psychology,* 35(2), 145-152.

TRIANDIS, H. C. (2002) Generic individualism and collectivism. IN GANNON, M. J. & NEWMAN, K. L. (Eds.) *The Blackwell Handbook of Cross-Cultural Management.* (16-45), Oxford, UK, Backwell.

TRIBAL COMMUNITY BOARDS PROJECT (1986) *Program Planning for Tribal Conciliation Systems,* San Francisco, Tribal Community Boards Project of the Northwest Intertribal Court System and Community Board Center for Policy and Training.

TROMPENAARS, F. (1993) *Riding the Waves of Culture. Understanding Cultural Diversity in Business,* London, Economist Books.

TROMPENAARS, F. (1996) Resolving international conflict: Culture and business strategy. *Business Strategy Review,* 7(3), 51-68.

VAN DIJK, T. A. (1987) *Communicating Racism: Ethnic Prejudice in Thought and Talk,* Newbury Park, CA, Sage.

WATSON-GEGEO, K. A. & WHITE, G. M. (Eds.) (1990) *Disentangling. Conflict Discourse in Pacific Societies,* Stanford, CA, Stanford University Press.

WELSCH, W. (2000) Transkulturalität. Zwischen Globalisierung und Partikularisierung. *Jahrbuch Deutsch als Fremdsprache,* 26, 327-351.

WHORF, B. L. (1936 [1956]) An American Indian model of the universe. IN CARROLL, J. B. (Ed.) *Language, Thought, and Reality. Selected Writings of Benjamin Lee Whorf.* (57-64), Boston, M.I.T. Press.

ZURN, C. (2000) Anthropology and normativity: A critique of Axel Honneth's 'formal conception of ethical life'. *Philosophy & Social Criticism,* 26(1), 115-124.

Usuluhishi. Terms and Concepts of Intercultural Mediation and Conflict Management from Tanzanian Perspectives

Claude-Hélène Mayer, Christian Martin Boness, Samuel Togolai Kussaga

Introduction

During the past decade, the interdisciplinary interest in theoretical approaches to intercultural mediation has increased (Busch and Schröder, 2006, Liebe and Gilbert, 1996, Mayer, 2005, 2006) without reaching a common definition on the topic of intercultural mediation (Augsburger, 1992, Myers and Filner, 1994, Mayer, 2008).

However, mediation can be viewed as the creative act of re-constructing conflict realities through third party intervention (Mayer, 2008a) and might be defined as a situation where one or two individuals or a group would take a third party in to provide support in communicating with each other between the parties (Mayer and Boness, 2004: 49).

In Sub-Saharan Africa, intercultural mediation and conflict management have grown in significance during the past decades. The contexts in which intercultural mediation has taken place are diverse: mediation across cultures has gained importance in the political arena in Sub-Saharan Africa (Algard, 2005, Purdecova, 2008), in international organizations (Mayer, 2008), in medical contexts between doctors and patients (Carlson 1990), in religious and spiritual contexts, such as mediations between individuals and ancestors and individuals who are possessed by spirits (Carlson, 1990: 297), in ethnic conflicts, such as in Kenya (Ajulu, 2002), or in school contexts (Boness, 2002), as well as in family interactions, such as joking relationships (Davidheiser, 2005).

In Tanzania, mediation—as a form of third-party-intervention—has traditionally played an important role in different contexts of society (Boness, 2002). However, also Western mediation influences have reached Tanzania and therefore Western and African forms of mediation and their combination have gained even more interest in different societal and juridical contexts during the past years.

Most of the recent literature on intercultural mediation in Sub-Saharan African and also in Tanzanian contexts has been written and published by non-African researchers (e.g. Davidheiser, 2005, Mayer, 2005 etc.) and tries to understand the emic perspectives. This article, also particularly focuses on an emic perspective of Tanzanian interviewees from different social contexts, such as school, churches, hotels and Ministries, on intercultural mediation and conflict management to improve the understanding of mediation in different socio-cultural contexts in the selected society.

The purpose of this article is to contribute to the intercultural discourse on concepts of intercultural mediation and conflict management through African eyes. Therefore, it presents approaches to terms and concepts of intercultural mediation and conflict management of selected Tanzanian interviewees from four selected organizational contexts.

The main aim of this article is to understand terms and concepts associated with conflict management and intercultural mediation from the emic perspective of Tanzanian interviewees.

To achieve the aims of the article, the following research questions will be answered:

- How do the interviewees define the terms 'conflict', 'conflict resolution', 'reconciliation', and 'mediation'?
- What kind of conflicts occur in the selected organisations
- How do the interviewees understand intercultural mediation?

The article contributes towards an in-depth understanding of intercultural mediation and conflict management processes in selected contexts in Tanzanian society. Therefore, it is necessary to explore the basic terms and concepts of conflict, conflict resolution, reconciliation and mediation from an emic perspective, to afterwards refer to the question of what kind of conflicts occur in the selected contexts. This leads the question of how interviewees define and understand intercultural mediation.

In the following order, this article presents a short overview of the literature on mediation in the Tanzanian context. Swahili (linguistic) terms and concepts of intercultural mediation and conflict management are presented and defined from a Tanzanian perspective. It then describes the research design and research findings according to the research questions stated above. Research findings will be discussed and a conclusion will be introduced. Finally, this will lead towards recommendations for future research on intercultural mediation and conflict management in the Tanzanian context.

Intercultural mediation in Tanzanian contexts

In intercultural situations, conflicts and value concepts are often managed through cross-cultural mediation. It is common sense, however, that particularly in cross-cultural mediation, culture-specific value-orientations are discussed. Cross-cultural mediation is the creative act of re-constructing conflict realities and values through third party intervention (Mayer 2008b). Intercultural mediation is defined as 'a situation where one or two individuals or a group would take a third party in to mediate between the parties' (see Mayer, 2005, Mayer and Boness, 2004). Müller-Jacquier (2002: 1) defines intercultural mediation as "a special, usually voluntary, discussion and consensual decision-making process in which one or more impartial persons—the mediator(s)—assist people, organizations, and communities in conflict to work toward a variety of goals. Parties in the mediation process are encouraged to:

- improve communication processes, understanding culture specific interaction rules, values, conflict resolution strategies and symbols;
- improve relationships and empathy;
- use mediation rules to minimize, avoid or enhance involvement in the legal/judicial system;
- work toward mutual understanding to resolve a problem or dispute in order to finally
- reach their own decisions, resolve underlying conflicts, and prevent problems from recurring."

The existing literature on intercultural mediation in Tanzanian contexts is quite limited. This exploratory case study begins to fill the void of reseach on intercultural mediation in Tanzania with regard to inter-personal relationships and thereby contribute to the intercultural debate on terms and concepts used in and about mediation in non-Western societies and different societal contexts. Only recently, the Tanzanian government published a handbook on mediation (Jamhuri, 2007) regarding mediation in labour conflicts with regard to the law on employment and relationships at work (*sheria ya ajira na mahusiano kazini*, 2004 in Jamhuri, 2007: 1). This law with regard to mediation was passed by the parliament (*Ubunge*) in 2004 and was implemented in Tanzania in 2007. On the basis of this law a lot of decrees were published by the Government. The publication comprises five decrees of which decrees number 66 and 67 of March 2007 deal with mediation and arbitration. Several ways to manage grievances (*malalamiko*) are presented (Jamhuri 2007: 83). If grievances can not be solved informally the manager of an enterprise is supposed to resolve them formally in a meeting where three types of conflict resolution are discussed:

- facilitation (*uwezeshaji*);
- mediation (usuluhishi); and
- arbitration (*uamuzi*).

In case where these types of resolution do not work successfully the above mentioned law on employment and relationships at work comes into action. The handbook of mediation (Jamhuri, 2007) is published in Swahili to empower workers and employees who are not familiar with English, which is the official language in Tanzania for legal texts.

Danish mediation systems have been analysed by Tanzanian experts and have now been implemented into the Tanzanian labour law to build the basis of official labour mediation in Tanzania. At the same time, South African concepts have been analysed and implemented by Tanzanian officials, as indicated by interviewees of this study and as referred to in Jamhuri (2007). Since the Danish legal system is said to be one of the best in the world and since South Africa's transformation from Apartheid to Post-Apartheid has been supported successfully by mediation, these two countries have been chosen as ideals for Tanzanian experts (as indicated in informal interviews in the Ministry of Labour, March 2009). The background to why mediation has been implemented in Tanzania by the government is based on the fact that labour court processes often take years until they come to a resolution. In contrast, mediation processes are limited to a maximum of 30 days of mediation and revision. If a conflict can not be settled through mediators within a period of 30 days, the case is forwarded to the arbitration section and will be resolved through arbitration procedures.

Research design

This case study is based on the post-modernist premise that no one true reality exists and that there is no absolute truth (Becvar and Becvar, 2006). It asserts that human beings inhabit different realities that are socially constituted and which may, therefore, vary quite dramatically across cultures, time and context (Gonzalez et al., 1994); and that multiple selves are socially constructed in the context of increasingly varied and constantly changing relationships (Becvar and Becvar, 2006). In this article, aspects of Tanzanian perspectives of intercultural mediation and conflict management are presented, analysed and discussed.

Research approach

Given the qualitative nature of this research, phenomenological and interpretative paradigms were considered the most relevant approaches (Collis and Hussey, 2003) thereto. Within these paradigms, the theoretical and methodological approaches used are founded on both the epistemological tradition of constructivism (Berger and Luckmann, 2000) and interpretative hermeneutics (Gadamer, 1990, Habermas, 1999). Various theoretical stances reflect a post-modern epistemology and can be grouped around terms such as constructivism or social constructivism, which share the notion of multiple realities.[1]

1 Here, constructivism is used as an umbrella term for both constructivism and social constructivism (McLeod, 1996) and is generally defined as postulating the objective world as a

Research method

While quantitative research is often based on analytical empiricism with a strong emphasis on objectivity, qualitative research focuses on exploring a research issue and gaining a deeper understanding of the research issue (Cheldelin et al., 2003), deep data and "thick description" (Geertz, 1987). In order to gain an understanding of the above-mentioned topics, an exploratory study approach was used. This approach was used to assess terms and concepts of intercultural mediation and conflict management in the Tanzanian context. Four contexts and organizations were chosen to be explored with regard to intercultural mediation, as shown in Table 1.

Tertiary sector	Organisations	Number of interviewees
Governmental	educational organisations	5
	governmental executive organisations	4
Non-governmenal	Ecclesiastical organisations	4
	private enterprises	5

Table 1: Interviews in organisations (source: authors' own construction).

An in-depth understanding regarding the above described topics and research questions was achieved making use of in-depth interviews. The interviews were guided by using predetermined research questions, which focused on the subjective experiences of interviewees. Thereafter, useful explanations were developed and interpretations of the described subject were given according to four levels of text reconstruction (Ricoeur, 1979, Wolff, 2000: 87), which are explained in the section on data analysis. The findings cannot be generalized, but they give an explorative in-depth insight into the described Tanzanian contexts and might be replicated in other African countries or in different contexts in Tanzania. Based on this exploratory study, a folllow-up research based on qualitative and quantitative research methods is planned.

The research method used in this case study approach is explained in the following by considering the research participants, measuring instrument, research procedure and data analysis.

---

construct of social interaction or, alternatively, as a process of the observed and the observer, the last giving meaning to what is observed (Jonassen, 1991). Constructivism, therefore, implies that all stories or interpretations are equally valid and that no single truth or interpretation exists (Dickerson & Zimmerman, 1996).

Research setting

The research was aiming at studying experiences of conflict and intercultural mediation in different societal organizations in the Tanzanian society. Therefore, governmental and non-governmental organizations were chosen as contexts in which to study the described phenomenon. The organizations in which intercultural mediation occurs were chosen based on the results of an earlier study that was conducted in Tanzania (Boness, 2002). One finding of this earlier study is that intercultural mediation is conducted in educational and ecclesiastical settings. This current study is to gain in-depth insight into the educational and ecclesiastical contexts and gain deeper insight into governmental organizations and private enterprises with regards to conflict and intercultural mediation to explore the issues from different social perspectives.

The selection of the organisations was based on the following criteria:

- importance of these societal contexts and organisations for the Tanzanian society and Tanzanian citizens with regard to intercultural mediation and conflict management,
- organisational structures in urban Tanzanian contexts,
- permissible access to the organizations chosen,
- representability of organisations in Tanzanian society.

With regard to this setting, the sample was chosen, as described below.

Sample

Data were gathered by means of in-depth individual and group interviews, in accordance with the interviewees involved and their preferences, from a sample of 18 persons selected by the authors by random sample, where every member of the population, who is involved in mediation processes within the organizations, stands a chance of being chosen for the sample. The interviews were conducted by a research team, consisting of the authors of this article.

Altogether 18 interviewees from three different urban centres—Arusha, Moshi and Dar-es-Salaam—working in the tertiary sector in Tanzania were interviewed. The sample comprised twelve male and 6 female interviewees. All interviewees are Tanzanian citizens of different ethnic backgrounds. The sample was recruited from governmental (educational, governmental executive) and non-governmental organizations (ecclesiastical organizations and private enterprises).

Within the governmental organizations, there are 5 persons from the educational (2 teachers, 3 heads of school) and 4 from the administration context (2 managing directors, 1 principal, 1 president). Looking at the non-governmental organizations, there are 4 persons from ecclesiastical (1 reverend, 1 chaplain, 1 director, 1 executive secretary) and 5 from hotel contexts (1 employee, 4 managing directors).

Data collection methods

Data were collected by using focus interviews. An interview structure was developed containing ten questions to explore the issues of this study. Ten interview questions were asked, referring to intercultural mediation and conflict management experienced in selected contexts. In parallel to the interviews, organizational documents and secondary literature were also analysed to guarantee triangulation of the data.

The focus interviews were recorded in full to ensure precise transcription. The transcripts were viewed as selective constructions that reproduced aspects of the conversation and which were transcribed, according to Von Steinke (2000: 327), in a "manageable" way which is "simple to write, easy to read, easy to learn and to interpret". The transcription procedure focused mainly on the verbal aspects of the communication in the interest of analysis and evaluation. Analytical data evaluation was included (as described in Data analysis, Level 4), subsequent to the texts being transcribed.

Four major concepts—conformability, credibility, transferability, and trustworthiness—were defined as criteria for judging this qualitative research. Johnson (1997) supports the approach that constructivism may facilitate the aim of qualitative research—which is fundamental to this research—to create a deeper understanding of the research objective with regard to changing multiple-reality constructions (Hipps, 1993).

Data analysis

After the data gathering procedure data were analysed according to four levels of text reconstruction (Ricoeur, 1979, Wolff, 2000: 87):

- Level 1: The interviewee perceives and experiences intercultural mediation and conflict management aspects in daily life situations.
- Level 2: The interviewee narrates his/her experiences during the interview.
- Level 3: The researcher transcribes the interview and categorises this transcribed text through content and key word analyses.
- Level 4: The researcher interprets the categorised text through content analysis (Mayring, 2003). Key terms are defined as words that occupy key positions in text through the import of their content, their significance in the text structure and conception or repetition or other emphasis. This culminates in the construction of categories.

Data analysis was conducted according to the five-step process of Terre Blanche, Durrheim and Kelly (2006: 322-326): Step 1: Familiarisation and immersion, Step

2: Inducing themes, Step 3: Coding, Step 4: Elaboration and Step 5: Interpretation and checking, to ensure a transparent process of data analysis and reconstruction. However, Terre Blance *et al.* admit that "in reality, interpretative analysis rarely proceeds in as orderly a manner as may be suggested by [their] step-wise presentation (Terre Blanche et al., 2006: 322-326). Following these steps in data analysis enhances the "thick description" (Geertz, 1973).

Content analysis comprises a subjective process between the text and the person coding the text: "Verifying the reliability of content analysis is primarily done by inter-individual and intra-individual verification" (Yin, 2002: 45), as in this explorative study. Objectivity in analysis should, therefore, be guided by inter-subjective validation, such as adhering to particular rules and regulations and/or verifying that the same (or similar) findings have been attained by different researchers. In this study, the coding of the text and its analysis and re-categorisation are considered this way.

Research findings

The research findings presented focus on the perspective of Tanzanian interviewees from the tertiary sector with regard to terms and definitions of conflict, conflict resolution, reconciliation and intercultural mediation in the selected governmental and non-governmental organisations as described above.

Terms in Swahili and English

With regard to the first research question on how interviewees define the terms of conflict, conflict resolution, reconciliation and intercultural mediation, the interviewees were asked what the English terms of conflict, conflict resolution, reconciliation and intercultural mediation mean in Kiswahili. In the following, this article presents how each of the words can be translated with regard to a selected English–Swahili Dictionary (Johnson, 1978) and referring to the statements of the interviewees:

- "Conflict" is equivalent to "*mapigano*": hitting each other and "*vita*": war (Johnson, 1995: 108). However, in most cases the interviewees translate "conflict" as "*migogoro*": obstacle, obstruction, difficulty, nuisance (Johnson, 1978: 277) or "*kutoelewana*": lack of mutual understanding (Johnson, 1978: 81), "*matatizo*": entanglement, complication, difficulty (Johnson 1978: 456) and lack of "*maridhiano*": lack of satisfaction (Johnson, 1978: 393). The official translation for "conflict" in publications by the Tanzanian Government is "*mgogoro*": obstacle, difficulty. Referring to these different translations, it can be assumed that the direct translation of "conflict" according to the dictionary is not usually used by the interviewees, because it alludes to "hot conflicts", like "hitting one another" or "making war". These expressions seem to be too strong for the interviewees and by avoiding these strong terms, the interviewees indicated in the interviewes that they prefer to use less strong words to "minimize the conflict": obstacle, difficulty and entanglement. For Suaheli speakers, the pronouncement of negatively connoted words might cause and provoke the occurrence of an incident through the "magic of the word" (Mbiti, 1991).

- Conflict resolution resembles according to the interviewees the Swahili words of "*kutatua*": disentangle, cut a knot, solve a difficulty (Johnson, 1978: 456) and "*kusuluhisha*": cause to agree, to reconcile (Johnson, 1978: 440), followed by words, such as "*mwafaka*": agreement, bargain, pact (Johnson, 1978: 4), "*makubaliano*": be on good terms (Johnson 1978: 225) and "*patanisho*": reconciliation, peace (Johnson, 1978: 369).
- Conflict resolution is understood as "*tatua tatizo*": to solve a difficulty (Johnson, 1978:456), "*suluhisha*": cause to agree (Johnson, 1978:440), and "*patanisha*": to reconcile (Johnson, 1978:369). The concept of conflict resolution is translated by the interviewees as being proximate to the real process of resolution. Swahili speakers seem to prefer to use positive denotatives with regard to conflict resolution and avoid special apotropeic expressions, as shown in the conflict-translation examples above.
- Reconciliation in Swahili is translated as "*kupatanisha*": reconcile (Johnson, 1978: 369) and "*kusuluhisha*": cause to agree (Johnson 1978: 440), "*kuunganisha*": cause to join each other (Johnson, 1978: 501), "*kubaliana*": be on good terms with one another (Johnson 1978: 225), and "*kuelewana*": mutual understanding (Johnson 1978: 81). The meaning of "*reconciliation*" in Swahili is translated as: making an agreement, cause to join each other and be on good terms with one another. All equivalent words in Swahili contain the grammatically relevant "reciprocal aspect" of reconciliation. Additionally, "*kuunganisha*" and "*kusuluhisha*" bear the morpheme –isha, the causative suffix meaning that a facilitating person is included in the interaction of the conflicting parties.
- The word intercultural is translated as "*uingiliano*": mutual entry/penetration with purpose (Johnson, 1978: 142) "*wa makabila*": of the tribes, "*utamaduni*": refinement, civilization (Johnson 1978: 448), "*mila*" (Johnson 1978: 280) "*na desturi*" (Johnson 1978: 72): customs and regular practice. The term intercultural is understood as an active, interwoven "penetration of tribes", "tradition and customs". There is no direct translation of the word and concept "intercultural" available in Swahili language. Referring to the term and concept of "culture", it is used in Swahili as follows:

- *Ukulima*: culture of agriculture;
- *Malezi*: culture of education;
- *Elimu*: culture of daily behavior including the concept of "*adabu*": politeness and "*ustaarabu*": civilized behaviour (Johnson, 1995: 129).

The concept of culture is connected to the "culture of agriculture", the "culture of education" and the "behavioural culture". The concept of "ethnic culture" is not explicitly mentioned. However, the concept of "*ustaarabu*" ("being civilized") seems to be closely connected to the "culture of education" and the "culture of behaviour". This concept is mainly important in the Arabic tradition in Tanzania—as the Arabic-Swahili term shows. The Swahili language has highly been influenced by Arabic which is particularly important on the Tanzanian coastal strip and the islands of Zanzibar, Pemba and Mafia which are dominantly influenced by Arabic cultures (for more contextual information on the Tanzanian society see Boness 2002).

- Mediation is translated to either "*upatanishi*": agreement, arrangement or "*usuluhishi*": reconciliation, as well as to "*urekebishaji*": put together, assemble (Johnson, 1978: 395), "*ukalimani*": interpretation, translation into and from another tongue (Johnson, 1978: 168), "*unganisha mawasiliano kwa njia ya mtu wa kati*": connecting the communication by a third party and the term "*maelewano*": mutual understanding.

Linguistically, mediation is connected to the terms and concepts of agreement, arrangement, reconciliation and interpretation by a person who is positioned in between the conflicting parties. Recently, the concept of mediation received official recognition from the government (see above) and is defined as "usuluhishi"—reconciliation (Jamhuri, 2007). This official Tanzanian concept refers to and is compatible with the ruling conflict management commissions in South Africa, where the Truth and Reconciliation Commission was responsible to listen to individuals and groups narrating their experiences from Apartheid regarding political or racial conflict of the former South African Apartheid regime.

Terms in English	Terms in Swahili
Conflict	migogoro—obstacles (7)[2] kutoelewana—lack of understanding (7) matatizo—entanglement (4) maridhiano—lack of satisfaction (2)
Conflict resolution	kutatua—disentangle (6) kusuluhisha—cause to agree (4), mwafaka—bargain (1), makubaliano—be in good terms (1), patanisho—reconciliation (1),
Reconciliation	kupatanisha—to reconcile (3) kusuluhisha—cause to agree (1), kuunganisha—cause to join each other (1), kubaliana—be in good terms (1), kuelewana—understand each other (1),
Intercultural	to uingiliano wa makabila- mutual penetration of tribes (1), utamaduni—civilisation (1), mila na desturi—customs and regular (1)
Mediation	upatanishi—reconciliation (6), usuluhishi—cause to agree (2), urekebishaji—put together, assemble (1), ukalimani—translation, interpretation (1), unganisha mawasiliano kwa njia ya mtu wa kati—connect the communication through a person who stands in between (1), maelewano- mutual understanding (1), usuluhishi- agreement (1)

Table 2: Terms in Swahili and English translations. Source: authors' own construction.

Referring to the use of verbs and nouns used to describe conflict, conflict resolution, reconciliation and intercultural mediation, the following is obvious: most of

2 The number behind the Swahili terms indicates the frequency with which the terms have been mentioned by the Tanzanian interviewees.

the Swahili translations include derivative verbs with formative suffixes. The "reciprocal aspect" (Ashton, 1989: 214) attracts suffix "-na". This suffix means "mutual", "one another" (Wilson, 1994: 194) or "associative" in English translation. This phenomen shows that the inter-relationship of individuals or groups involved in conflict and its resolution and mediation practices needs to be understood and interpreted in the context of human relationships, interaction and interdependence (Ashton, 1989: 240), as is visible in the words *kutoelewana*, *maridhiano*, *makubaliano* and *upatanisho*.

After the consideration of the relevant terms the second research question about what kinds of conflict occur in the selected organizations will be answered.

Conflicts in the selected organisations

In the following section, the research question about what kinds of conflicts occur in the selected organization will be addressed.

In total, 40 conflicts were narrated by 18 interviewees. These conflicts were narrated relating to the different organizational contexts of:

- Educational organizations (10 narrations)
- Governmental excecutives (nine narrations)
- Ecclesiastical organisations (six narrations)
- Private enterprises (15 narrations)

The interviewees from the Ministry of Labor and the Ministry of Education and Culture narrated four conflicts. They experience conflicts regarding salaries and benefits, crime with regard to responsibilities and "forged signatures" and labour contracts. In all these conflicts, mediation was used to resolve the conflict. However, the interviewees mention explicitly that the conflicts are not intercultural conflicts. They define these conflicts as pure work or labour-related conflicts without any cultural or ethnic background. The interviewees from the Ministry of Education and Culture deal with conflicts related to personal resources, such as shortage of teachers in particular areas in Tanzania, as well as education, for example how students should be taught in different subjects or how teachers should be trained. Due to cultural diversity and differences in religious behaviour and customs in the country, they also deal with aspects of religion, which sometimes cause conflict particularly with regard to religious belief. Finally, conflicts occur which are based on international relations and cooperations in educational contexts, which include a high conflict potential with regard to organizing international school partnerships and establishing contacts with teachers and students from other countries.

Organisation	Field of conflict	Topic of conflict
Ministry of Labor	payment	claims on benefits and salaries (i7)[3]
	crime	forged signature (i12.1)
	law	cartoonist's contract, (i12.2)
Ministry of Education	personal resources	shortage of teachers, (i13.3)
		no educational questions, (i13.2)
	culture diversity	hijab covering, (i11.1)
	international relations	school partnership with Finland, (i11.2)

Table 3: Governmental executives. Source: authors' own construction

The interviewees from ecclesiastical organisations narrate intercultural conflicts regarding Christian family ethics. These conflicts focus on the question of polygyny and marrying two wives as well as concerns about infertility in marriages and the consequences thereof.

Other conflictual issues deal with employment, highlighting aspects of nepotism and dismissal due to misconduct. Finally, there are conflicts in ecclesiastical contexts regarding the structure of organizations: one conflict is about the fight of two church groups and their differences in faith about God's truth. The other conflict is about a dioceses which falls apart.

Organisation	Field of conflict	Topic of conflict
Ecclesiastical organisations	Christian family life	marrying two wives, (i8.1)
		couple without child, (i8.2)
		nepotism, (i15.1)
	employment	dismissal due to misconduct, (i15.2)
	organization structure	revival group versus established church, (i3)
		Pare diocesan conflict (i6)

Table 4: Ecclesiastical organizations. Source: authors' own construction.

3 i7 indicates, e.g. interview number 7, i12.1, for example, refers to interview number 12, conflict narration 1. The interview number is indicated behind the conflict topics to guarantee transparance.

The interviewees working in private enterprises in Tanzania experience specific conflicts in intercultural interactions. These are based on service delivery, financial issues, external impacts, such as electricity shortcuts or overbookings, as well as crime.

Four out of ten conflicts refer to service issues, mainly grievances and complaints from clients who were described as "international tourists". Three conflicts are connected to the field of finances e.g. membership fees, rates and private training. Two conflicts are based on external impacts, which are, for example, electricity shortcuts caused by the national electricity supplier and a tourist company in Moshi, which overbooked travel packages for Kilimandjaro tours. Finally, crime is narrated with regard to theft of passport and personal belongings in a hotel.

Organisation	Field of conflict	Topic of conflict
Private enterprises	service	service delivery in hotel, (i1.1) impatience of service, (i4.3) dissatisfaction with service, (i14.2) dissatisfaction with standard, (i14.1)
	finances	rates, (i2.2) membership fees, (i4.2) private trainings, (i4.4)
	external impact	shortcut, (i9.1) Kilimanjaro overbooked, (i9.2)
	possession	theft of passport, (i2.1)

Table 5: Private enterprises. Source: authors' own construction

Interviewees from educational organizations narrate conflict on territory, diversity and education and socialization. One interviewee from educational organizations narrates a conflict that is connected to territory and the use of a governmental school compound: a group of Maasai has occupied a piece of land of a governmental college to use it for religious purposes. Four conflict narrations focus on cultural diversity. Two conflicts deal with the outer appearance of students, particularly with religious clothing and the Muslim hijab, as well as culture-specific clothing, such as the Western fashion style. Both types of clothing are discussed ideologically and are experienced as conflictual in three interviews. Finally, five conflicts focus on education and socialization, especially with regard to aspects of achievement and performance of teachers and gender-specific conflicts in educational organisations and society. Interviewees highlight the problems of female students who have to prostitute themselves for food. They also describe the abuse of female students and that female students are often barred from studying when they, for example, fall pregnant. Interviewees see here a conflict between traditional gender ethics and modern ways of life.

Organisation	Field of conflict	Topic of conflict
Educational organisations	Territory	Maasai on school compound (i5)
	Culture diversity	eating from the floor, (i9) decorated hijab, (i16.5) hijab, (i18.1) Western fashion style, (i18.2)
	Education and Socialization	girls don't study, (i16.1) girls prostitution for food in a secondary school, (i16.2) poor performance of teachers, (i16.3) socialization on race, (i17) priest abuses student, (i16.4)

Table 6: Educational organizations. Source: authors' own construction

Except for the governmental excecutives, most of the interviewees announced that the experienced conflicts were "intercultural" conflicts. According to the content analysis, these "intercultural conflicts" can be subcategorised into conflicts with ethnic background (7), gender-related conflicts (7), religious-based (8), organizational (9) and international conflict (15). Therefore, most of the interviewees from the educational contexts define "intercultural" implicitly as "international" conflicts. At the same time intercultural conflicts include conflicts that are based on organizational culture, religious-, gender- and ethnic motivated background. This result shows that interviewees from the ecclesiastical, the governmental and the private enterprises define'intercultural' rather in a broad sense that includes various aspects of diversity.

After having focused on the conflicts that occur in the selected organizations, concepts and characteristics of intercultural mediation will be addressed.

Concepts and characteristics of intercultural mediation

Finally, the third research question will be answered, focusing on what the concepts and characteristics of intercultural mediation are in the selected organizations. The concepts of intercultural mediation and conflict management comprise the following characteristics, indicated by the interviewees:

- types,
- aims,
- values,
- structure, and
- mediators and their qualifications.

These conceptual aspects will in the following be introduced with regard to emic Tanzanian perspectives.

Types of intercultural conflict

Five types of intercultural conflicts can be categorized referring to the 40 interviews. Interviewees define intercultural conflicts as ethnic, religious, gender, organizational, or internationally-based conflicts.

Which type of intercultural conflict is defined is partly bound to the organizational occurrence:

- In educational organizations the ten collected narrations mostly show ethnic, religious and gender types of intercultural conflicts.
- Governmental executives mostly mediate in organizational and labour conflicts.
- Ecclesiastical organizations deal with ethnic, religious and gender types of intercultural conflicts.
- Private enterprises are confronted with international conflicts.

Aims of intercultural mediation

The aims of intercultural mediation mentioned by the interviewees vary between the organizations. The most frequently quoted aims are introduced in the following table.

Organization	Aims of intercultural conflict mediation
Educational organizations	Maintain and build peace Consensus Shape good relationship

Educational organizations	Maintain and build peace Consensus Shape good relationship Promote understanding and tolerance Reconciliation Eradication of segregate ideologies
Governmental executives	Make peace Promote school exchange activitiesast conflict resolution according to law Resume former relationship
Ecclesiastical organizations	Build peace, harmony and acceptance Consent Strengthen unity of churches

Table 7: Aims of intercultural conflict mediation. Source: authors' own construction.

The aims of intercultural mediation are related to the main functions of the organization, as results show:

- Interviewees of educational organizations connect the aims of intercultural mediation to the objectives of the curricula, such as peace building, consensus, tolerance and fighting against segregating ideologies, for example, "*ubaguzi wa ngozi*" which means "racial discrimination".
- Interviewees of governmental executive organizations prefer to pursue their organizational objectives in parallel with aims of intercultural mediation: one of the selected organizations aims at promoting activities of a particular project. A second governmental executive organization implements intercultural conflict resolution through their programme to accelerate conflict resolution procedures in accordance with the laws and legislation.
- Interviewees of ecclesiastical organizations pursue the aim of unifying the church under "the word of God". In accordance with this aim the interviewees emphasize peace, harmony, consent and unity in intercultural mediation processes.
- Profit maximization is indicated as main aim by the interviewees from private enterprises. They highlight avoiding conflicts, providing safety for the clients, satisfying conflicting parties and achieving consensus.

Values in intercultural conflict

Intercultural conflict and mediation is based on values constellations, which vary situationally and according to the context.

With regard to the educational context, interviewees mention values such as understanding, respect, peace, tolerance and non-violence which people negotiate in intercultural mediation settings. Of particular importance in the educational context is the value of humility. This concept includes the idea that a person interacts with others in a humbled way with respect.

Interviewees from governmental organizations highlight the values of harmony, neutrality, peace and fairness, which are usually mediated in mediation sessions across cultures. Intercultural mediation which is performed within governmental organizations is based on the values of the Tanzanian law and therefore always in accordance to it. Values that are not in accordance with the law are not accepted in intercultural mediation situations.

The interviewees from ecclesiastical organizations emphasize an array of spiritual values. These values that are negotiated in intercultural mediation include the word of God and the dignity of human beings as basic values. Other values, such as unity, reconciliation, the enlightening of the mind and humanity are basic values in mediation processes within the ecclesiastical context. Particularly, the concept of "*utu*" which can be translated as "humanity" is of major importance. This concept is understood as the philosophy of mankind. This means that in intercultural mediations in this specific context, the way people define themselves as group members and in relation to God and spiritual forces is the basic value throughout mediation sessions. Through this basic value and the negotiation of inter-relationships on human and spiritual levels, energy is released and conflicts are resolved.

Values cited by interviewees of private organizations, encompass appreciation, unity, sharing, safety, trust, patience and forgiveness. The values of unity, sharing and forgiveness are based on a specific conception of humanity: particularly in conflict situations, conflicts should be resolved by behaviour and attitudes, which express the value of unity, sharing and forgiveness. Intercultural mediation sessions in this context of private enterprises are therefore based on this forgiving attitude.

Very specific to this context is the mediation of values, which deal with the treatment of clients and the protection of customer's rights. In the view of interviewees from private enterprises, customers and clients are viewed as needing to be treated "like kings". This value often leads to conflict with regard to how clients and customers are treated in intercultural communication situations.

The structure in intercultural mediation

The structure of intercultural mediations in Tanzanian contexts is related to the process of (re-)building relationships. Referring to educational and ecclesiastical contexts and private enterprises the structure of mediation can be (re-)defined according to the needs of the individuals involved. In contrary, in mediation sessions in government organizations, such as the Ministries, mediation is based on a particular phase model which derives from Western concepts of mediation.

Interviewees from educational contexts explain the structure of intercultural mediation with regard to the following concept. The structure of mediation is based on how the mediator guides the conflict parties according to their needs and the underlying values of the mediation process. Basically, mediations are viewed as a special kind of team building process, as a negotiation or counselling situation. Elements of negotiation and counselling are part of intercultural mediation sessions. This means that the mediator can change the role of being a mediator to the role of being a negotiator or counselor. The transitions from one role to the other are flowing.

Interviewees explain that the following structural elements are followed throughout mediation processes in educational contexts:

- bring people involved to one table,
- identify key persons in the conflict,
- create a safe environment,
- treat parties equally, and
- challenge mutual understanding.

In intercultural mediations, many individuals who define themselves as being part of the conflict or as being involved are invited to the mediation process. Then, the mediator identifies the individuals who are particularly involved in the conflict and its resolution. These "eminent individuals" often hold a key position in the conflict and are therefore defined as "leaders".

Interviewees state that governmental excecutive organizations have elaborated a strictly structured process of intercultural mediation. Three interviewees of two Tanzanian ministries emphasize that they follow a 5 step-model which recently was introduced by "invited experts from Denmark" as one of the interviewees quoted (i12). In this process, interviewees describe the following phases that they follow:

- Introduction,
- Information gathering,
- Option seeking,
- Conlusion and consensus,
- Sign agreement.

Even the interviewees from governmental organizations emphasize that counselling and guiding are basic aspects of the mediation process. The introduction phase is used to "get to know each other and the process". Information is collected in the second phase and options to resolve the conflict are discussed with the mediator. The mediator is expected to give advice with regard to finding an adequate solution. A conclusion will finally be given by the mediator, conflict parties need to agree with consensus and an agreement needs to be reached which is sealed by the parties shaking hands and hugging.

The interviewees from ecclesiastical organizations emphasize the following structural elements of mediation sessions:

- sit together,
- talk and exchange issues, ideas and differences at a round table.

One interviewee proposes that to "shape familiarity", "create lobe"—meaning to get sensitized for the thoughts, feelings and needs of the other party, "appeal to Christian unity" and "make the mediation a learning process for the attendants" are structural elements of mediation processes in ecclesiastical environments. Mediations need to create a "welcoming and familiar atmosphere" which builds the ground for the participants to be able to listen to each other. Unity—in the sense of a Christian unity—is viewed as being the base of mediation, on the one hand, and being the aim of mediation, on the other hand, and therefore structures the process of mediation.

Interviewees of private enterprises obviously use different structural elements in intercultural mediation processes as they indicate: intercultural mediation encompasses:

- listening to each other at a round table,
- managing problems without judging,
- co-operating directly, and
- "win or lose in small extent".

The structure of the mediation is based on active listening processes and on what participants bring into the mediation session. Problems should be managed in a practical way and different worldviews, perceptions and attitudes should not be judged. A co-operative attitude should influence the entire mediation process. Finally, the mediation should end with a "win or lose in small extent" which means that a mediation process is not necessarily aiming at a win-win-solution. It rather accepts different outcomes of the mediation which can be either a win-win-solution or a win-lose solution. Mediators and conflict parties take into account that a win-win-solution can not always be achieved by all parties involved. Therefore, conflict parties are prepared from the beginning of the mediation session that they might assign their claims or allow the claims of the other parties.

Interviewees from private enterprises state that if the option of intercultural mediation is turned down by one of the parties or if the mediation process is unsuccessful, the police are called in to take over and resolve the conflict.

Mediators and their qualifications

With regard to the statements in the interviews, interviewees highlight that the person who is guiding the conflict parties through the mediation process needs to have special characteristics and qualifications. According to the specific contexts, interviewees describe the roles and qualifications of the mediator differently.

The interviewees in educational organizations prefer individuals in specific positions as mediators. The most accepted individuals in the role of mediators are those in special positions with high social status, such as principals, heads of schools, leaders, and board members. Besides these individuals, persons from governmental administration, including police officers, are accepted to mediate. These mediators are expected to being qualified in the following way: they should not be biased, they should be in a good and healthy condition should be able to accept both parties and should be efficient in resolving the conflict. With regard to their attitude, they should be responsible, perform their duties and be scrupulous, educated and convincing. Referring to the personality of the mediator, characteristics, such as being self-confident, wise, empathetic and sensitive to gender issues are mentioned. Mediators should be able to respect the conflict parties and be impartial. With regard to the characteristics of mediators, being wise is of great importance. Therefore, old people who have already retired from their jobs are often chosen as mediators, because they are expected to have the knowledge and experience to resolve conflicts.

According to the interviews conducted in governmental executive organizations, mediators have to undergo specific training to qualify for the position of mediator. The government usually prefers to employ postgraduate trainees, lawyers, religious elders, retired government employees and individuals who work in high positions. Interviewees in the governmental context highlight on the one hand that the government prefers mediators with experience in so called "Western mediation". On the other hand, the government is interested in lawyers, religious and elders who have worked in government positions and who mediate on the base of "traditional African values" and on an "experienced person's wisdom". These mediators are expected to force parties to agree to particular solutions and accept the mediator's ideas about resolving the conflict.

The government states in various internal documents that the qualifications for being a mediator include being impartial, being forceful, advising, being knowledgeable and acting according to key ethics. These key ethics include values such as honesty, independence and fairness, which should guide the mediator and influence the communication during the mediation process. Additionally, mediators should be willing to support the conflict parties, committed to their job, facilitating with regard to all aspects of the mediation, tolerant, sympathetic and humbled.

The interviewees from ecclesiastical organizations appreciate pastors, parish leaders, bishops, "faithful people" and "retired persons from various social and ecclesiastical groups" as mediators. The concept of "faithful people" is based on the assumption that these individuals can guide the conflicting parties through the conflict by using their "spiritual aura" and their "connection to God". Also pastors, parish leaders and bishops are epected to be able to conduct the mediation in connection with God and in a spiritual atmosphere.

The mediators should be qualified by "emanating experience", having gained wisdom throughout their lives, having gained respect in society, trust, reliability, credibility, integrity and patience. They should have a "good character". Throughout the process of mediation they should "not blame the conflict parties for what they have been doing" and should listen to what the conflict parties have to say.

Preferably elderly, retired individuals are requested to conduct intercultural mediations. These kinds of mediator are expected to be highly experienced, patient and to be the "best listeners".

Private enterprise interviewees use mediators from different professional backgrounds in intercultural mediations. They usually rely on managers (particular from middle or top management), human resource officers, pastors, advocates, lawyers, "elders of the court" and police officers to mediate in the experienced conflicts. Mediators, in their opinion do not need to be independent persons, but can be employed by a governmental or ecclesiastical organization or can even be employed in the private enterprise in which the conflict occurs.

Interviewees view mediation as a practical tool to resolve conflicts in a pragmatic way, to resolve conflicts effectively. These interviewees state that mediators, in their opinion, need the following personal characteristics: mediators need to have a remarkably high IQ, they "definitely need a sense of humor" and they need "*huruma*" which can be translated as "mercy" or "compassion". The requirement of "having a high IQ" expresses the value of education and the assumption that mediators need to be educated to resolve conflicts in an adequate way. Interviewees are of the opinion that mediators need to be "psychologically competent" and "trained in communication".

Besides these qualifications, mediators in intercultural contexts are expected to be understanding, guiding, honest, caring, authoritative, responsible, humorous and patient. All of these qualities which a mediator should have are based on a conception of man which relates back to the philosophy of "*utu*" which highlights the importance of "good mutual relationships", "humour" and "joy of life".

Conclusion

Many terms, definitions and aspects of intercultural mediation are mentioned in different organizational contexts and have been presented in this paper, which gives an overview of the research results a study of intercultural mediation.

It can be concluded that terms and concepts of intercultural mediation vary across the different organizational contexts within Tanzanian society. Concepts of conflict, conflict resolution and intercultural mediation differ from the English concepts. The interviewees generally try to use terms of translation, which prefer a rather more positive connotation than the English terms, as refered to above (see also Mbiti, 1991).

Referring to the described conflicts experienced in the different organizational contexts, the following can be summarized: Interviewees from educational organizations experience conflicts with students, teachers, parents and socio-cultural and structural aspects, such as food supply or the teacher's performance.

Conflicts narrated by government excecutives are mostly bound to labour-conflicts or are crime-related. Interviewees explicitly state that the conflicts they deal with are not "ethnic or cultural conflicts".

In contrast, conflicts in ecclesiastical organisations are connected to the negotiations around Christianity, Christian lifestyles or spiritual aspects of life.

Interviewees from private enterprises experience mainly "international conflicts" with their international clients and customers.

Finally, concepts and characteristics of intercultural mediation are defined by the interviewees from the educational, governmental, ecclesiastical and private enterprise contexts with regard to the types of intercultural mediation, aims, values, structure and the role of the mediator and their expected qualifications. Conflict resolution concepts are variously defined by the interviewees, including aspects of "Western mediation", particulary by government representatives, as well as African values and mediation concepts. All interviewees refer to intercultural mediations as religious, gender, social and/or ethnic mediation. Thereby the value of harmony is very important regarding mediation sessions.

In conclusion, this research gives a highly diverse insight into intercultural mediation concepts and definitions in selected organizations in the Tanzanian context. It leads to recognizing the fact that a concept of "Tanzanian mediation" does not exists, but rather highly context and organization specific terms and concepts are used with regard to intercultural mediation. One aspect that is similar in all described intercultural mediation settings refers to the fact the mediator should be a wise and experienced person, particularly when mediating between individuals or groups from different cultures.

Practical and theoretical implications

Finally, based on the outcome of this research and the limitation of not being able to generalise from the qualitative research methodology, the following can be recommended for future research on intercultural mediation in Tanzanian contexts:

- to replicate this study in a couple of different organisations based in Tanzania to gain deeper insight into and understanding of a culture-specific point of view on intercultural mediation;
- to conduct a study on intercultural mediation by using different methods to gain a broader view and deeper insights and results which can be generalised with regard to various contexts in the Tanzanian society;
- to develop a study on the abovementioned topics by using qualitative and quantitative research approaches to deepen and widen the focus of research.
- to replicate this study within organisations in different countries to gain insight into culture-specific and/or culture-general issues of intercultural mediation in different national cultures within and outside of Africa; and
- to evaluate intercultural mediation processes through discourse analysis with regard to culture-specific communication processes in intercultural mediation sessions in various contexts.

In conclusion, it is of great importance for research in intercultural mediation to broaden the view of mediation by identifying and highlighting similarities and differences in intercultural mediation concepts according to different socio-cultural contexts, such as educational, ecclesiastical, governmental and private enterprises within a national setting. Future research should focus on evaluating and emphasizing the complexity of conflict management and intercultural mediation processes in various social contexts, instead of rigidifying the stereotypic assumption that an overall concept of Tanzanian mediation exists across cultures.

References

AJULU, R. (2002) Politicised Ethnicity, Competitive Politics and Conflict in Kenya: A Historical Perspective, *African Studies*, 16(2): 251-268.

ALGÅRD, A. (2005) *Does the Gacaca system in Rwanda provide an effective remedy in compliance with international norms and standards?,* Lund, University of Lund, http://www.mrforum.se/upload/files/1/Utbildning%20och%20forskning/Victims%20rights%20in%20Rwanda.pdf [last accessed: 01-08-2009].

ASHTON, E. O. (1989) *Swahili Grammar.* Essex, UK, Longman.

AUGSBURGER, D.W. (1992) *Conflict mediation across cultures*, Kentucky, John Knox Press.

BECVAR, D.S. & BECVAR, R.J. (2006) *Family therapy: A systemic integration* (6th ed.), Boston, MA, Allyn & Bacon.

BERGER, P.L. & LUCKMANN, T. (2000) *Die gesellschaftliche Konstruktion der Wirklichkeit. Eine Theorie der Wissenssoziologie* [The societal construction of reality] (17th ed.). Frankfurt: Fischer.

BONESS, C. (2002) Kritische Situationen in Begegnungen zwischen Tansaniern und Europäern. Eine Felduntersuchung im Sekundarschulsystem Tansanias. *Europäische Hochschulschriften,* Reihe 11, Pädagogik, Band 859. Frankfurt, Peter Lang.

BUSCH, D. UND SCHRÖDER, H. (2006) (Eds.) *Interkulturelle Mediation in der Grenzregion. Studien zur Interkulturellen Mediation 2,* Frankfurt, Peter Lang.

CARLSON, R.G. (1990) *Banana beer, reciprocity, and ancestor and propitiation among the Haya of Bukoba, Tanzania,* hier fehlen noch Ort und Verlag. Ethnology.

CHELDELIN, S., DRUCKMAN, D. & FAST, L. (2003) *Conflict: from analysis to intervention,* New York, Continuum.

COLLIS, J. & HUSSEY, R. (2003) *Business research: A practical guide for undergraduate and postgraduate students* (2nd ed.), New York, Palgrave Macmillan.

DAVIDHEISER, M. (2005) Special Affinities and Conflict Resolution: West African Social Institutions and Mediation. *Beyond Intractability.* In: GUY BURGESS & HEIDI BURGESS (Eds.) *Conflict Research Consortium.* Colorado, University of Colorado, Boulder, http://www.beyondintractability.org/essay/joking_kinship/ [last accessed: 01-08-2009].

DICKERSON, V.C. & ZIMMERMAN, J.L. (1996) Myths, misconceptions, and a word or two about politics. *Journal of Systemic Therapies, 15*(1), 79-88.

GADAMER, H.G. (1990) *Wahrheit und Methode. Grundzüge einer philosophischen Hermeneutik.* (6th ed.), Tübingen, Mohr/Siebeck.

GEERTZ, C. (1973) *The interpretation of cultures,* New York, Basic Books.

GEERTZ, C. (1987) *Dichte Beschreibung. Beiträge zum Verstehen kultureller Systeme* [Thick descriptions. Contribution to understand cultural systems], Frankfurt, Suhrkamp.

GONZALEZ, N., MOLL, L.C., FLOYD-TENERY, M., RIVERA, A., RENDON, P., GONZALES, R. & AMANTI, C. (1994) *Funds of knowledge: Learning from language-minority households. ERIC Digest. Retrieved from the World Wide Web on 19 July 2008 at* http://www.ericfacility.net/databases/ERIC_Digests/ed367146.html, last accessed: 01-08-2009.

HABERMAS, J. (1999). *Theorie des Kommunikativen Handelns* [Theory of the communicative action] (3rd ed.), Frankfurt, Suhrkamp.

HIPPS, J.A. (1993) *Trustworthiness and authenticity: Alternate ways to judge authentic assessments.* Paper presented at the annual meeting of the American Educational Research Association, Atlanta, American Educational Research Association.

JAMHURI YA MUUNGANO WA TANZANIA (2007). *Kanuni za ajira na mahusiano kazini (kanuni za utendaji bora) mwaka.* Dar-Es-Salaam, Chuo Kikuu cha Dar es Salaam.

JOHNSON, B.R. (1997) Examining the validity structure of qualitative research. *Education, 118*(3), 282-292.

JOHNSON, F. (1978) *A standard Swahili-English Dictionary,* Nairobi, Oxford University Press.

JOHNSON F. (1995) *A standard English-SwahiliDictionary,* Nairobi, Oxford University Press.

JONASSEN, D.H. (1991). Evaluating constructivistic learning. *Educational Technology, 28*(11), 13-16.

LIEBE, F. & GILBERT, N. (1996) Interkulturelle Mediation—eine schwierige Vermittlung. Eine empirische Annäherung zur Bedeutung von kulturellen Unterschieden. *Berghof Report Nr. 2.*, Berlin, Berghof Forschungszentrum für konstruktive Konfliktbearbeitung.

MAYER, C.-H. (2005) *Artificial walls. South African narratives on conflict, difference and identity. An exploratory study in post-apartheid South Africa* Stuttgart, Ibidem.

MAYER, C.H. (2006) *Trainingshandbuch Interkulturelle Mediation und Konfliktlösung. Didaktische Materialien zum Kompetenzerwerb,* Münster, Waxmann.

MAYER, C.-H. (2008a). *Managing conflict across cultures, values and identities. A case study in the South African automotive industry*, Marburg, Tectum.

MAYER, C.-H. (2008b) Identity and health in transcultural mediation. The model of Culture-Synergetic Transcultural Mediation and its impacts. *Journal of Intercultural Communication*, 17, June 2008, http://www.immi.se/intercultural/ [last accessed: 01-08-2009].

MAYER, C.-H. & BONESS, C. (2004*) Interkulturelle Mediation und Konfliktbearbeitung. Bausteine deutsch-afrikanischer Wirklichkeiten*. Münster: Waxmann.

MAYER, C.-H., BONESS, C.M. & LOUW, L. (2008). 'The Impact of Value-Orientations on Cross-cultural Encounters and Mediation. A Survey in Tanzania's Educational System', *African Journal on Conflict Resolution*, 8(1), 39-76, http://www.accord.org.za/downloads/ajcr/ajcr_2008_1.pdf [01-08-2009].

MBITI, J. (1991) *African Religions and Philosophy,* Oxford, Heinemann.

MCLEOD, J. (1996) The emerging narrative approach to counselling and psychotherapy. *British Journal of Guidance & Counselling, 24*(2), 173-195.

MYERS, S. AND FILNER, B. (1994) *Mediation across Cultures. A Handbook about Conflict and Culture,* Amherst, Amherst Educational Publishing.

ONLINE SWAHILI-ENGLISH DICTIONARY (2009) http://africanlanguages.com/swahili/ [last accessed: 01-08-2009].

PURDECOVA, A. (2008) *Repatriation and Reconciliation in Divided Societies: The Case of Rwanda's 'Ingando'*, Oxford, University of Oxford.

RICOEUR, P. (1979) Der Text als Modell: hermeneutisches Verstehen [The text as model: hermeneutic understanding]. IN BRUEHL, W.L. (Ed.). *Verstehende Soziologie. Grundzuege und Entwicklungstendenzen*. München, Nymphenburger Verlag.

TERRE BLANCHE, M., DURRHEIM, K. & KELLY, K. (2006) First steps in qualitative data analysis. IN TERRE BLANCHE M., DURRHEIM, K. & PAINTER, D. (Eds.), *Research in practice. Applied methods for the social sciences,* 321-344.

VON STEINKE, I. (2000) Gütekriterien qualitativer Forschung [Criteria of qualitative research]. IN FLICK U.V., KARDOFF, E. & VON STEINKE, I. (Eds.) *Qualitative Forschung. Ein Handbuch*, 219-331). Hamburg, Rowohlts Enzyklopädie.

WILSON, P.M. (1994) *Simplified Swahili,* Essex, UK, Longman.

WOLFF, S. (2000) Clifford Geertz. IN FLICK U.V., KARDOFF, E. & VON STEINKE, I. (Eds.) *Qualitative Forschung. Ein Handbuch* [Qualitative research. A handbook.], 84-96. Hamburg, Rowohlts Enzyklopädie.
YIN, R.K. (2002) *Case study research: Design and methods* (2nd ed.), London. Sage.

Intercultural Mediation: Asian and Western Conflict Lens

Stella Ting-Toomey

Intercultural conflict is defined in this chapter as the perceived or actual incompatibility of cultural values, situational norms, goals, face orientations, scarce resources, processes, and/or outcomes in a face-to-face (or mediated) context (Ting-Toomey and Oetzel, 2001). The greater the cultural distance between the two conflict parties, the more likely the assessment of the conflict interaction process would be misconstrued. The cultural membership distances can include deep-level differences such as historical grievances, cultural worldviews, and beliefs. Concurrently, they can also include the mismatch of applying different normative expectations in a particular conflict episode.

Intercultural conflicts can cover a wide range of conflict topics, for example, from intercultural marital and family disputes, intercultural business partnership conflicts, international students' roommate disagreements, interethnic neighborhood fights, to international frictions on the global level. Oftentimes, many initial disagreements escalate to full-blown, polarized conflicts because the conflict parties have lost the art of communicating with and relating to one another. In addition, in an *intercultural* conflict situation, many disputants lack the necessary culture-sensitive knowledge, motivation, and operational skills to handle their conflicts appropriately and effectively.

A culturally-sensitive mediator, in mediating an intercultural conflict situation, serves as a "bridge person" in mediating the substantive, relational, process, and culture-level identity differences between the two intercultural conflict parties. From the transformative mediation framework (Bush and Folger, 2005), mediation is a facilitative communication process by a mutually-acceptable third party whereby the disputants learn to transform their thinking, viewing, and reacting to the conflict topic and to each other and, in the process, creating their own agreed upon outcome. Intercultural mediation means that some elements of cultural-based or ethnic-based group membership differences make an impact on the mediation developmental process. In an intercultural mediation session when two parties are from two contrastive cultures, their entering point in the mediation, their assumptions about the mediation process, and their expectancies of the mediator' role will all have a strong impact on the symbolic exchange and meaning construction process of the mediation session.

This chapter aims to introduce a theoretical framework, namely, the conflict face-negotiation theory framework (Ting-Toomey 1988, 2005a) in connection with a discussion of some of the possible differences between an East Asian lens (drawing from some of the research findings in China, Japan, Korea, Taiwan, and Hong Kong) and a Western lens (drawing from the predominant U.S.-based research literature) in viewing a mediation session. The essay is organized in three sections. First, key assumptions from the conflict face-negotiation theory will be summarized and the four culture-based conflict approaches are connected with the Asian and Western views of the mediation process. Second, intercultural mediation competence is discussed and some specific guidelines are offered in communicating competently with Asian and Western disputants appropriately and effectively. Third, a mindful transformation perspective is outlined and some critical reflective questions concerning the development of mindful transformation are suggested.

The Conflict Face-Negotiation Theory

Intercultural conflict often involves different face losing and face saving behaviors. Face refers to a claimed sense of desired social self-image in a relational or international setting (Ting-Toomey, 2005a). Face loss occurs when we are being treated in such a way that our identity claims are either being directly or indirectly challenged or ignored. Face-loss can occur either on the individual level or the identity group level, or both. Repeated face-loss and face-threat often lead to escalatory conflict spirals or an impasse in the conflict negotiation process (Wilmot and Hocker, 2007).

Culture-Based Facework: Core Theoretical Assumptions

In response to the heavy reliance on the individualistic Western perspective in framing various conflict approaches, Ting-Toomey (1988) and Ting-Toomey and Kurogi (1998) developed an intercultural conflict theory, namely, the conflict face-negotiation theory to include a collectivistic Asian perspective to broaden the theorizing process of various conflict orientations. In a nutshell, Ting-Toomey's (2005a) conflict face-negotiation theory assumes that: (1) people in all cultures try to maintain and negotiate face in all communication situations; (2) the concept of face is especially problematic in emotionally-threatening or identity vulnerable situations when the situated identities of the communicators are called into question; (3) the cultural value spectrums of individualism-collectivism (Cai and Fink, 2002, Triandis, 1995) and small/large power distance (Carl et al., 2004) influence facework concerns and conflict styles; (4) individualism and collectivism value patterns shape members' preferences for self-oriented facework versus other-oriented facework; (5) small and large power distance value patterns shape members' preferences for horizontal-based facework versus vertical-based facework; (6) the value dimensions, in conjunction with individual, relational, and situational factors influence the use of particular facework behaviors and conflict tactics in particular cultural scenes; and (7) intercultural facework and conflict competence refers to the optimal integration of knowledge, mindfulness, and communication skills in managing vulnerable identity-based conflict situations appropriately, effectively, and adaptively. For a detailed review of research findings in testing the conflict face-negotiation theory, readers can consult Ting-Toomey (2005a) and Ting-Toomey and Takai (2006). For a review of extensive research findings that reflect a Western lens on various conflict approaches and conflict styles, consult Putnam (2006) and Nicotera and Dorsey (2006).

More generally, for example, in a direct empirical test of the theory (Oetzel et al., 2001, 2008, Oetzel and Ting-Toomey, 2003), the research program tested the underlying assumption of the face-negotiation theory that face is an explanatory mechanism for cultural membership's influence on conflict behavior. A questionnaire was administered to 768 participants in 4 national cultures (China, Germany, Japan, and the U.S.) in their respective languages asking them to recall and describe a recent interpersonal conflict. The major findings of the study are as follows: First, cultural individualism-collectivism had direct effects on conflict styles, as well as mediated effects through self-construal personality (i.e., whether the person's personality trait is independent-inclined or interdependent-inclined; see Markus & Kitayama, 1991, 1998) and face concerns. Second, self-face concern was associated positively with dominating and competing conflict styles and other-face concern was associated positively with avoiding and compromising styles. Third, German respondents reported the frequent use of direct and confrontational facework strategies and did not care much for avoidance facework or apology tactics; Japanese reported the use of different pretending strategies to act as if the conflict situation does not exist; Chinese engaged in a variety of avoiding, obliging, and also passive aggressive facework tactics; and U.S. Americans reported the use of upfront expression of feelings and remaining calm as facework strategies to handle problematic conflict situations. Fourth, multiple Asian cultural groups (Japan, Hong Kong, Thailand, and Vietnam) also see themselves as using the preferred integrative, problem-solving conflict style in trying to resolve the conflict problem (Onishi and Bliss, 2006). In another research study, Kim et al (2007) also uncovered the following differences between the Koreans, Chinese, and Japanese: Korean respondents tend to use more compromising conflict strategies than both Chinese and Japanese in dealing with conflicts with their supervisors; Japanese respondents, however, tend to use much more obliging and compliance conflict strategies in accommodating to their supervisors' wishes than both Korean and Chinese respondents. In sum, Asian respondents tend to use indirect, high-context conflict approach with the emphasis of the importance of understanding the embedded self-in-role-contexts conflict viewpoint. Comparatively, Western respondents appear to emphasize the "logical" separation of substantive issue and relational issue in conflict and practice a direct, low-context conflict style in dealing with the conflict task at hand (Hall, 1983; Ting-Toomey, 1988). While some common conflict style patterns have been found under the broad "Asian" cultural umbrella, distinctive differences and variations also exist between the different Asian cultural communities--especially pending on various culture-based situational appraisal factors such as ingroup-outgroup parameters, meaning constructions, and what constitute appropriate and inappropriate conflict behaviors. Furthermore, country-of-origin, immigration experience, acculturation pattern, generational level, host culture's language mastery, family socialization norms, and ethnic identity salience factors also create tremendous distinctions between and within these multiple groups (Ting-Toomey et al., 2000).

Cultural Value Conditioning Patterns

As cultural beings, we are socialized by the values and norms of our culture to think and behave in certain ways. Our family, peer groups, educational institutions, mass media system, political system, and religious institutions are some of the forces that shape and mold our cultural and personal values. Two such conditioning value patterns are individualism-collectivism and small-large power distance (Hofstede, 2001). Indeed in the recent GLOBE (stands for "Global Leadership and Organizational Behavior Effectiveness") empirical research project, researchers (House et al., 2004) have provided additional evidence that the foundational constructs of individualism-collectivism and small/large power distance permeate 62 countries (and with a sample size of 17,370 middle managers from three industries) at the societal, organizational, and individual levels of analysis. Basically, individualism refers to the broad value tendencies of a culture in emphasizing the importance of the "I" identity over the "we" identity, individual rights over group interests, and individuated-focused emotions over social-focused emotions. In comparison, collectivism refers to the broad value tendencies of a culture in emphasizing the importance of the "we" identity over the "I" identity, ingroup interests over individual desires, and other-identity concerns over self-identity concerns (Ting-Toomey, 1988).

Individualistic and collectivistic value tendencies are manifested in everyday interpersonal, family, school, and workplace social interactions. Individualistic and collectivistic value tendencies also influence why disputants from Germany and the mainstream U.S. cultures tend to use more upfront and confrontational conflict tactics, while the Japanese and the Chinese cultural groups tend to use more accommodating to even avoiding conflict tactics. While Western cultural respondents seem to emphasize self-face concern in conflict, Asian cultural respondents seem to emphasize other-face concern above and beyond self-face concern. Self-face concern is the protective concern for one's own identity image when one's own identity image is threatened in the conflict episode. Other-face concern is the concern for accommodating the other conflict party's identity image in the conflict situation. In addition, mutual-face concern is the concern for both parties' images and the image of the relationship. In a mediation session, a competent mediator oftentimes spends his or her commitment and energy in moving the communication session forward between the two disputants, from their respective self-face concern defensive positions to a mutual-face validation process. She or he also attempts to facilitate a productive dialogue between the disputants in achieving a harmonious outcome.

In discussing various relationship harmony models in various East Asian countries, Leung et al. (2002) propose a dual model of harmony in explaining the interplay between a value harmony motivation and an instrumental harmony motivation among the various Asian cultural groups. Harmony is "he" in Chinese, "wa" in Japanese, and "jowha" in Korean, and generally connotes "a balanced, peaceful heart and a comfortable, harmonizing relationship." In addition, for example, a state of "he" can be attained in Chinese if one maintains appropriate role relationships, is other-oriented, and accepts the established hierarchy (Gao & Ting-Toomey, 1998). In the context of Asian conflict ideology, a value harmony motivation reflects the ideal that genuine harmony and peace should be pursued and that conflict should be tone down in order to preserve ingroup cohesiveness and interdependent functioning. In comparison, instrumental harmony motivation reflects the aim of how a conflict-free relationship may be used to achieve a particular goal above and beyond the actual conflict situation itself. Leung et al. (2002) also view the two approaches as exist on a bi-dimensional model so that individuals in a cultural community can emphasize a "balancing" conflict mode (i.e., high on both value harmony and instrumental harmony motivations and reflecting a Neo-Confucianism position), a "disintegrating" conflict mode (i.e., low on both value harmony and instrumental harmony motivations), an "aligning" conflict mode (i.e., high on value harmony motivation, low on instrumental harmony motivation, and thus, the need to align intrinsic harmony value with overt behavior), and a "smoothing" conflict mode (i.e., low on value harmony motivation, high on instrumental harmony motivation, and thus, smoothing over or coddling the relationship for surface peace). Thus, a culturally competent mediator needs to understand both the cultural-based conflict assumptions and the harmony-based assumptions that differentiate the Western and Asian lens, and the individual harmony ideologies and preferences of the disputants in a particular mediation scene.

Interestingly also, whether the conflict interaction is with members of the ingroup (i.e., members with strong emotional ties and interdependent fate) or outgroup (i.e., members with no emotional ties or strangers) also clearly influences how East Asian collectivists manage conflict. Chinese and Japanese, for example, are more likely to pursue a conflict with peripheral outgroup members and less likely to pursue a conflict with familiar ingroup members than U.S. Americans. They also use strong win/lose competitive to aggressive tactics when competing with peripheral outgroup members in a task project as versus with familiar ingroup members (Leung and Tjosvold, 1998, Ting-Toomey and Takai, 2006). Meanwhile, mainstream U.S. Americans tend not to draw a sharp distinction between the boundary of ingroup and outgroup conflicts and tend to engage in upfront, competitive conflict tactics in workplace disputes in comparison to East Asian collectivists.

Cultural Values' Integrative Complexity: Mediation Implications

Beyond individualism-collectivism, another important value dimension that is critical in understanding workplace conflict interaction is the value dimension of *power distance* (Carl et al., 2004). Power distance, from the workplace values' analysis standpoint, refers to the way in which a corporate culture approaches and deals with status differences and social hierarchies. Indeed, individuals in *small power distance* corporate cultures tend to value equal power distributions, symmetrical relations, a mixture of positive and negative messages in feedback sessions, and equitable reward and cost distributions based on individual merits. Individuals in *large power distance* corporate cultures tend to accept unequal power distributions, asymmetrical relations, authoritative feedback from the experts or high-status individuals, and rewards and sanctions based on rank, role, status, age, and perhaps even gender identity.

In combining both individualism-collectivism and small/large power distance value patterns, we can discuss four predominant corporate value approaches along the two grids of individualism-collectivism continuum and small-large power distance continuum: impartial, status-achievement, benevolent, and communal (Ting-Toomey and Oetzel, 2001). The impartial approach reflects a combination of an individualistic and small power distance value orientation; the status-achievement approach consists of a combination of an individualistic and large power distance value orientation; the benevolent approach reflects a combination of a collectivistic and large power distance value orientation; and the communal approach consists of a combination of collectivistic and small power distance value orientation (see Figure 1). Overall, managers and employees around the world have different expectations of how a workplace conflict episode should be interpreted and resolved—pending on whether the workplace culture emphasizes impartial, status-achievement, benevolent, or communal conflict interaction rituals (see Kaushal and Kwantes, 2006, Merkin, 2006).

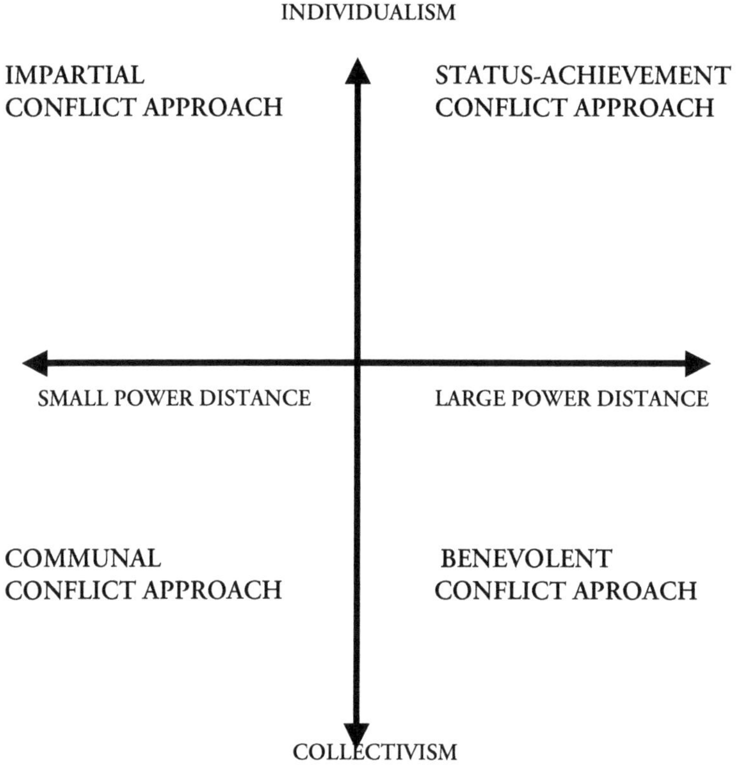

Figure 1: Culture-Based Value Patterns' Grid: Four Conflict Approaches.

More specifically, for example, in the impartial approach (a combination of individualism and small power distance) to workplace conflict, the predominant values of this approach are personal freedom and equal treatment (Smith et al., 1998). From the impartial conflict approach lens, if an interpersonal conflict arises between a manager and an employee, the manager has the responsibility to deal with the conflict in an objective, upfront, and decisive manner. The employee is sometimes invited to provide feedback and reactions to the fact-finding process. He or she can also ask for clear justifications and evidence from the manager. In an equal-rank employee-employee conflict, the manager would generally play the "impartial" third-party role and would encourage the two employees to talk things over and find their own workable solution. Managers in large corporations in Denmark, the Netherlands, Sweden, and Norway appear to practice the impartial conflict communication approach (Hofstede, 2001).

The impartial conflict approach will have a strong impact on the expectations of the horizontal individualists (i.e., individuals with strong preference for impartial rules and objective guidelines for conflict resolution) in entering a mediation session. They would expect a truly neutral, objective third-party to mediate a conflict and that facts and evidence should drive the mediation case. They would also watch closely for any sign of the mediator's playing favoritism. They would expect a fair and equitable outcome at the end of a mediation session.

Alternatively, from a *status-achievement approach* (a combination of individualism and large power distance) to conflict, the predominant values of this approach are personal freedom and earned inequality. For example, in France, employees often feel that they have the freedom to voice directly and complain about their managers in the workplace (Storti, 2001). At the same time, they do not expect their managers to change much because they are their bosses and, thus, by virtue of their titles hold certain rights and power resources. The managers, meanwhile, also expect conflict accommodations from their subordinates. When the conflict involves two same-rank co-workers, the use of upfront conflict tactics to aggression tactics is a hallmark of the status-achievement approach. Ting-Toomey and Oetzel (2001) also observed that U.S. management style often follows a conjoint impartial approach and a status-achievement approach because the larger U.S. culture emphasizes that via individual hard work, personal ambition, and fierce competitiveness, status and rank can be earned and status cues can be displayed with pride and credibility.

If self-perceived high-status managers (or vertical individualists) enter a mediation session, they would expect the mediator to have the necessary credentials and expertise to mediate the case. They would also expect some special recognition for their names or status positions and their busy time schedule. The culturally astute mediator needs to pay mindful attention to power imbalance and subtle power coercion issues between the two disputants (especially mediating a high-status/low-status employee conflict case) and to make sure that talk times and interruption times are managed appropriately and effectively. During the conjoint problem-solving phase, the mediator needs to make sure that both of the conflict parties have equal input and feedback on the outcome agreement.

Based on the empirical work of the GLOBE project (Carl et al., 2004), many managers in other parts of the globe also tend to see themselves as interdependent and at a different positional status level than others by virtue of their ranks or years of work experience. That is, these managers think of themselves as individuals with interlocking connections with others and as members of a hierarchical network. They practice the *benevolent approach* (a combination of collectivism and large power distance value patterns) in approaching a conflict problem. The term "benevolent" implies that many managers play the authoritative parental roles in approaching or motivating their employees. Two values that pervade this approach are obligation to others and asymmetrical interaction treatment. Countries and large corporate cultures that predominantly reflect the benevolent approach include most Latin and South American nations (e.g., Mexico, Venezuela, Brazil, Chile), most Asian nations (e.g., India, Japan, China, South Korea), most Arab nations (e.g., Egypt, Saudi Arabia, Jordan), and most African nations (e.g., Nigeria, Uganda) (Hofstede, 2001). Of course, tremendous diversities and layered historical, political, ethnic, religious, linguistic, and regional complexities also exist within each nation-state (Oetzel et al., 2006).

The philosophy of Confucianism or Neo-Confucianism, for example, strongly shapes proper facework rituals and conflict interaction performance in many East Asian societies (e.g., China, Taiwan, Singapore, Korea, and Japan). For example, for the Chinese, the notion of face is embedded in two concepts: *mian zi* and *lien*. While *mian zi* refers to social image, social position, social reputation, and social prestige, *lien* refers to moral face or integrity face. While having or not having *mian zi* is externalized and conditioned by how successful one is in meeting established social rules, *lien* refers to the internal moral character and personal integrity of an individual in upholding her or his dignity or causing shame to oneself. Likewise, the Koreans used the term *che-myon* or face with multilayered meanings. According to Lim and Choi (1996), while the Western concept of face is mostly the image of personal and psychological self, the Korean face is about the image of sociological self more than that of personal self. In fact the Korean *che-myon* concept is a double-faced concept. On the one hand, it is "the image of personal self that is claimed and negotiated through social interactions. On the other hand, it is the image of the sociological self that is defined by the society and must be protected by passing the normative standards of positiveness of relevant social values" (p. 124). When Koreans lose *che-myon*, they feel like an utter failure in that society and that they cannot lift their face to others because of shame. This sense of shame is closely tied to the traditional root of Confucian ethics.

Confucius was a Chinese philosopher of practical ethics who lived from 551 to 479 B.C. His practical code of conduct emphasizes hierarchical societal structure (i.e., large power distance) and appropriate family role performance. Some core Confucian values include: a dynamic long-term orientation, perseverance, ordering relationships by status, having a sense of shame, and emphasizing collective face-saving (Gao and Ting-Toomey, 1998). An interdependent sense of shame includes the constant awareness of other people's expectations of one's own or ingroup performance and the particular sensitivity for mutual face-saving, face-losing, and face-giving (i.e., give-and-take face-enhancement process) behaviors in conflict interaction process. For many of the large East Asian corporations, for example, Confucian-driven hierarchical principles tend to promote a parent-child relationship between the manager and the subordinate.

Under the benevolent conflict approach, while a manager can confront their employees in order to motivate them to work harder, it is very rare that subordinates will directly challenge the manager's authority during a conflict interaction process. However, they might opt for using passive aggressive or sabotage conflict strategies to deal with the workplace tensions or frustrations. In dealing with low-premium conflicts, managers would consider using the "smooth over" relational tactics or subtle face-pressuring tactics to gain employees' compliance. However, in dealing with high-premium conflicts, benevolent managers could act in a very directive or autocratic and controlling manner. They might also practice preferential treatment or particularistic value by treating senior employees more favorably than junior employees, or family network friends more generously than peripheral workplace members.

From the benevolent cultural value angle, the Asian vertical collectivists who enter a mediation session would expect that the mediator should be more directive and controlling in moving the mediation process forward. They would also expect that the "expert" mediator would tell them what to do with clear directions and instructions and that the mediator as leader should come up with concrete solutions to solve their problem. They might be caught off guard to realize that they themselves have to come up with creative options or implementation plans.

Lastly, the *communal approach* (a combination of both collectivism and small power distance value orientation) is the least common of the four conflict workplace approaches. The values that encompass this approach are authentic interdependent connection to others and genuine equality via respectful communication exchange at all levels. Costa Rica is the only country found to fit this approach (Hofstede, 2001) on a national values' analysis level. Non-profit mediation centers or successful start-up small businesses also appear to practice some of the communal decision-making behaviors and participatory democracy so that everyone has a say, and also taking turns to rotate democratic leadership. In the communal approach or for the horizontal collectivists, personalized respectful treatment and equality of turn-taking are expected of all disputants. In a mediation session, the participants themselves would expect to spend more time in relationship-building and community-building (Barge, 2006, Domenici and Littlejohn, 2006). They would value both factual and emotional data inputs in the mediation process. They would also look at the mediator's role as a co-participant or interactional facilitator more so than an authoritative figure as in the benevolent corporate conflict orientation. They would also expect to have more free time to explore and discover the conflict issues themselves and dialogue directly with one another.

Understanding the unspoken value clashes and the misconstrued assumptions between the Western and East Asian approaches to conflict and a mediation session would serve *as a good first step* to reconcile some of the possible cultural differences. Digging deep into our own ethnocentric lens and coming to the realization that our cultural and personal value patterns shape our mediation lens would help us to become a more mindful intercultural mediator. We engage in an ethnocentric perspective when we view our own cultural way of communicating as the most proper and correct way of communicating, and we view the unfamiliar communication practices of other cultural groups as improper and incorrect (Ting-Toomey and Chung, 2005). Ethnorelativism, on the other hand, means the capacity to view communication behaviors from the other person's cultural frame of reference and understand why people behave the way they behave from their cultural values' standpoint (Bennett, 2009, Bennett and Bennett, 2004).

Intercultural Mediation: Facework Competence

According to Assumption 7 of the conflict face-negotiation theory, intercultural facework competence refers to the optimal integration of knowledge, mindfulness, and communication skills in managing vulnerable identity-based interaction scenes appropriately, effectively, and adaptively. Canary and Lakey (2006), for example, argue for the importance of the twin criteria of "appropriateness" and "effectiveness" in assessing conflict competence. They comment that "communication can be judged as competent only within the context of a relationship or situation because the context determines the standards of appropriateness that must be met" and that "communication can be appropriate without being effective and effective without being appropriate" (p. 187). Likewise, mediation competence can also borrow from the twin standards of communication appropriateness and effectiveness (see Spitzberg & Cupach, 1984, 1989). An intercultural mediator has acted appropriately when both cultural disputants view that the mediator has communicated skillfully and displayed adaptive facilitation styles so that both disputants feel included in the mediation session. Concurrently, the mediator also has moved the conflict parties forward productively or effectively and helped them to reach a doable, mutual-interest outcome.

To behave appropriately in a mediation session, competent mediators need to have the relevant value knowledge patterns of the larger cultures of both conflict parties. They also need to apply culture-sensitive situational norms in understanding the holistic conflict story. To be perceived as effective mediators, the intercultural mediators need to have linguistic, verbal, and nonverbal elastic skills to confront, to conjure, and to know when to "manage" the mediation process and when to "let go" of the mediation process and let the disputants take over the process. They also need to have "differentiating" knowledge in understanding that both cultural-based and personal-based motives operate in a mediation session. More important, appropriateness and effectiveness criteria are positively interdependent. When the mediator uses a culture-sensitive approach to mediate the mediation session, the "good faith" respectful behaviors can induce cooperative and effective outcome. Likewise, when the mediator skillfully moves the disputants from one stage of the mediation process to another stage, her or his effective facilitation skills can elicit respect from both the disputants toward each other and toward the mediator herself or himself.

Intercultural Mediation Knowledge: Asian and Western Conflict Viewpoints

According to the conflict face-negotiation theory (Ting-Toomey, 2005a), culture-sensitive knowledge, mindfulness, and constructive communication skills constitute the key features of intercultural facework competence. Of all the components, knowledge is the most important component that underscores the other components of competence. Knowledge here refers to developing an in-depth understanding of relevant intercultural concepts (e.g., cultural value patterns and preferred conflict communication styles) and culture-sensitive mediation process work that can help to manage the mediation episode flexibly and adaptively.

A typical mediation process often involves the following developmental stages: Introduction, storytelling, negotiating joint problem-solving, resolution (Domenici & Littlejohn, 2001). In the "introduction" stage, the mediator explains the process, establishes the communication guidelines, clarifies the mediator's role, and ensures confidentiality. In the "storytelling" stage, the mediator invites each disputant to tell his or her conflict story and tries to facilitate a genuine understanding process of the identity, relational, substantive, and process issues of the conflict case. By empathetic listening, meaning clarification, probing questions, and reframing skills, the mediator tries to move the dialogue process forward. In the "negotiating joint problem-solving" stage, the mediator helps the disputants to find common interests that underlie their positions, encourages them to brainstorm solutions, and generates inclusive criteria to assess the various solutions. In the "resolution" stage, the mediator facilitates an agreement that is satisfactory to all conflict parties, writes up the final agreement, and compliments the commitment and creative efforts put forth by all disputants in willing to "struggle with" each other in arriving at a common-ground solution.

In mediating conflicts with Asian cultural members, mediators may want to heed the following guidelines: (1) Asian disputants may emphasize a strong benevolent conflict approach in entering a mediation session; (2) they may expect that the mediator is there to serve as a benevolent, authoritative figure and who is there to give them the solution to a conflict problem; (3) Asian disputants are oftentimes face-sensitive in disclosing private information—they may not feel comfortable engaging in direct conflict storytelling and self-disclosure unless some emotional ties or trust have been established; (4) they may not see the distinction between substantive conflict issue and relational conflict issue—they may tend to see both data sets as an integrative whole; (5) they may not feel comfortable with the free-wheeling brainstorming techniques especially under time pressure; (6) they may need to claim "face victory" in front of their own ingroups.

To address the above issues, culture-sensitive mediators must learn to "*give face*" or "honor and uplift" the face images of the Asian disputants via the following strategies. First, they need to spend more time in the "introduction" stage of the mediation to clearly define the meaning of mediation, the mediator's role, and to emphasize the confidentiality of the process in terms that privately-disclosed information will not spill over to any ingroup or outgroup members beyond the boundary of the mediation session. Second, they need to use more patience in generating the ground rules that govern the mediation process especially from the reticent Asian members. They need to tolerate silence and hesitations and engage in more high-context probing questions and clarification questions. They may want to engage in more metaphorical and analogical probes in inviting the Asian disputants to open up their deeply-guarded emotions. Third, they need to encourage the Western disputants to learn to listen and not to interrupt. They need to use a stronger coaching, facilitation technique to explain what does "brainstorming" mean in the mediation context and give some concrete examples. They need to emphasize that there is no right or wrong answer in the initial brainstorming stage and that regardless of rank or age, all disputants should feel free to bring forth their creative ideas without evaluative judgments. They need to emphasize both value harmony motivation and instrumental harmony motivation. They can persuade the Asian disputants via the dual-harmony motivation model. The intercultural mediators, for example, can emphasize that indeed, when the mediation agreement is signed, the Asian disputants and their families can finally enjoy some tranquil moments after a successful mediation session and that surface peace may entice improved neighborly relationship in the long run.

On the other hand, competent intercultural mediators must also learn to "*validate the face*" or social self-images of the Western disputants via the following strategies. First, they need to spend more time in the "introduction" stage to educate the Western disputants about the importance of displaying cultural sensitivity to all conflict parties in the mediation session. They can also address the possibility that individuals in the room may have different conflict style approaches and preferences. They can also emphasize that indeed their role is neutral, impartial, and objective so that they can match the expectancies and concerns of disputants who subscribe to a strong "impartial" or "status-achievement" conflict approach. Second, mediators should make sure to serve as well-balanced traffic conductors in balancing the talk times between the Western individualists and reticent Asian collectivists. They should also make sure that the Western disputants understand why some Asian disputants, once they start talking, they spend so much time in "contexting" their conflict story and not get to the point head-on because of their high-context communication tendencies. Third, they need to role-model adaptive communication styles so that both the Asian and Western disputants can observe first-hand how to engage in appropriate and respectful culture-sensitive dialogue. They may also want to team up with other intercultural experts and conduct co-mediation sessions when there are strong linguistic and deep-rooted cultural animosities exist among the cultural group members.

Intercultural Mediation: Mindfulness and Skills

Knowledge and an open-minded attitude are closely intertwined and reciprocally influence one another. To be an astute decoder of a complex conflict situation, an intercultural mediator must develop a mindful, layered systems outlook in assessing the macro- and micro-level features of a culture clash episode. *Mindfulness*, from the intercultural conflict competence framework, means the willingness to attend to one's internal cultural and personal communication assumptions, cognitions, and emotions and, at the same time, becoming exquisitely attuned to the other's communication assumptions, cognitions, and emotions (LeBaron, 2003; Ting-Toomey, 1999). Mindful fluency requires us to tune into our own cultural and personal habitual assumptions in scanning a problematic interaction scene. It also refers to the willingness to learn from the unfamiliar other. To be mindful of intercultural differences, individuals have to learn to see the unfamiliar behavior from multiple cultural angles, which means understanding the underlying value dimensions of the unfamiliar culture *as a starting point*.

Constructive communication skills refer to our operational abilities to manage a conflict situation appropriately and effectively via skillful verbal and nonverbal behaviors. Many communication skills are useful in enhancing intercultural mediation competencies. Of the many possible operational competence skills (see Ting-Toomey, 2004), for example, skills such as deep listening, mindful reframing, de-centering, face-sensitive respectful dialogue skills (e.g., for a review of the dialogue approaches, see Barge, 2006; and face-sensitive skills, see Domenici & Littlejohn, 2006), and facilitating collaborative conflict negotiation skills (e.g., the skill set of the "A.E.I.O.U." negotiation that stands for "Attack, Evade, Inform, Open, Unite," developed by Coleman & Raider, 2006) across cultural and ethnic/racial lines are critical practices.

Mindful Transformation: A Big Picture View

Mindful transformation is the incremental awakening process in understanding how our own cultural worldviews and value system shape our conflict responses and gut-level reactions, and simultaneously, realizing that there are alternative worldviews and value system that frame our cultural disputants' conflict lens and meanings and that of our own lens. According to Senge, Scharmer, Jaworski, and Flowers (2004), to engage in transformative change, individuals need to practice a "U-movement" downward swing characterized by "transforming our habitual way of seeing" and then back up the U, and "transforming the source of our awareness" (p. 224).

To transform "our habitual way of seeing," the competent mediators need to intentionally shift their frame of focus from their habitual angle of seeing things to seeing things from a "third culture" viewpoint. They need to reposition their own cultural standpoints and be ready to code-switch between an individualistic and a collectivistic viewfinder, or a small power distance and a large power distance perspective (Molinsky, 2007). In committing to transform "the source of our awareness," the competent mediators need to intentionally examine the grounded assumptions and premises that drive their disputants' conflict meaning-making process within embedded historical and immediate cultural contexts.

Mindfulness: Eastern and Western Orientations

According to Langer's (1989, 1997) concept of mindfulness, mindfulness can include the following characteristics: (a) learning to see behavior or information presented in the conflict situation as novel or fresh, (b) learning to view a conflict situation from several vantage points or perspectives, (c) learning to attend to the conflict context and the person in whom we are perceiving the behavior, and (d) learning to create new categories through which conflict behavior may be understood. Applying this Western mindfulness orientation to intercultural conflict, the perspective suggests a readiness to shift one's frame of reference from an ethnocentric lens to an ethnorelative lens, and the possibility to understand a conflict episode from the other person's cultural frame of reference.

On the other side of the spectrum, mindfulness, from an Eastern Buddhist orientation, means "empting our mindset" and learning to listen deeply without preconceived notions, judgments, and assumptions. Through an Eastern philosophical lens (Chogyam, 1976; Kabat-Zinn, 1994; Thich, 1998), mindfulness means learning to observe an unfolding conflict episode with one-pointed wakefulness and watchfulness. It means being fully present—attending fully to our own arising emotions and the cultural disputants' conflict assumptions, worldviews, positions, interests, and arising emotions. It also means listening deeply with all our senses open and all our perceptual filters unclogged.

In fact, the Chinese character for "*listening*" refers to the term "*ting*" which means "listening with one-pointed attention with our ears, eyes, and a focused heart." Thus, mindful listening in any conflict situation means listening to the hidden value assumptions, expectancies, words, tones, nonverbal nuances, multilayered meanings, and contexts that underlie the symbolic exchange process. This layered way of listening via culture-sensitive paraphrasing, perception-checking, and reframing is of great benefit in an intercultural tug-and-pull mediation session. It slows down the antagonistic, polarized conflict process between the disputants. It increases the chance of mutual, authentic understanding along the various mediation developmental stages. It essentially involves a gradual shift of worldview or cultural perspective as viewed from an alternative lens. It evokes mutual respect and creates a third space for the disputants to tell a complete conflict story without interruptions and judgments.

Conflict Transformative Questions

We can also use some critical reflective questions to guide our conflict transformative "U" learning process (Fisher-Yoshida, 2005, Mezirow, 2000). For example, if a disputant in an intercultural mediation session was constantly using "silence" or indirect response to every question a mediator asked during the conflict storytelling phase, the mindful transformative questions that the mediator can process within herself or himself are: First, what are my cultural and personal assessments about the use of "silence" in this particular mediation scene? (a content reflection question). Second, why do I form such assessments and what are the sources of my assessments? (a process critical reflection question Third, what are the underlying assumptions or values that drive my evaluative assessments? (a premise-value question). Fourth, how do I know that they are relevant or valid in this conflict context? (a premise-self-challenge question). Fifth, what reasons might I have for maintaining or changing my underlying conflict premises? (an identity transformation question). Sixth, how should I shift my cultural or personal premises into the direction that promotes deeper intercultural understanding? (a mindset transformation question). Seventh, how should I behaviorally swing adaptively to the other person's preferred conflict competence responses in order to facilitate a productive mutual-interest outcome? (a behavioral transformation question). The first three questions are based on Fisher-Yoshida's work (2005) concerning the importance of engaging in deeper double-loop thinking in analyzing the role of self-in-conflict context. The last four questions are an extension of Ting-Toomey's (1999, 2005b) mindful identity transformation work. These seven questions can be applied to our own transformational process in dealing with diverse individuals in the mediation process.

The mindful intercultural conflict negotiator is one who is nimble and flexible enough to engage in a code-switching figure-8 dance during a protracted mediation session. She or he can integrate the best practices of both individualistic and collectivistic value tendencies, and the equality treatment and respect-humility attributes of both small and larger power distance value tendencies. She or he can reconcile the value dilemmas in the developmental mediation session and using the strengths of both spectrums and intentionally transform the relationship between the disputants and their cultural lens in viewing the original conflict episode. She or he can create a transformative learning experience for the disputants and, simultaneously, building a bridge and a safety net for diverse voices be heard and multiple stories be told, with mutual face-sensitive respect and dignity.

References

BARGE, J.K. (2006) Dialogue, conflict, and community. IN J. OETZEL & S. TING-TOOMEY (Eds.) *The Sage Handbook of Conflict Communication: Integrating Theory, Research, and Practice*, 517-548. Thousand Oaks, CA, Sage Publications.

BENNETT, J.M. (2009) Transformative training: Designing programs for culture learning. IN M.A. MOODIAN (Ed.) *Contermporary Leadership and Intercultural Competence: Exploring the Cross-Cultural Dynamics Within Organizations*, 95-110). Los Angeles, CA, Sage.

BENNETT, J. M., & BENNETT, M. J. (2004) Developing intercultural sensitivity: An integrative approach to global and domestic diversity. IN D. LANDIS, J. BENNETT, & M. BENNETT (Eds.) *Handbook of Intercultural Training* .3rd ed., 147-165. Thousand Oaks, CA, Sage.

BUSH, R.A., & FOLGER, J. P. (2005) *The Promise of Mediation: The Transformative Approach to Conflict*, San Francisco, Jossey-Bass.

CAI, D. A., & FINK, E. L. (2002) Conflict style differences between individualists and collectivists. *Communication Monographs*, 69, 67-87.

CANARY, D., & LAKEY, S.G. (2006) Managing conflict in a competent manner: A mindful look at events that matter. IN J. OETZEL & S. TING-TOOMEY (Eds.) *The Sage Handbook of Conflict Communication*, 185-210. Thousand Oaks, CA, Sage Publications.

CARL, D., GUPTA, V., & JAVIDAN, M. (2004) Power distance. In R. House, P. Hanges, M. Javidan, P. Dorfman, & V. Gupta (Eds.), *Culture, Leadership, and Organizations: The GLOBE Study of 62 Societies*. 513-563. Thousand Oaks, CA: Sage Publications.

CHOGYAM, T. (1976) *The Foundations of Mindfulness*, Berkeley, CA, Shambhala.

COLEMAN, S., & RAIDER, E. (2006) International/intercultural conflict resolution training. IN J. OETZEL & S. TING-TOOMEY (Eds.) *The Sage Handbook of Conflict Communication*, 663-690. Thousand Oaks, CA, Sage Publications.

DOMENICI, K., & LITTLEJOHN, S. (2001) *Mediation: Empowerment in conflict management, 2nd ed.*. Long Grove, IL, Waveland Press.

DOMENICI, K., & LITTLEJOHN, S. (2006) *Facework: Bridging Theory and Practice*. Thousand Oaks, CA, Sage.

FISHER-YOSHIDA, B. (2005) Reframing conflict: Intercultural conflict as potential transformation. *Journal of Intercultural Communication, 8*, 1-16.

GAO, G., & TING-TOOMEY, S. (1998). *Communicating Effectively with the Chinese*. Thousand Oaks, CA, Sage.

HALL, E. T. (1983) *The Dance of Life*. New York, Doubleday.

HOFSTEDE, G. (2001) *Culture's Consequences: Comparing Values, Behaviors, Institutions, and Organizations across Cultures*, 2nd ed. Thousand Oaks, CA, Sage.

HOUSE, R., HANGES, P., JAVIDAN, M., DORFMAN, P., & GUPTA, V. (Eds.) (2004) *Culture, Leadership, and Organizations: The GLOBE Study of 62 Societies*. Thousand Oaks, CA, Sage.

KABAT-ZINN, J. (1994) *Wherever You Go There You Are: Mindfulness Meditation in Everyday Life*, New York, Hyperion.

KAUSHAL, R., & KWANTES, C. (2006) The role of culture and personality in choice of conflict management strategy. *International Journal of Intercultural Relations, 30*, 579-603.

KIM, T.-Y., WANG, C., KONDO, M., & KIM, T.-Y. (2007) Conflict management styles; The differences among the Chinese, Japanese, and Koreans. *International Journal of Conflict Management, 18*, 23-41.

LANGER, E. (1989) *Mindfulness*, Reading, MA, Addison-Wesley.

LANGER, E. (1997) *The Power of Mindful Learning*, Reading, MA, Addison-Wesley.

LEBARON, M. (2003). *Bridging Cultural Conflicts: A New Approach for a Changing World*, San Francisco, Jossey Bass/John Wiley.

LEUNG, K., KOCH, P.T., & LU, L. (2002). A dualistic model of harmony and its implications for conflict management in Asia. *Asia Pacific Journal of Management, 19*, 201-220.

LEUNG, K., & TJOSVOLD, D.W. (Eds.) (1998). *Conflict Management in the Asia Pacific*, Singapore, Wiley.

LIM, T.-S., & CHOI, S.H. (1996) Interpersonal relationships in Korea. IN W. GUDYKUNST, S. TING-TOOMEY, & T. NISHIDA (Eds.) *Communication in Personal Relationships across Cultures*, 122-136. Thousand Oaks, CA, Sage.
MARKUS, H. R., & KITAYAMA, S. (1991), Culture and self: Implication for cognition, emotion, and motivation. *Psychological Review, 98,* 224-253.
MARKUS, H. R., & KITAYAMA, S. (1998) The cultural psychology of personality. *Journal of Cross-Cultural Psychology 29,* 63–87.
MERKIN, R. (2006) Power distance and facework strategies. *Journal of Intercultural Communication Research, 35,* 139-160.
MEZIROW, J. (Ed.) (2000). *Learning as Transformation: Critical Perspectives on a Theory in Progress,* San Francisco, CA, Jossey-Bass.
MOLINSKY, A. (2007) Cross-cultural code-switching: The psychological challenges of adapting behavior in foreign cultural interactions. *Academy of Management Review, 32(2),* 622-640.
NICOTERA, A., & DORSEY, L. (2006) Individual and interactive processes in organizational conflict. IN J. OETZEL & S. TING-TOOMEY (Eds.) *The Sage Handbook of Conflict Communication*, 293-325. Thousand Oaks, CA, Sage.
OETZEL, J., ARCOS, B., MABIZELA, P., WEINMAN, A.M., & ZHANG, Q. (2006) Historical, political, and spiritual factors of conflict: Understanding conflict perspectives and communication in the Muslim world, China, Colombia, and South Africa. IN J. OETZEL & S. TING-TOOMEY (Eds.) *The Sage Handbook of Conflict Communication*, 549-574. Thousand Oaks, CA, Sage.
OETZEL, J. G., GARCIA, A., & TING-TOOMEY, S. (2008) An analysis of the relationships among face concerns and facework behaviors in perceived conflict situations: A four-culture investigation. *International Journal of Conflict Management, 19*, 382-403.
OETZEL, J. G., & TING-TOOMEY, S. (2003) Face concerns in interpersonal conflict: A cross-cultural empirical test of the face-negotiation theory. *Communication Research, 30,* 599-624.
OETZEL, J. G., TING-TOOMEY, S., MASUMOTO, T., YOKOCHI, Y., PAN, X, TAKAI, J., & WILCOX, R. (2001) Face behaviors in interpersonal conflicts: A cross-cultural comparison of Germany, Japan, China, and the United States. *Communication Monographs 68,* 235–258.
ONISHI, J., & BLISS, R.E. (2006) In search of Asian ways of managing conflict: A comparative study of Japan, Hong Kong, Thailand and Vietnam. *International Journal of Conflict Management, 17,* 203-225.
PUTNAM, L. (2006). Definitions and approaches to conflict and communication. IN J. OETZEL & S. TING-TOOMEY (Eds.) *The Sage Handbook of Conflict Communication,* 1 - 32. Thousand Oaks, CA, Sage.
SENGE, P., SCHARMER, C., JAWORSKI, J., & FLOWERS, B. (2004) *Presence: Human Purpose and the Field of the Future*, Cambridge, MA, The Society for Organizational Learning, Inc.

SMITH, P., DUGEN, S., PETERSON, M., & LEUNG, K.(1998) Individualism, collectivism and the handling of disagreement: A 23 country study. *International Journal of Intercultural Relations, 22,* 351-367.

SPITZBERG, B., & CUPACH, W. (1984) *Interpersonal communication competence.* Beverly Hills, CA, Sage.

SPITZBERG, B., & CUPACH, W. (Eds.) (1989) *Handbook of Interpersonal Competence Research.* New York, Springer.

STORTI, C. (2001) *Old World/New World,* Yarmouth, ME, Intercultural Press.

THICH, N.H. (1998) *Mindful Living,* Berkeley, CA, Parallax Press.

TING-TOOMEY, S. (1988) Intercultural conflicts: A face-negotiation theory. IN KIM, Y.Y. & GUDYKUNST, W. (Eds.) *Theories in Intercultural Communication,* 213–235. Newbury Park, CA, Sage.

TING-TOOMEY, S. (1999) *Communicating across Cultures,* New York, Guilford.

TING-TOOMEY, S. (2004) Translating conflict face-negotiation theory into practice. IN LANDIS, D., BENNETT, J., & BENNETT, M. (Eds.) *Handbook of Intercultural Training,* 3rd ed.,217-248. Thousand Oaks, CA, Sage Publications.

TING-TOOMEY, S. (2005a) The matrix of face: An updated face-negotiation theory. IN GUDYKUNST, W. B. (Ed.) *Theorizing about Intercultural Communication,* 71-92. Thousand Oaks, CA, Sage Publications.

TING-TOOMEY, S. (2005b) Identity negotiation theory: Crossing cultural boundaries. IN GUDYKUNST, W. B. (Ed.) *Theorizing about intercultural communication,* 211-234. Thousand Oaks, CA, Sage.

TING-TOOMEY, S., & CHUNG, L. C. (2005) *Understanding Intercultural Communication,* Los Angeles, CA, Roxbury Publications/Oxford University Press.

TING-TOOMEY, S., & KUROGI, A. (1998) Facework competence in intercultural conflict: An updated face-negotiation theory. *International Journal of Intercultural Relations 22,* 187-225.

TING-TOOMEY, S., & OETZEL, J. G. (2001) *Managing Intercultural Conflict Effectively.* Thousand Oaks, CA, Sage.

TING-TOOMEY, S., & TAKAI, J. (2006) Explaining intercultural conflict: Promising approaches and directions. IN OETZEL, J. & TING-TOOMEY, S. (Eds.) *The Sage Handbook of Conflict Communication,* 691 -723. Thousand Oaks, CA, Sage.

TING-TOOMEY, S., YEE-JUNG, K., SHAPIRO, R., GARCIA, W., WRIGHT, T., & OETZEL, J. G. (2000) Ethnic/cultural identity salience and conflict styles in four U.S. ethnic groups. *International Journal of Intercultural Relations, 24,* 47–81.

TRIANDIS, H. (1995) *Individualism and Collectivism,* Boulder, CO, Westview Press.

WILMOT, W., & HOCKER, J. (2007) *Interpersonal Conflict,* 7th ed., Boston, McGraw-Hill.

Is Cross-Cultural Mediation a Technique? Theoretical/Methodological Frameworks and Empirical Evidence from Interaction

Claudio Baraldi

The search for good practices in mediation

In recent years, many studies have tried to indicate the "good practices" of mediation (e.g. Bowling and Hoffman, 2000, Bush and Folger, 1994, Picard and Melchin, 2007, Winslade and Monk, 2008). In these studies, mediation is described mainly as a technique, i.e. a selection of adequate actions. Mediation is primarily analysed as being a successful technique.

Three important issues should be considered in analysing this approach. Firstly, techniques do not have any sense or relevance without methodology. Methodology has the function of fixing the ways of observing (Luhmann, 1990), while techniques are the operational implementations of methodology. In the specific case of mediation, the methodology sets out the ways in which mediation is successfully achieved. Methodology is a stable presupposition of mediation, and techniques may vary because it is the methodology that provides internal coherence. Secondly, techniques do not have any meaning or relevance without a theory that explains the function of mediation. Theory has the function of indicating what is observed (Luhmann, 1990). While methodology specifies how mediation can be performed, theory defines what mediation is. Thirdly, techniques do not have any meaning or relevance without empirical observation. In most studies, techniques are presented as prescriptions, as a recipe for solving problems. In fact, their feasibility and affordability need to be carefully tested in specific conditions and situations. Empirical research is essential for this purpose, while experiential exemplifications and normative prescriptions are not only insufficient but also detrimental to an adequate understanding of mediation.

The understanding of cross-cultural mediation requires an accurate investigation into its theoretical and methodological bases, in particular into its relationship with the contexts in which it finds a function, on the features of this function, on its achievement in interaction, and finally on the features of its successful achievement.

The reasons for the theory and methodology of mediation

The concept of mediation originates from the need for new forms of conflict resolution, which take the name of Alternative Dispute Resolution (ADR). According to Winslade, "mediation, by its very nature, is about weaving a path through contents and contradictions" (2006: 507). Mediation is generally defined as a third neutral position in a conflict, with the function of helping the conflicting parties in managing their relationships, in particular of coordinating the parties' autonomous and shared solutions of their conflicts, solutions which should satisfy both of them.

In managing conflicts, mediation renounces to judgements based on right/wrong distinctions (e.g. Carnevale and Pruitt, 1992, Mulcahy, 2001). Mediators "flourish when they please all parties, when they oppress anybody" (Zeldin, 1998: 161). Therefore, mediation is based on the critical observation of the function of judgment in conflict resolution. The problem with the definition of mediation as "alternative dispute resolution" is: what are the "alternative" features of conflict management? In defining these features, particularly the features of cross-cultural mediation, one meets four main problems.

1. The function of mediation is observed in facilitating communication between conflicting parties (e.g. Bowling and Hoffman, 2000, Sahah-Kazemi, 2000). In particular, cross-cultural mediation facilitates intercultural communication. Communication is observed as intercultural whenever the creation of a single, shared culture is prevented (Carbaugh, 2005), i.e. whenever communication includes differences on the level of presumably shared symbols. In the literature, intercultural communication is frequently explained through cultural variability, i.e. through the existence of different cultures which might be compared and contrasted (e.g. Hofstede, 1980, Triandis, 1995). In communication, participants show their cultural identities (Carbaugh, 1999), which are We-identities (Tan and Moghaddam 1999, Ting-Toomey, 1999). In this sense, cross-cultural mediation requires knowledge of different cultures and should achieve their bridging (Gudykunst, 1994). We may note two problems with this approach. Firstly, intercultural communication seems to produce above all cultural hybridisations (Nederveen Pieterse, 2004, 2007) which cancel original cultural heritages. Consequently, cultural differences are unstable (Verschueren, 2008): cultures change and their differences may be reduced by hybridisation. Secondly, cultural differences are constructed via communication processes (Gumperz, 1982, Gumperz and Roberts, 1991), not within pre-existing "groups", and their construction is always unpredictable. Problem: cross-cultural mediation may encounter difficulties in dealing with the "cultural" aspects of the conflicting parties.

2. In some cases of cross-cultural mediation, conflicts are not visible at all. In international settings, mediation can be easily observed as conflict management, which frequently concerns cultural identities (e.g. Brigg, 2003, Coleman and Lowe, 2007, Jeong, 2008). In national settings, different cultural identities may be involved in mediation; however, in many situations conflicts are not visible because

national policies of both assimilation and recognition try to avoid them. This is the consequence of a long-term persistence of multicultural societies, which implies a certain success in the political management of cross-cultural relationships and processes of hybridisation. Determining the disappearance of clear-cut cultural identities, hybridisation decreases the potential for intercultural conflict. Therefore, in healthcare services, schools and other public services, only occasionally is conflict management the explicit and visible function of cross-cultural mediation. In these situations, conflict is only an abstract horizon. Moreover, the literature on intercultural conflicts often associates mediation with conflict avoidance (e.g. Ting-Toomey, 1999, Ting-Toomey and Kurogi, 1998). Conflict avoidance is considered positive in co-operative and relational-oriented interactions, as it avoids destructive escalations and defends relationships from stressful and unnecessary disputes (Tjosvold and Sun, 2002). The relevance of conflict management in cross-cultural mediation is controversial because in some cases conflicts are not relevant and in other cases they can be more fruitfully avoided. Problem: the definition of mediation as alternative conflict management does not satisfy all the empirical conditions in which cross-cultural mediation is considered relevant and is practised.

3. Mediators' neutrality is associated with their authoritativeness, which is based on the parties' trust in their role and probably in their person: neutrality should assure trust (Siniver, 2006). However, in recent years mediation has been increasingly seen as a form of active participation. According to Winslade and Monk, "mediators are never neutral, as conventional mediation theory requires" because a mediator "cannot avoid being positioned discursively in the conflict, even as he is mediating it" and he chooses "a set of positions and not others" (2008: 113). Mediators actively intervene as distributors of opportunities to talk, inducing parties to introduce and deal with particular issues, reinforcing certain roles and identities, making some outcomes more likely than others. They construct new narratives (Winslade and Monk, 2000, 2008) and they systematically use and treat emotions (Katz Jameson, Bodtker and Jones, 2006, Maiese, 2006). Problem: neutrality cannot entail the absence of active contributions to mediation.

4. The effectiveness of cross-cultural mediation in achieving meaningful changes, particularly in promoting symmetrical power relations within broader social contexts, is contested. It has been observed that while mediation can effectively lead to temporary progress in social relationships and agreements about specific issues or goals, it de-emphasises the importance of the broader social context, of the durability of the relationships between parties, of their reciprocal stable recognition (Gwartney, Fessenden and Landt, 2002). Connections between mediation and its social context are seen as "outside the parameter of the mediator's responsibility" (Schoeny and Warfield, 2000: 254): in this way, mediators "become de facto agents

of the status quo invested in maintaining the stability of the current social system and stopping the conflict before it moves beyond the affected institutions' control" (Welsh and Coleman, 2002: 345-46). Problem: is mediation effective in changing the status quo of social systems, and in empowering the less influent participants?

In social practices, mediation is frequently considered useful and satisfying. However, its theoretical definition is insufficient. This gap between theory and practice may have negative methodological consequences; i.e. it may create a gap between the urgency of intervention and opportunities for reflection. Consequently, mediation needs a theoretical and methodological framework, supported by empirical analysis.

Contextualising mediation

The first theoretical statement is that mediation supports important social functions, e.g. political, medical, educational and juridical functions, which are implemented in differentiated social systems within society (Luhmann, 1997). Mediation is implemented whenever these social functions do not work appropriately and generate problems of communication. Mediation supports decisions in the political system, business and economics, educational processes, the provision of healthcare services, the implementation of rights. As its realisation depends on poor communication, mediation must adapt to the presuppositions of existing communication processes within differentiated social systems.

These social systems set the prerequisites for the implementation of mediation. These prerequisites are the cultural presuppositions (Gumperz, 1992) of communication within social systems. Mediation depends on these cultural presuppositions, created within the social systems which contextualise it. Cultural presuppositions are specific sets of expectations (Baker, 2006b, Luhmann, 1984). For example, in healthcare systems, expectations concern the treatment of illness and the recovery of health, medical roles and actions, and patients' adaptation to treatment. In education systems, expectations concern the shaping of children personality, namely children's achievement of knowledge, competence and abilities, teachers' actions and students' experience of teaching, control of success and feasibility of personality shaping, therefore assessment which requires children's actions (e.g. answering teachers' questions).

Some cultural presuppositions may be differentiated within the social system itself. For example, in healthcare systems, expectations may concern doctor-centred communication or patient-centred communication (e.g. Barry et al, 2001, Heritage and Maynard, 2005, 2006, Mishler, 1984). Doctor-centred communication is characterised by expectations of medical role performances based on scientific knowledge and technical competence, and patients' acceptance of medical diagnoses and adaptation to medical prescriptions. In patient-centred communication, on the other hand, the patients' perspectives and emotional expressions and the doctors' affective involvement are expected as the primary achievement: the patient's emotional expression of her/his life-world is encouraged, while doctors' affiliation substitutes medical control of patients' adaptation to medical prescriptions. In this context, we may observe expectations regarding cross-cultural mediation. On the one hand, mediators are asked to help doctors to explore patients' problems and to inform patients of relevant aspects regarding their illness and its remedy. On the other hand, they are asked to give patients the opportunity to explain their problems and express their perspectives on medical treatments. The difference between patient-centred and doctor-centred patterns of expectations also enhances differences in the ways of mediating. In education systems, we may observe different patterns of expectations with regard to roles and results. On the one hand, education may be observed and practised as the transmission of knowledge in a hierarchical interaction between experts (teachers) and persons in a developmental phase (learners) in need of experts' guidance. On the other hand, education may be observed and practised as the facilitation of children's agency and active participation (e.g. Baraldi, 2008, James and James, 2004, James, Jenks and Prout, 1998, Jans, 2004, Prout, 2000) with teachers considered "organisers of learning" (Holdsworth, 2005). In this context, cross-cultural mediation may be coherent both with the emphasis on children as social agents and with the model of transmission of knowledge and assimilation to the dominant culture.

The differentiation among contextualising social systems explains the lack of correspondence between mediation and conflict management. Open conflicts are not always the main problem of contextualising social systems. In many of these systems, such as the healthcare system and education system, mediation deals with problems of understanding, information and participation rather than conflicts, or it is required for the prevention or avoidance of conflicts in order to assure the problem-free course of communication.

Finally, contextualisation explains the specificity of cross-cultural mediation. Intercultural communication topicalises and gives meaning to cultural presuppositions that are not accepted by all participants (Baraldi, 2006a, 2006b). Cross-cultural mediation deals with the difference between cultural presuppositions.

Historically, ethnocentrism has been the most widespread way of creating meanings for these cultural differences (Pearce, 1989). Ethnocentrism means the interpretation and evaluation of participants' actions through a guiding distinction between a positive Us and a negative Them. Ethnocentrism gives meanings to cultural differences through the attribution of group belonging (collectivism): participants in communication are considered in terms of their being "members" of a cultural group and having a cultural identity based on normative expectations, i.e. expectations of conservation and stability. However, the increasing insensitivity to group appurtenance and cultural identities has enhanced the pluralism of perspectives, the relevance of role performances (individualism) and relevance of personal expressions. Today, cross-cultural mediation frequently deals with the differences between pluralism, individualism and personal expression on the one hand, and hierarchies, collectivism and denial of personal expression on the other. It is expected that ethnocentrism be avoided in intercultural communication, therefore to avoid the advocacy and separation of We-identities. However, the risk of cross-cultural mediation is the production of a new form of ethnocentrism, evaluating and refusing any cultural presuppositions deemed as threats to pluralist participation, individual freedom of speech, or rights of personal expression. It is the risk of adopting an Us-perspective by limiting the parties' voices in the name of pluralism and freedom of choice. The risk of cross-cultural mediation is the promotion of only one version of cultural diversity, while speaking in the name of humanity and projecting universal definitions of rights and needs.

This risk seems to be avoidable through the bridging (Gudykunst, 1994) of different cultural presuppositions, which creates intercultural competence (Spitzberg, 1997) and intercultural sensitivity (Yamada and Singelis, 1999). In this perspective, cross-cultural mediation is a transcultural form of communication (Milhouse, Asante and Nwosu, 2001) which must promote conjunction and harmonisation of different cultural presuppositions, and the co-construction of a "third culture" (Casmir, 1999, Chen and Starosta 1998) as an effect of the hybridisation of preexistent cultural presuppositions. Transcultural mediation should enhance cross-cultural adaptation (Kim, 2001), i.e. the dissolution of cultural boundaries which are considered causes of ethnocentric conflicts; it should also open up to other channels of cultural expression.

Transcultural mediation should promote the overcoming of diversity together with its respectful conservation; i.e. it should promote the simultaneity of the conservation of cultural differences and the creation of a new culture. Transcultural mediation should preserve and simultaneously change cultural presuppositions. Moreover, transcultural mediation is based on selected cultural presuppositions (guiding values) which should be shared by the parties. In the light of these ambivalences, the effectiveness of transcultural mediation in limiting ethnocentrism may be questioned.

The function of mediation

The first theoretical statement is that mediation is carried out differently in different contextualising social systems. The second is that, in all contextualising social systems, mediation is expected to facilitate communication through the promotion of active participation and the coordination of reflection.

Individuals participate in communication both by acting and understanding (Lumhann, 1984). However, communication may be observed only through participants' actions. Therefore, active participation is essential for communication and also for the solution of communication problems. In their attempts to facilitate communication, mediators promote the parties' active participation: promotion meaning the creation of opportunities for active participation. Facilitation of communication requires the promotion of the parties' active participation (Ayoko, Härtel and Callan, 2002).

The function of mediation depends on the recognition of increasing difficulties in promoting active participation in social systems, for example in involving children in schools, in gaining the trust of patients in healthcare services, in obtaining the satisfactory distribution of rights and wrongs in courts, in reaching agreements between conflicting parties in international politics. Whenever these difficulties create serious conflicts, or the fear of conflict is high, mediation is considered important. The "power" of conflicts in fostering social worries is the reason for the frequent association between mediation and conflict management.

A widespread term used to indicate the function of the promotion of active participation is empowerment. According to Bush and Folger (1994), mediation mainly promotes the participants' empowerment in defining issues and autonomously deciding about them. Bush and Folger think that in this way mediation can create change, i.e. it is transformative mediation. Transformative mediation is different from problem-solving mediation, which simply resolves specific conflicts through a short-term settlement: the idea of transformative mediation opens up the opportunity to think about effective changes to social systems, and this opportunity is linked to empowerment. The concept of empowerment embodies two meanings of change: on the one hand empowerment is change which is enhanced by mediation (empowering participants), on the other hand empowerment is the means by which participants may enhance change (empowered participants).

The function of the promotion of active participation is also recognised by Winslade and Monk (2000, 2008) in their concept of narrative mediation. Baker (2006a) defines narratives as social constructions, in which the observed world is interpreted and "storied". Narrative mediation is the construction of alternative narratives with respect to the existing ones, and in particular to existing narratives in which one party is subjugated to or emarginated from the other. Mediators actively intervene as distributors of opportunities to communicate, soliciting the parties to introduce and deal with particular issues, giving voice to their own stories. Narrative mediation is based on the creation of opportunities for the parties to introduce their own stories as first person stories, and gives importance to recovering unstoried experiences. According to Winslade (2006), narrative mediation has three goals: (1) creating the conditions for the growth of alternative stories, (2) building on these stories as incompatible with hierarchical forms of relationship, and (3) providing room for shifts in participants' discursive positioning, towards "positive" positioning. In particular, the creation of alternative narratives encourages the parties to see relationships in other ways and to consider new ways of dealing with different perspectives (Winslade, Monk and Cotter, 1998); therefore, thickening alternative stories is important in narrative mediation. Narrative mediation deals with the parties as active producers and editors of their own stories. Empowerment is not considered the main feature of narrative mediation, which is observed in terms of re-authoring stories (Winslade and Monk, 2008). However, it is easy to observe that this re-authoring requires the recognition and promotion of the parties' active participation, i.e. empowerment. The distinction between re-authoring and empowerment seems to be only analytical, as empowerment is necessary for authorship.

The promotion of active participation (empowerment and re-authoring) is not sufficient to facilitate communication between the parties. Facilitation needs coordination, i.e. the creation of space for different voices which do not hinder each other. Coordination follows the promotion of active participation, allowing inclusion of the parties' voices in a new reflexive phase. According to Luhmann (1984) reflexivity means observation in communication of other communication processes. Reflexivity enhances the observation of ways of communicating in the system, but not observation of the meaning of the system. Observation of the meaning of the system requires reflection. According to Luhmann (1984), reflection is a process through which social systems observe the meanings of their internal 'reality', indicating it as a unit and dealing with this unit in communication, i.e. creating its identity (e.g. the medical treatment of illness, education, mediation, etc.). Reflection topicalises narratives which have been produced in previous communications, allowing for their change. Both reflexivity and reflection require coordination; however, the coordination of reflection is the most important process in the system. Therefore, the coordination of reflection is a second important function of mediation. The coordination of reflection provides mutual recognition of perspectives, which sustains empowerment (Bush and Folger, 1994) and the thickening of alternative stories through the identification of openings to alternative stories, encouragement of these stories and building on stories of cooperation (Winslade and Monk, 2008).

The promotion of active participation may create conflicts between different positions, and reflection gives the opportunity to manage these conflicts effectively. In this sense, conflict management is a possible third function of mediation. In another sense, conflict management may mean the prevention or avoidance as well as the resolution of conflicts; therefore, this third function could become essential. In fact, while resolution requires a conflict to be open, avoidance means that conflicting positions do not find answers, and prevention means that conflicting positions do not appear. If mediation is interpreted as conflict avoidance or prevention, however, it is difficult to observe its function in terms of conflict management, while the promotion of participation and the coordination of reflection on its results are always observable.

To sum up, the function of mediation is a combination, in a sequence, of (1) the promotion of active participation and (2) the coordination of reflection, (3) occasionally enhancing conflict management.

As satisfaction is generally considered a positive indicator of mediation, the promotion of active participation and the coordinating of reflection should be satisfactory for the parties. However, reasons for individual satisfaction are difficult to detect and generalise. The most convincing way of measuring the success of mediation is not detecting individual satisfaction, but the effective promotion of active participation (e.g. Maoz, 2001, 2005).

The success of these functions of mediation depends on choices which are made in the contextualising social systems. For example, in healthcare systems and education systems, the promotion of active participation is considered important because it enhances respectively patient-centred communication and children's agency. A different perspective in contextualising systems may change the function of mediation.

Dialogic mediation

The first methodological consideration which follows these theoretical statements is that mediation which promotes active participation and the coordination of reflection is based on dialogue, i.e. it is dialogic mediation. The adjective "dialogic" explains the methodology of mediation. Dialogic mediation is not prescriptive or ideal, it is an option available to reach results which are considered important for the contextualising social systems. The features of dialogic mediation may be identified by looking at the ways of promoting participation and coordinating reflection successfully.

Although in some approaches communication is always considered dialogic (Weigand, 1994), the concept of dialogue may be interpreted as a specific form of communication, based on specific cultural presuppositions. According to Wierzbicka, in dialogue participants make efforts to understand each other and make themselves understood; dialogue "implies that each party makes a step in the direction of the other", while it does not imply "that they reach a shared position or even mutual warm feelings" (2005: 692). Participants' positions are intentionally questioned and negotiated, in order to reach a coordinated positioning.

Dialogic mediation is based on peculiar cultural presuppositions (patterns of expectations). These cultural presuppositions determine: 1) the promotion and fair distribution of active participation in interaction (equity); 2) the display of sensitivity towards the interlocutors' interests and/or needs (empathy); 3) treatment of disagreements and alternative perspectives as enrichments in communication (empowerment). Dialogic mediation requires equity and empathy as premises for empowerment. Firstly, dialogic mediation requires an equal distribution of opportunities for active participation and personal expression. It implies expression and the acknowledgement of different perspectives: each party is led to observe and take into account the other's competent and legitimised perspective. Secondly, dialogic mediation requires empathy, i.e. showing interest in the parties' personal expressions and sensitivity to their needs. Empathy may be observed as addressing the parties' interests and/or needs through an integration of attention towards the contents of communication and sensitivity towards personal expressions in communication. Empathy means appreciation for emotions and needs, based on the ability to understand them.

Dialogic mediation evokes the other side of a distinction: monologue. In its more usual version, monologue is intended as a one-sided discussion: speakers talk and their interlocutors cannot respond, passively listening to them. However, we may also see monologue as a form of communication which ignores the difference of perspectives in interaction. In monologue, "language use is regarded from the perspective of the speaker"; this means that "the meanings of words and utterances are seen as resulting from the speakers' intentions or strategies alone, while co-present people are seen as recipients of the units of information prepared by the speaker" (Wadensjö, 1998: 8). Monologue is based on expectations of the unequal distribution of participation, a lack of sensitivity for the interlocutors' actions, and treatment of disagreements and alternative perspectives as irrelevant or dangerous. In this sense, monologue is a disempowering form of communication. Monologue is not the absence of understanding or consideration for interlocutors; rather it is a particular form of understanding and consideration for them. In monologue, speakers give more value to their own action than to their interlocutors' understanding, display certainty of their own understanding, attribute errors to their interlocutors, show indifference towards the consequences of their own actions on their interlocutors, and a lack of attention to their interlocutors' perspectives. Monologue means a preference for hierarchical relationships: in a monologue, speakers claim the right to control the distribution of opportunities for action.

It appears that mediation cannot take the form of a monologue. Nevertheless, monologic mediation can be provided under certain conditions, depending on the cultural presuppositions of the contextualising social systems. In fact, what from a prescriptive perspective is considered a mistake or a non-sense may be perfectly understandable if we look at the cultural presuppositions of the contextualising social systems. For example, mediation which explains the parties' perspectives, rather than giving voice to them, can be considered monologic; nevertheless, it aims to help the parties to express themselves. Cross-cultural monologic mediation is ethnocentric: while apparently a non-sense, it is in fact an empirical reality (Baraldi and Gavioli, 2008).

Mediation may promote both intercultural and cultural coordination, whereas intercultural coordination actually looks at the possibility of favouring the expression of different cultural presuppositions and dealing with it, and cultural coordination simply promotes the reproduction of the cultural presuppositions of the system inside which mediation takes place. Dialogic cross-cultural mediation promotes intercultural coordination, on the basis of contextualising cultural presuppositions which favour participants' agency and personal expression. Dialogic cross-cultural mediation enhances empowerment and the recognition of cultural diversity; it is supposed to abolish ethnocentric boundaries and promote cross-cultural adaptation. However, dialogic cross-cultural mediation does not necessarily promote conjunctions, harmonisation, and third cultures; these are only possible and not necessarily desirable outcomes of this form of mediation. Therefore, it may be questioned whether dialogic cross-cultural mediation is "transcultural", mediators should be experts of "cultures" and explaining different cultural meanings to the parties is dialogic mediation. In dialogic cross-cultural mediation, opening up spaces to express different cultural presuppositions may favour reciprocal acknowledgement between the parties and possibly promote change of the dominating cultural presuppositions within the contextualising systems. The failure to open up such space inevitably leads to the reproduction of dominating cultural presuppositions. On the other hand, cultural coordination is enhanced by monologic mediation and is successful when contextualising systems appreciate assimilation to their existent cultural presuppositions.

Interaction and re-contextualisation

A second important methodological statement is that prescriptive patterns of mediation must be tested in empirical cases of mediation in communication, as mediation requires the achievement of interaction in order to exist. It is important to distinguish between the premises of mediation and its practical accomplishment. The difference is mainly observed between prescriptive politics and performances in interactions. Mediation requires policy decisions which determine its orientation and the conditions of its implementation. These decisions are both organisational premises (e.g. the way in which mediators may be hired, the kind of tasks which may be assigned to mediators, the quantity of work required, etc.) and prescriptions regarding the function of mediation (e.g. promotion of participation or conflict resolution). The latter create the narrative of "ideal" mediation which may or may not be observed in empirical interactions. Observation of mediation is allowed by both prescriptions, i.e. guiding values which shape expectations, and interactions in which these expectations can or cannot be accomplished. The question is how mediation is accomplished in interactions. The answer implies an analysis of communication in the interaction.

Probably, the most useful methodology of investigation into empirical processes of communication in interactions is Conversation Analysis (CA). CA provides "a perspective within which language, culture and social organization can be analyzed (...) as integrated elements of coherent courses of action" (Goodwin and Heritage, 1990: 301). CA identifies a social organisation of sequences in turn-taking: the minimal unit in this organisation is the adjacency pair, based on "the rule that a current action (...) requires the production of a reciprocal action" (Goodwin and Heritage, 1990: 287), and the turn-taking sequence, based on a mechanism of next positioning, which means that the "current action may project (...) one among a range of possible next actions" (Goodwin and Heritage, 1990: 288). Turn-taking takes place on a turn-by-turn basis so that after each completed turn, the next speaker arrives at a point of possible change (Sacks, Schegloff and Jefferson, 1974). CA emphasises the possibility for all participants to act or take a turn.

CA implies that social organisation is interaction. However, as we have seen, interactions, for example mediation, can be only explained within contextualising social systems. This means that we need an integration of two different approaches in order to analyse mediation (Baraldi and Gavioli, 2007a). The first approach describes cultural presuppositions, i.e. expectations regarding guiding values (e.g. the treatment of illness or the shaping of personalities), participants' contributions (e.g. roles), the results of communication (normative order, change, personal expression). The second approach concerns the organisation of specific interactive sequences, including (1) adjacency pairs and the projection of actions, and (2) linguistic (verbal and non-verbal) forms signalling the main cultural presuppositions (contextualization cues in Gumperz, 1992). According to Ayoko, Härtel and Callan, mediators' actions are aimed at "promoting conversation, offering speaking turns, using conversational repairs, or even choosing familiar and non-threatening topics" (2002: 169).

Interactions may produce re-interpretations of cultural presuppositions and may have significant effects on contextualising social systems, e.g. on the expectations of guiding values, role performances and personal expression, and the results of communication. On the one hand, cultural presuppositions shape interaction, while on the other, interaction may renew cultural presuppositions precisely by re-interpreting them within the local context. Therefore: 1) interaction is contextualised by a set of cultural presuppositions (expectations); 2) such contextualisation derives from social systems which contextualise interactions and which are significant in society by virtue of their functions (e.g. healthcare and education); 3) interactions may possibly change these cultural presuppositions; that is, they may re-contextualise (Baker, 2006b) the contextualising systems; 4) contextualisation and re-contextualisation are made evident through particular linguistic cues in interactions; 5) both intercultural and cultural coordination of reflection can promote the re-contextualisation of the contextualising system.

Dialogic actions

The social and cultural preference for dialogic mediation is linked to the tendency in society to give increasing value to personal expression in interactions, for example in healthcare and education systems. As a consequence, it becomes increasingly important to understand what actions may enhance dialogic mediation in interactions. These dialogic actions do not determine communication processes. To be successful in communication, they need to be understood and accepted by the parties; consequently, their success is observable only in the organisation of the turn-taking sequence during activities of mediation. However, it is possible to observe whether and under what conditions specific dialogic actions may enhance dialogic mediation in their projecting the parties' actions.

The detailed features of dialogic actions have been frequently described in the literature (e.g. Ayoko, et al, 2002, Bohm, 1996, Coleman, Hacking, Stover, Fisher-Yoshida and Nowak, 2008, Gergen, McNamee and Barrett, 2001, Gudykunst, 1994, Kim, 2001, Littlejohn, 2004, Pearce and Pearce, 2003, Picard & Melchin, 2007, Poitras, 2005, Royce, 2005, Winslade and Monk, 2008). Here I will try to make a summary of the features which seem more interesting for dialogic cross-cultural mediation, with the help of some examples extrapolated from research on naturally occurring interactions in mediation in different contextualising social systems (see also Baraldi, 2006b, 2008, Baraldi & Gavioli, 2007b).

The examples are transcriptions of audio or video recorded interactions within: 1) international multicultural meetings planning activities for children (case A); 2) international multicultural camps involving adolescents (case B); 3) multicultural classes of children (case C); 4) multicultural classes of preadolescents (case D); 4) interpreter-mediated interactions in healthcare services (case E). In cases A and B, the participants speak English as a lingua franca. In cases C and D, the participants speak Italian and transcriptions have been translated in English. In case E, the participants speak different languages and the transcription has been translated in English. The mediators involved are professionals only in cases D and E. Mediation should not be considered only a specific professionalised field. It can be performed in all situations in which the facilitation of communication is possible and the promotion of active participation and coordination of reflection are considered important. All people having tasks which regard communication may be mediators, such as the educators in cases A, B and C.

The following are the most important dialogic actions which were observed in these interactions, exemplified by few and short extracts which should give at least an idea of their meaning.

1. Active listening to the parties' personal expressions. Active listening shows sensitivity to the parties' needs and feelings, through signals of involvement in communication, both verbal (e.g. continuers, echoes) and non-verbal (glances, postures, smiles, gestures). In particular, "double listening" (Winslade and Monk, 2008) shows sensitivity to both sufferance and hope, for both explicit stories and opportunities for opening alternative stories.

In extract 1, case B, a female adolescent from Argentina (Farg) proposes her perspective (turns 1, 4) regarding an activity. In turns 3 and 5, the Greek female mediator (MFgre) shows her sensitivity for this proposal through continuers (mm mmm, yeah). These responses stimulate Farg's checking of the mediator's understanding (turn 8), which is confirmed by MFgre's positive answer (turn 9).

1. Farg: Ah for example (...) ah:m he can't see ah we put like an activity that he, he, he (?) can't do, only he can do and I need to (.) to: (.) to cross ahm one place without ahm falling with some objects and the other ahm, the other participants in that group have to tell him what [where he have to go

2. Mdan: [where he can go

3. MFgre: mm mmm

4. Farg: so that he doesn't fall and in that way they are helping him.

5. MFgre: yeah.

6. Farg: ahm although she can't see.

7. Fita: ok.

8. Farg: do you understand?

9. MFgre: yeah, I understood.

In extract 2, case D, the mediator (M) actively listens to the preadolescents' proposals through echoes which demonstrate his active listening (turns 51, 53, 55). In the literature on person-centred counselling (Mearns and Thorne, 1999), echoes are considered particularly useful in reflecting the interlocutors' positions and promoting their active participation, as it is demonstrated also in this extract.

49. M: what is the meaning of friendship for you? Being a friend?

50. Mita: staying together all the time, playing together all the time.

51. M: staying together all the time, playing together all the time.

52. Mita: being like brothers

53. M: being like brothers

54. Fmor: to trust each other.

55. M: to trust each other.

2. Formulation of the meanings of the parties' previous turns. Formulation consists in reacting to the interlocutors' actions with the explicit intention of clarifying their meanings and effects. They consist in "summarising, glossing, or developing the gist of an informant's earlier statement" (Heritage, 1985: 100). Formulations make explicit, gloss or develop the interlocutor's personal expressions. In this sense, the gist of the prior utterance is developed by focusing personal expressions and formulations that may (1) develop and emphasise personal expressions, (2) select what in the previous reports permits the inference of the interlocutor's self-positioning, and (3) re-present the gist of these reports in order to permit their focusing, topicalisation and elaboration in the subsequent interaction.

In extract 3, case E (italics means Arabic), a Moroccan female patient (Fmor) introduces a possible start (turn 11), which is immediately responded to by the mediator (M) who echoes the patient's turn encouraging her to go on (turn 12). In turn 13, the patient's statement projects a translation of what was previously said by the doctor (D), i.e. that there is nothing to worry about (turn 14). In turn 15, the patient introduces her problem, and the mediator again echoes the patient (turn 16). A dyadic sequence is then constructed where the patient is encouraged to express her worries and concern. By echoing the patient and providing feedback to her, the mediator supports the patient's tentative emotional expressions (turns 12, 16), helping her to go on. In turn 20, the mediator displays her active listening. In the following turns, the mediator formulates her understanding of the gist of this dyadic sequence. In turn 21 the interpreter summarises the patient's words, while in turns 23 and 25 she redevelops and makes inferences about the gist of the patient's narrative: the reason why she is there to tell that story. Her formulation "translates" the patient's narrative, giving voice to her emotions in the interaction with the doctor. This leads to the doctor's active listening (turn 24) and involvement (turn 26).

11. Fmor: *now* –12. M: *now* -13. Fmor: *I feel nothing wrong.*

14. M: *this (.) If everything is alright your period is okay and you feel nothing wrong (.) then she says there's no need for a check.*

15. Fmor: *now it's been a month and I haven't had it.*

16. M: *a month and you haven't had it.*

17. Fmor: *precisely a month.*

18. M: *isn't it that -*

19. Fmor: *I felt nothing wrong.*

20. M: *ah (.) okay then.*

21. M: she says that pain (.) means something is wrong as she hasn't had it (.) She says she's alright.

22. DFita: ah.

23. M: her menstruation is abundant (..) The only thing, probably the reason why she came

24. DFita: mmh.

25. M: is that this month she hasn't had her period (..) ((smiling)) and she is a bit worried.

26. DFita: so (.) in that case there's only one thing to do (.) Let's do a pregnancy test.

This extract also demonstrates that interpreting is mediation. Interpreters "cannot avoid functioning as intercultural mediators" (Wadensjö, 1998: 75) and their translation activity is "a form of cross-cultural encounter" (Davidson, 2000: 381). In interpreter-mediated interactions, mediators are the only participants who can effectively understand all the contents and the intentions uttered in communication; consequently, they can promote the parties' active participation and coordinate their interaction. Interpreting may empower the parties' voices and promote mutual recognition between them. Interpreting may introduce new and unpredicted narratives to the interaction. First, acting as responders in dyadic sequences with one party, mediators can give voice to this party's narratives in the interaction; second, through translation, mediators can solicit the other party's concern for the interaction. Therefore, translation is an opportunity for the parties to express the cultural world which they feel as an important personal heritage. Cross-cultural adaptation is made possible if this personal expression is adequately supported in communication. Support of personal expression includes (1) narration of stories in dyadic sequences in the first language with a party, and (2) effective translation (formulation) of the gist of these stories in the second language, allowing the involvement of the other party (Baraldi and Gavioli, 2007b). Interpreters' mediation can promote alternative stories in monolingual dyadic sequences (supporting a party's voice) and can thicken these stories through their translations, in this way projecting the other party's support and creating cross-cultural adaptation.

3. Confirmation and support of the parties' personal expressions. Confirmation and support can demonstrate acceptance and acknowledgement, and create positive connotations of the parties' positions.

In extract 4, case A, MDan (Danish male) is supporting the active participation of Find (Indonesian female) and Mcan (Canadian male) through acknowledgement tokens (turns 64, 66), a formulation which emphasises acceptance of their proposals (underlined statements indicate particular emphasis) and non-verbal behaviour such as smiling and nodding (turn 68). This support is welcomed by the participants (turn 69).

63. Find: maybe it doesn't need, all the leaders can talk to their delegation

64. Mdan: yeah.

65. Find: during delegation time, °that is easier°

66. Mdan: good.

67. Mcan: so they can explain

68. Mdan: <u>or</u>:! <u>Everybody, all the leaders</u> can just talk to their delegation, during delegation time! ((nodding and smiling))

69. Many participants: yeah! ((laughing))

4. Appreciation of the parties' actions, experiences and positions. Dialogic actions are effective only if they do not produce a negative evaluation of the parties' actions and if they avoid identifying them as problematic people. For this reason, appreciation for the parties' contributions is particularly important. Appreciation concerns the fact of contributing, not necessarily the contents of contributions. For this reason, appreciation does not imply passing up on a personal perspective on the contents.

In extract 5, case C, the mediator (M) emphatically appreciates (turn 4) the children's coordination in organising the assigned task (turns 1, 2, 3).

1. Fita: I'll write the whole story.

2. Fita ((to Fger)): wait a moment (.) Would you like be in the story?

3. Fger: yes, but I would like to say that while we are drawing, we should also give her ((Marta)) some ideas.

4. M: <u>what a beautiful idea. Fantastic!</u>

5. Narration of personal stories, i.e. deliberate self-positioning (van Langenhove & Harré, 1999). This action enhances narrative mediation which allows legitimate expressions of the parties' perspectives.

In extract 6, case C, in turns 21 and 25 the mediator (M) narrates his story with the intention to promote the children's agency and coordination regarding a task (writing a story). This story creates the conditions for the children's active participation and coordination in decision-making (turns 24, 26, 27, 29), supported by the mediator's appreciation (turn 28).

> 21. M: I remember when I was with a group of friends and we always went to the mountains together. At first we planned a series of trips around the mountains. We met on Sunday mornings, we walked along the path together and the (.) we reached the mountain hut, and came back home. But once the group started to fight: let's go this way, no, the other way. So do you know what we did?
>
> 22.Fita: erm, no -
>
> 23. M: we decided to [find –
>
> 24. Mita: [to find an agreement
>
> 25. M: an agreement which was—(.) a group went one way, another group went on the other one, then we met at the mountain hut and everybody had done what they wanted, but everybody met at the mountain hut. Does this suggest something to you?
>
> 26. Mita: I understand: she does the [text—
>
> 27. F2ita: [and then we meet at the mountain hut with the text!
>
> 28. M: what do you mean? (..) Look, you had a beautiful idea: I like this idea!
>
> 29. F2ita: I'll do the text, if they don't want to do the text, I'll do it by myself and then (.) we'll look at it together, we'll read it and:

6. Narration of stories which include the parties' perspective. The construction of inclusive stories indicates that diverse positions are taken into account, avoiding stereotypes, paying attention to the terminology concerning the identities and the expression of meanings about these identities, avoiding utterances which can interrupt communication, such as status assertions and other forms of dominant behaviours or the ignoring of particular topics (Ayoko, et al., 2002).

In extract 7, case D, the mediator (M) tries to include the Moroccan girl's perspective in the conversation (turns 93, 96, 99), defending her from her classmates' charges. The mediator reports what Fmor is saying indirectly, supporting her position through his authoritativeness and managing a conflict in this way involving Fmor, Fita (Italian female) and Mita (Italian male).

92. Fita: in my opinion, we cannot draw these distinctions between males and females, because each individual has a different personality and that's it, you cannot say females are so and so, males are so and so because -

93. M: she is not saying 'I feel in this way' because she is a female but probably she feels so and so not because she is a female but because this is her personality right? It is because her personality makes her like that, not because she is different from me. Do you want to say something?

94. Mita: I agree also with Michela but I would just like to underline a moment what Rawan said because when I was near her and I asked her for something she didn't lend it to me.

95. Fmor: this is not true.

96. M: she says that it is not true, perhaps -

97. Mita: no, it is that you ask her for a pencil, a rubber, these things, and she says yes to one out of ten.

98. Fmor: it is not true.

99. M: she says that it is not true.

7. Asking for feedback on the effects of actions in terms of the parties' understanding, acceptance and positioning. Asking for feedback enhances the parties' contributions to the communication process and clarifies the possible effects of dialogic actions.

In extract 8, case A, Mdan first explains some activities (turn 13), then presents a problem about an activity and asks for a feedback (turn 15), introduced by "but", which is a cue for self-disclaiming, i.e. disclaiming his own position as a speaker. This self-disclaimer promotes the interlocutors' personal contributions, through a mitigation of the speaker's authoritativeness, opening to the request for support ("so maybe have any ideas?"). Musa aligns with this request trying to find an alternative proposal, which seems to be successful (turn 17).

13. Mdan: erm regarding to you:, some name games regarding tonight, we're gonna start with the lion hunt, performed by yours truly, and (04) yeah, and then mini banana, and then erm: we're also ((reading from a sheet)) going to: to do some games, and I wish (run) one of those.

((many participants appreciate the proposal))

14. Mdan: and then I will run the, we have twenty minutes (as) last time, we just wrote energisers but (they're) just too (plain) just do energizers for twenty minutes, so maybe, so maybe have erm: any ideas? do maybe really good name games (the time that lasts the activity), last erm

15. Musa: (??) different erm translations, as time maybe (??) that time you left. ↓

16. Some leaders: yeah.

8. Constructing alternative stories (re-authoring) through asking promotional questions. Asking questions can promote the parties' authorship and editing of alternative stories, without impositions. Questions can achieve the goal of re-authoring stories towards a positive positioning of the parties, favouring their self-positioning within new narratives.

In extract 9, case D, the mediator's turns are all promotional questions (turns 1, 3, 5, 7, 9, 11, 13, 15, 18) with the effect of promoting the preadolescents' active participation in defining the meaning of the interaction.

1. M: well, do you know what we are going to do today? Did you make up some idea? Somebody did make up an idea?

2. M1ita: that you help to speak with our classmates, to solve our problems, also with other cultures, the other gender.

3. M: and how did you make up this idea?

4. M1ita: because there were many questions about this topic.

5. M: in the questionnaire?

6. M1ita: yes.

7. M: and before the questionnaire what was your idea? Did your teachers talk with you?

8. M1ita: not much.

9. M: not much, but did you make up an idea before the questionnaire?

10. M1ita: no.

11. M: No. Did someone else did make up an idea? Different? Similar? It is not sure that what your classmate said will be what we'll do. Now we'll see. Do you think you have problems? That there are problems which need a solution?

12. M1ita: no, as a group it seems to me that we get along well.

13. M: other ideas? What would you like to do together?

14. M1ita: what would we like to do together?

15. M: yes today, what would you like? What do you expect?

16. (02)

17. M2ita: to try to understand the way we are.

18. M: to try to understand the way you are?

19. M2ita: yes, meaning what we do. Looking at the questionnaires, I must say that many questions concerned out thoughts, what we're like.

A slightly more integrated example of mediation is shown in extract 9, case B. The Canadian mediator (MFcan) coordinates the adolescents' reflection through promotional questions (turns 1, 5); she fosters active listening through echoes (turns 3, 13); non-verbal behaviour (turn 8), and a continuer (turn 9); she promotes acknowledgment of diversity through a formulation of the different proposals (turn 11), and she promotes the adolescents' opportunity to decide autonomously (turn 11). MFcan's actions succeed in getting the adolescents involved, in promoting the expression of their ideas and also in promoting coordination between them (turns 6-7, 14-15).

1. MFcan: what do you think? (03) Your idea was to have two, like you would say maybe commoner and something else?

2. Fbra: ah::m I, I was thinking special.

3. MFcan: special/perfect.

4. Fbra: yeah, special and it doesn't have to be perfect, we are perfect as we are.

5. MFcan: what do you guys think? Did you hear what she said? Hh, did you guys listened to that?

6. Fbra: is perfect, but (.) He's perfect but we are also perfect, like for us we are perfect.

7. Mdan: we are perfect selves.

8. ((MFcan smiles))

9. MFcan: ok.

10. Fbra: but the commoners (?) it.

11. MFcan: so we have two ideas: we can call it special/perfect or the common-commoner (03) it's up to you guys, whatever you think.

12. Mita: special/common.

13. MFcan: special/commoner?

14. Mdan: let's do that.

15. Fbra: yeah::hhh.

The analysis of dialogic actions leads to an understanding of the possibility and effectiveness of dialogic mediation in empirical situations, which concern the promotion of participation, coordination of reflection and possibly conflict management.

Conclusions

In this paper, I have tried to highlight some theoretical, methodological and empirical requirements to understand, describe and explain mediation, in particular cross-cultural mediation. My concern is that the present debate is entrapped in the search for techniques which could be prescribed in order to obtain effective mediation as conflict resolution. The fear of intractable conflicts and the passion for simple technical solutions may lead to the exclusion of the most important theoretical, methodological and empirical clarifications of mediation.

A theoretical perspective leads us to observe that mediation (1) is contextualised in different social systems and depend on their cultural presuppositions; (2) in these systems, it facilitates communication through the promotion of active participation and coordination of reflection. Methodologically, this function requires a dialogic form of mediation which can be tested in specific interactions in which mediation is performed. Therefore, the analysis of interactions is important in order to understand the dialogic actions which can effectively implement the function of mediation. This analysis allows for observation of the empirical forms of mediation, rather than its ideal and prescribed models.

In this paper, I could not explore exhaustively the empirical meanings of dialogic mediation. In the shown extracts, the parties' active participation is promoted and coordinated. Only in some of these cases are the mediators professionals. The examples concern only some social systems. Other and more complex examples, in other social systems, would be useful for a wider understanding of the ways mediation can work in empirical interactions. Furthermore, I have not shown failures in mediation and monologic forms of mediation which are analogously interesting in order to understand its achievement. For example, in interpreter-mediated interactions, monologic mediation has been frequently observed (e.g. Baraldi and Gavioli, 2008, Bolden, 2000, Davidson, 2000, Mason, 1999).

The analysis demonstrates that dialogic mediation can create the conditions for participants' empowerment because it enhances the parties' autonomous decision-making, based on the recognition of their agency. It creates new narratives because it enhances the parties' coordinated stories.

The main theoretical and methodological problems in analysing mediation have found some solutions. Firstly, as the examples demonstrate, dialogic cross-cultural mediation does not mean that personal expressions are conducive of cultural identities; rather it means that the parties have the opportunity to express their personal perspective and therefore also their cultural identities, if they wish. Secondly, mediators' neutrality is never inactivity; on the contrary, dialogic actions are the most important component of mediation. Although these actions are never elements of advocacy, confirmation and support, appreciation of the parties' positions in communication are usual; therefore, the term "neutrality" is too ambiguous to seem effective in explaining dialogic actions. Thirdly, as the theoretical perspective explains and as has been confirmed in the examples, dialogic mediation does not necessarily have the function of managing conflicts, if we do not intend conflict management as "prevention", i.e. the facilitation of communication which prevents the emergence of conflicting positions.

Fourthly, it may be questioned whether dialogic mediation can create changes in contextualising systems, i.e. whether it can re-contextualise them. The change of the course of interactions may not seem important to those who think of change as the reform, revolution or evolution of contextualising social systems. This approach, however, underestimates that changes in social systems often (if not always) require changes in interactions. The effects of interactions in re-contextualising social systems are evident in international political mediation (e.g. Saunders, 2003, Siniver, 2006). Moreover, these effects may be preceded and accompanied by other, less evident interactional achievements (e.g. Kelman, 2005, Maoz, 2001, 2005, Maoz, Steinberg, Bar-On and Fakhereldeen, 2002). Dialogic mediation can re-contextualise families, the distribution of rights in courts, school practice, ways of treating illness, business exchanges. Furthermore, in dialogic mediation the way of achieving change is particularly important. In critical theories, change is important in itself as a fight against inequalities in the distribution of power and forms of oppression. The concept of dialogic mediation does not deny the existence and relevance of unequal power distribution. However, in dialogic mediation the process of promoting participation and coordination is more important than its final result, which is always unpredictable. Therefore, the most important changes concern processes rather than results: we should not forget that change may be achieved also through monologic mediation which can promote separation and we-identities. Moreover, dialogic mediation can also avoid and prevent changes: if it is coherent with the contextualising cultural presuppositions, it can preserve them and this would not seem to be a problem in itself.

Finally, my conclusion is that mediation is not a technique; consequently, it is not possible to write a manual which describes all the effective practices of mediation. This kind of manuals, frequently proposed to practitioners in helping professions, is misleading, as it entraps practices in prescribed patterns which are always excessively simplified and thus risky in terms of their accomplishment. Mediators may be advised to adopt a theoretically and methodologically guided "double listening" approach to both the contextualising system and the ongoing interaction. This double listening is a real help for mediators, and learning about its theoretical and methodological bases is the most important aspect of their training.

References

AYOKO, O.B., H, C.E., & CALLAN, V.J. (2002) Resolving the puzzle of productive and destructive conflict in culturally heterogeneous workgroups: A communication accommodation theory approach. *International Journal of Conflict Management,* 13(2), 165-195.

BAKER, M. (2006a) *Translation and Conflict. A Narrative Account*, London, Routledge.

BAKER, M. (2006b) Contextualization in translator- and interpreter-mediated events. *Journal of Pragmatics,* 38, 321-337.

BARALDI, C. (2006a) New forms of intercultural communication in a globalised world. *International Communication Gazzette,* 68(1), 53-69.

BARALDI, C. (2006b) Diversity and adaptation in intercultural mediation. IN BUSCH, D. (Ed.) *Interkulturelle Mediation in der Grenzregion* (pp. 225-250), Frankfurt/Main, Peter Lang.

BARALDI, C. (2008), Promoting self-expression in classrooms interactions. *Childhood,* 15(2), 239-257.

BARALDI, C., and GAVIOLI, L. (2007a) The relevance of interactions in functionally differentiated society: the contribution of conversation analysis to the theory of social systems. *Soziale Systeme,* 13, 125-135.

BARALDI, C. and GAVIOLI, L. (2007b) Dialogue interpreting as intercultural mediation. An analysis in healthcare multicultural settings. IN GREIN, M. and Weigand, E. (Eds.) *Dialogue and Culture* (pp. 155-175), Amsterdam, John Benjamins

BARALDI, C. and GAVIOLI, L. (2008) Cultural presuppositions and re-contextualisation of medical systems in interpreter-mediated interactions. *Curare. Journal of Medical Anthropology,* 31(2+3), 193-203.

BARRY C.A., STEVENSON F.A., BRITTEN N., BARBER N., and BRADLEY C.P. (2001) Giving voice to the lifeworld. More human, more effective medical care? A qualitative study of doctor-patient communication in general practice. *Social Science & Medicine,* 53, 487-505.

BOLDEN, G.B. (2000) Toward understanding practices of medical interpreting: interpreters' involvement in history taking. *Discourse Studies,* 2(4), 387-419.

BOH, D. (1996) *On Dialogue*. London: Routledge.

BOWLING, D., and HOFFMAN, D. (2000) Bringing peace into the room: the personal qualities of the mediator and their impact on the mediation. *Negotiation Journal,* 16(1), 5-28.

BRIGG, N. (2003) Mediation, power, and cultural difference. *Conflict Resolution Quarterly,* 20(3), 287-306.

BUSH, R.A.B., and FOLGER, J.P. (1994) *The Promise of Mediation: Responding to Conflict through Empowerment and Recognition*, San Francisco, Jossey-Bass Publishers.

CARBAUGH, D. (1999) Positioning as display of cultural identity. IN HARRÉ R. and VAN LANGENHOVE, L. (Eds.), *Positioning Theory* (160-177), Oxford, Blackwell.

CARBAUGH, D. (2005) *Cultures in Conversation*, New York, Lawrence Erlbaum.

CARNEVALE, P.J., and PRUITT, D.G. (1992) Negotiation and mediation. *Annual Review of Psychology, 43*, 531-582.

CASMIR, F. (1999) Foundations for the study of intercultural communication based on a third-culture building model. *International Journal of Intercultural Relations,* 23, 91-116.

CHEN, G., and STAROSTA, W. (1998) *Foundations of Intercultural Communication*, Needham Heights/Ma, Allyn & Bacon.

COLEMAN P. T., HACKING, A. G., STOVER, M. A., FISHER-YOSHIDA, B. and NOWAK, A. (2008) Reconstructing ripeness I: A study of constructive engagement in protracted social conflicts. *Conflict Resolution Quarterly,* 26(1), 3-42.

COLEMAN, P. T. and LOWE K. J. (2007) Conflict, identity, and resilience: Negotiating collective identities within the Israeli and Palestinian diasporas. *Conflict Resolution Quarterly,* 24(4), 377-412.

DAVIDSON, B. (2000) The interpreter as institutional gatekeeper: The social-linguistic role of interpreters in Spanish-English medical discourse. *Journal of Sociolinguistics,* 4/3, 379-405.

GERGEN, K., McNAMEE, S., & BARRETT, F. (2001) Toward transformative dialogue. *International Journal of Public Administration,* 24, 697-707.

GOODWIN, C., and HERITAGE, J. (1990) Conversation analysis. *Annual Review of Anthropology* 19, 283-307.

GUDYKUNST, W.B. (1994) *Bridging Differences. Effective Intergroup Communication*, Thousand Oaks, Sage.

GUMPERZ, J. (1982) *Discourse Strategies*, Cambridge, Cambridge University Press.

GUMPERZ, J. (1992) Contextualization and understanding. IN DURANTI, A. and GOODWIN C. (Eds.) *Rethinking Context: Language as an Interactive Phenomenon* (229-253), Cambridge, Cambridge University Press.

GUMPERZ, J. and ROBERTS, C. (1991) Understanding in intercultural encounters. IN BLOMMAERT, J. and VERSCHUEREN, J. (Eds.) *The pragmatics of Intercultural and International Communication* (51-90), Amsterdam, John Benjamins.

GWARTNEY, P., FESSENDEN, L., and LANDT, G. (2002) Measuring the long-term impact of a community conflict resolution process. *Negotiation Journal*, 18(1), 51-74.

HERITAGE, J. (1985) Analysing news interviews: Aspects of the production of talk for an overhearing audience. IN VAN DIJK, T. (Ed.) *Handbook of Discourse Analysis, Vol. 3. Discourse and Dialogue* (95-117), London, Academic Press.

HERITAGE, J. and MAYNARD D.W. (Eds.) (2005) *Communication in Medical Care: Interactions Between Primary Care Physicians and Patients,* Cambridge, Cambridge University Press.

HERITAGE, J. and MAYNARD D.W. (2006) Problems and prospects in the study of physician-patient interaction: 30 years of research. *Annual Review of Sociology,* 32, 351-374.

HOFSTEDE, G. (1980) *Culture's Consequences*, Beverly Hills, Sage.

HOLDSWORTH, R. (2004) Taking young people seriously means giving them serious things to do. IN MASON, J. and T. FATTORE, T. (Eds.), *Children Taken Seriously. Theory, Policy and Practice* (139-150), London, Jessica Kingsley Publishers.

JAMES, A. and JAMES A. (2004) *Constructing Childhood. Theory, Policy and Social Practice*, Houndmills, Palgrave.
JAMES, A., JENKS, C. and PROUT, A. (1998) *Theorizing Childhood*, Oxford, Polity Press.
JANS, M. (2004) Children as citizens. Towards a contemporary notion of child participation. *Childhood*, 11(1), 27-44.
JEONG, H-W. (2008) *Understanding Conflict and Conflict Analysis*. Los Angeles: Sage.
KATZ-JAMESON, J., BOTKER A.M. and Jones, T.S. (2006) Like talking to a brick wall: implications of mediation metaphors for mediation practice. *Negotiation Journal* 22(2), 199-207.
KELMAN, H. (2005) Interactive problem solving in the Israeli-Palestinian case: Past contributions and present challenges. IN FISHER, R. (Ed.) *Paving the Way: Contributions of Interactive Conflict Resolution to Peacemaking* (41-64), Lanham (MD), Lexington Books.
KIM, Y.-Y. (2001) *Becoming Intercultural. An Integrative Theory of Communication and Cross-Cultural Adaptation*, London, Sage.
LITTLEJOHN, S. W. (2004) The transcendent communication project: Searching for a praxis of dialogue. *Conflict Resolution Quarterly*, 21(3), 327-359.
LUHMANN, N. (1984) *Soziale Systeme*, Frankfurt a. M., Suhrkamp.
LUHMANN, N. (1990) *Die Wissenschaft der Gesellschaft*, Frankfurt a. M., Suhrkamp.
LUHMANN, N. (1997) *Die Gesellschaft der Gesellschaft*, Frankfurt a. M., Suhrkamp.
MAIESE, M. (2006) Engaging the emotions in conflict intervention. *Conflict Resolution Quarterly*, 24(2), 187-195.
MAOZ, I. (2001) Participation, control, and dominance in communication between groups in conflict: Analysis of dialogues between Jews and Palestinians in Israel. *Social Justice Research*, 14(2), 189-208.
MAOZ, I. (2005) Evaluating the communication between groups in dispute: Equality in contact interventions between Jews and Arabs in Israel. *Negotiation Journal, 21(1)*, 131-146.
MAOZ, I., STEINBERG, S., BAR-ON, D. and FAKHERELDEEN, M. (2002) The dialogue between the "Self" and the "Other": A process analysis of Palestinian-Jewish encounters in Israel. *Human Relations*, 55(8), 931-962.
MASON, I. (Ed.) (1999) Dialogue interpreting. *The Translator*, Special Issue 5(2).
MEARNS, D. and THORNE, B. (1999) *Person-Centred Counselling in Action*, London, Sage.
MILHOUSE, V., ASANTE, M.K. and NWOSU, P. (Eds.) (2001) *Transcultural Realities. Interdisciplinary Perspectives on Cross-Cultural Relations*, Thousand Oaks, Sage.
MISHLER, E.G. (1984) *The Discourse of Medicine. The Dialectics of Medical Interviews*, Norwood, NJ, Ablex.
MULCHAY, L. (2001) The possibilities and desirability of mediator neutrality—Towards an ethic of partiality? *Social & Legal Studies*, 10(4), 505-527.
NEDERVEEN PIETERSE, J. (2004) *Globalization & Culture*, Lanham, Rowman & Littlefield.
NEDERVEEN PIETERSE, J. (2007) *Ethnicities and Global Multiculture. Pants for an Octopus*, Lanham, Rowman & Littlefield.

PEARCE, B. W. (1989) *Communication and the Human Condition*, Carbondale, Southern Illinois University Press.
PEARCE, B. W. and PEARCE, K.A. (2003) Taking a communication perspective on dialogue. IN ANDERSON, R., BAXTER, L.A. and CISSNA, K., (Eds.) Dialogue: Theorizing difference in communication studies (39-56) Thousand Oaks, CA, Sage.
PICARD, C.A. and MELCHIN, K.R. (2007) Insight mediation: A learning-centered mediation model. *Negotiation Journal*, 23(1), 35-53.
POITRAS, J. (2005) A study of the emergence of cooperation in mediation. *Negotiation Journal*, 21(2), 281-300.
PROUT, A. (2000) Children's participation: Control and Self-realisation in British late modernity. *Children & Society*, 14, 304-315.
ROYCE, T. (2005) The negotiator and the bomber: Analysing the critical role of active listening in crisis negotiation. *Negotiation Journal*, 21(1), 5-27.
SACKS, H., SCHEGLOFF, E. and JEFFERSON, G. (1974) A simplest systematics for the organization of turn taking for conversation. *Language*, 50, 696-735.
SAUNDERS, H. H. (2003) Sustained dialogue in managing intractable conflicts. *Negotiation Journal*, 19(1), 85-95.
SCHOENY, M. and WARFIELD, W. (2000) Reconnecting system maintenance with social justice: A critical role for conflict resolution. *Negotiation Journal*, 16(3), 253-268.
SHAH-KAZEMI, S.N. (2000) Cross-cultural mediation: A critical view of the dynamics of culture in family disputes. *International Journal of Law, Policy and the Family*, 14, 302-325.
SINIVER, A. (2006) Power, impartiality and timing: Three hypotheses on third party mediation in the Middle East. *Political Studies*, 54, 806-826.
SPITZBERG, B. (1997). A model of intercultural communication competence. IN SAMOVAR, L. and PORTER (Eds.) *Intercultural Communication. A Reader* (379-391), Belmont, Wadsworth.
TAN, S-L. and MOGADDHAM, F.M. (1999) Positioning in Intergroup Relations. IN HARRÉ, R. and VAN LANGEHOVE, L. (Eds.) *Positioning Theory* (174-194), Oxford, Blackwell.
TING-TOOMEY, S. (1999) *Communication across Cultures*, New York, The Guilford Press.
TING-TOOMEY, S. and KUROGI, A. (1998) Facework competence in intercultural conflict: An updated face-negotiation theory. *International Journal of Intercultural Relations*, 22, 187-225.
TJOSVOLD, D. and SUN H.F. (2002). Understanding conflict avoidance: Relationship, motivations, actions, and consequences. *International Journal of Conflict Management*, 13(2), 142-164.
TRIANDIS, H. (1995) *Individualism and Collectivism*, Boulder (CO), Westview Press.
VAN LANGENHOVE, L. and HARRÉ, R. (1999) Introducing positioning theory. IN HARRÉ, R. and VAN LANGEHOVE, L. (Eds.) *Positioning Theory* (14-31), Oxford, Blackwell.
VERSCHUEREN, J. (2008) Intercultural communication and the challenges of migration. *Language and Intercultural Communication*, 1(8), 21-35.
WADENSJÖ, C. (1998) *Interpreting as Interaction*. London: Longman.

WELSH, N.A. and COLEMAN, P.T. (2002) Institutionalized conflict resolution: Have we come to expect too little? *Negotiation Journal,* 18(4), 345-350.

WEIGAND, E. (1994) Discourse, conversation, dialogue. IN WEIGAND, E. (Ed.), *Concepts of Dialogue* (49-70). Tübingen: Niemeyer.

WIERZBICKA, A. (2006) The concept of 'dialogue' in cross-linguistic and cross-cultural perspective. *Discourse Studies,* 8(5), 675-703.

WINSLADE, J. (2006) Mediation with a focus on discursive positioning. *Conflict Resolution Quarterly,* 23(4), 501-515.

WINSLADE, J. and MONK G. (2000) *Narrative Mediation: A New Approach to Conflict Resolution,* San Francisco, Jossey-Bass.

WINSLADE, J. and MONK, G. (2008) *Practicing Narrative Mediation: Loosening the Grip of Conflict,* San Francisco, Jossey-Bass.

WINSLADE, J, MONK G. and COTTER, A. (1999) A narrative approach to the practice of mediation. *Negotiation Journal,* 14(1), 21-42.

YAMADA, A.-M. and SINGELIS, T. (1999) Biculturalism and self-construal. *International Journal of Intercultural Relations,* 23, 697-709.

ZELDIN, T. (1998) *An Intimate History of Humanity.* London: Vintage.

Human Social Behavior, Cultural Perspectives, and Conflict Mediation: A Multi-Variate Analysis of Gambian Dispute Processing

Mark Davidheiser

Introduction

The rapid growth of the field of conflict resolution since the latter part of the 20th century has produced a rich and growing literature on conflict mediation. While our understanding of mediation has blossomed, addressing socio-cultural diversity remains an outstanding challenge. Despite a surge in publications and courses on the subject, the research record remains lacking—particularly in regard to systematic and empirical studies—and questions remain.

The following paper uses descriptive and empirical data on conflict mediation collected from different populations in The Gambia to investigate socio-cultural variation in conflict mediation. Several mediation activities, such as caucusing, evaluating and assigning blame, and negotiating substantive issues, are used as benchmarks to exemplify the variance in mediation preferences uncovered in the study.[1] In addition to contributing rich empirical and descriptive data to the research record, the project underscores the multidimensional complexity of socio-cultural patterning and the need for further research. Accordingly, the paper provides suggestions for research design along with a discussion of the implications of the study findings.

Culture and mediation

There has been much discussion of how to define "mediation," but "third-party facilitated negotiation" has been widely used (cf. Doob, 1993, Mitchell, 1981). A literature review suggests at least three reasons why cultural dimensions of conflict and mediation are significant. First, intercultural conflicts are frequently considered exceptionally intense because divergent communication styles may impede disputants from establishing mutual understanding (Hall, 1976, Ting-Toomey, 1985). Second, variations between parties' shared values and norms may reduce the effectiveness of the standard problem-solving approach to mediation, as values cannot be negotiated easily (Kriesberg et al., 1998).

---

1 For a discussion of additional mediation activities, see Davidheiser, 2005.

Third, many authors have noted the rich traditions of conflict mediation found among the peoples of the Global South (e.g. Folberg and Taylor, 1984). As it emerged in the North Atlantic nations, the professional field of Alternative Dispute Resolution (ADR) drew early inspiration from descriptions of dispute settlement processes among the Kpelle of Liberia and others (Gibbs, 1963). That inspiration was a matter of general encouragement about resolving disputes outside of courts, however, and it did not extend to consideration or incorporation of specific techniques or procedures (Nader, 1989, 1991). Investigating strategies for conflict management among different groups may therefore provide a wide range of potential approaches for practitioners to choose from, according to the case characteristics. Alternatively, existing conflict resolution models may be enhanced by hybridization with other methodologies or by integrating techniques from other approaches. Finally, extending the socio-cultural wellsprings of ADR processes like mediation is particularly relevant in the early 21st century, when ADR is being exported to the Global South as a cutting edge approach to legal reform (cf. Menkel-Meadow, 2003).

As this paper should indicate, much of the existing research is limited by an overly broad treatment of cultural differences. Researchers have used binary oppositional categories such as individualist versus collectivist cultures (Hofstede, 1980) and high- and low-context communication styles (Hall 1969, Hall, 1976) to analyze societal influences in mediation (e.g. Cohen, 1996, Galtung, 1997). Such explanatory frameworks imply a dichotomy between North Atlantic perspectives and those of other societies (Augsburger, 1992).

Several concerns can be raised about such approaches. Can cultural variation worldwide really be reduced to a small number of specific factors? Additionally, assuming the existence of a shared culture based on ethnic or other collective identities is questionable; monolithic worldviews should not be conflated with ethnicity, religious affiliation, or any other collective identity.

Accordingly, Avruch (2003, 1998) argues that cultural influences on conflict mediation should be explored using descriptive models that are much more complex than previous versions of cultural dimensions (see Hofstede, 1980 as an example). In a similar vein, Wehr and Lederach (1996) note that conflict mediation research should focus on the interaction's procedural character and minimize ethnocentrism.[2] A broad conceptualization of mediation as simply third-party dispute

2 Standard definitions of mediation exclude all procedures without outsider/neutral third-parties, for instance. The preference for insider/partial interlocutors is very widespread outside the North Atlantic region, which problematizes the prevailing prescription for outsider/neutrals and exemplifies how narrow definitions of mediation may be ethnocentric and exclusivist.

interventions and peacemaking, which occur outside the state arena is thus employed here.

In a recent analysis, Handwerker (2002) emphasizes the need to recognize variation in individuals' life experiences and to consider how a person's experiences may impact their worldview. He notes how membership in particular sectors of society and factors--such as occupation, gender, and age—can affect people's experiences, and therefore their outlook and "configuration of cognitions, emotions, and behavior" that undergird cultural perspectives (Handwerker, 2002: 106).

There is much to recommend Handwerker's view. Cultural perspectives emerge through cognitive processing, and interpretive frameworks are constituted at the level of the individual. Cognitive filters, thought patterns, expectations, and behavioral patterns are linked to socialization and to experience; therefore they have both shared and idiosyncratic dimensions.

Following these assumptions about culture, LeBaron (2003, 1998) presents a model to account for the complexity of potential cultural influences on conflict and conflict mediation. To do this, LeBaron presents a variety of descriptive approaches to cultural diversity, suggesting that a combination of these concepts may emerge as the most suitable description of cultural influences on any level of conflict mediation under analysis. Avruch's (2003, 1998) and LeBaron's (2003, 1998) analyses pave the way for anthropological research on the influence of culture that may serve as a cumulative starting point for broader anthropological studies.

While many authors would generally agree with the necessity of taking complexity into consideration, empirical research so far remains sparse. Many authors discuss the issue, but their own research usually rests on the basis of data that are interpreted in a general manner (Avruch, et al. 1991, Bercovitch, 1996, Merry, 1987, Witty, 1980) or are generated on highly subjective grounds of personal observations in academic settings (Irani, 1999). This paper offers a detailed case study based on empirical data collected and analyzed using systematic, anthropological methods.

The "Smiling coast" of West Africa and Southwestern Gambia

The Gambia is a small country of 11,300 square kilometers with approximately 1.4 million inhabitants located on the coast of West Africa. Prior to the colonial era, parts of The Gambia were subsumed into various regional kingdoms and polities, such as the kingdoms of Kombo and Kaabu and the Wolof states. Other areas were governed by village headmen and women or councils of elders (cf. Faal, 1999, Sonko-Godwin, 1997). The Gambia was a colony of the United Kingdom from 1816 to 1965; however, outside of urban areas the colonial infrastructure was very limited.

	MANDINKA	JOLA	MANJACO
RELIGIOUS IDENTITIES NB: The two Abrahamic faiths are syncretized with local belief systems and practices.	Muslim (non-Muslims very rare)	Mixed (increasing Islamization, significant Christian populations)	Predominantly Christian (small numbers of Muslims in other parts of the country)
SOCIAL STRATIFICATION and HISTORICAL PATTERNS OF GOVERNANCE & SOCIAL ORGANIZATION	Highly stratified Hierarchical, precolonial kingdoms and caste systems	Relatively little stratification Acephalous, segmentary lineage kinship systems	Some stratification Some state-level societies in modern day Guinea-Bissau Formal authority structures largely absent in Gambian migrant communities
PRIMARY SOURCES OF LIVELIHOODS	Agriculture, some domestic animals	Agro-pastoralism & forest products	Palm and cashew products, significantly less reliance on agro-pastoralism

Table 1: General differences between the Mandinka, Manjaco and Jol of Southwestern Gambia.

Seven ethno-linguistic groups are considered indigenous to The Gambia: the Mandinka, Fula, Jola, Wolof, Serahule, Manjaco and Aku. In 1993, 95% of Gambians self-identified as Muslim, 3.5% as Christian, and 1.5% as animist (Frederiks, 2003). Animist and Christian populations are clustered in urban coastal regions and the southwest of the country.

This study was based in the southwestern corner of The Gambia, arguably the most diverse rural area in the country with a higher proportion of Manjacos, Jolas, and non-Muslims than other rural locales. Sample populations were drawn from the Mandinka, Jola, and Manjaco inhabitants of the region, and the study data were collected in villages dominated by one of these three groups. These groups were chosen because of their differentiation in three significant areas: religious affiliations, historical socio-political systems, and primary livelihood (Sagnia, 1983, Sonko-Godwin, 1986, 1997). Table 1 summarizes general characteristics and differences between the three ethno-linguistic identity groups.

The Mandinka are the most numerous of the ethnic groups considered to be indigenous to The Gambia, and their eponymous language is the predominant trade language in rural areas. Prior to colonialism, the Mandinka established highly stratified state-level agrarian societies or kingdoms, with populations divided into occupational castes. Patrilineage remains a significant Mandinka social consideration, and it impacts social, political, and religious leadership. Virtually all Mandinka self-identify as Muslims, and they are popularly considered the group that spearheaded the Islamicization of the southwest.

The Jola and the Manjaco are national minorities whose modes of social organization distinguish them from the other, more vertically stratified ethnic groups of the country. Precolonial Jola social organization featured relatively low levels of social stratification and followed the segmentary lineage kinship model, in which there is little centralization.[3] The Jola are the only indigenous Gambian group historically associated with acephalous governance systems. Village heads (*alkalos*) were imposed on the Jola during the colonial era; however, contemporary *alkalos* in Jola villages are generally less influential than their Mandinka counterparts, and more of their authority is shared with councils of elders. The Jola are also more religiously diverse than the Mandinka. Although the Mandinka forcibly converted many of them to Islam, others identify themselves as Christian and/or make offerings at shrines situated at the base of large trees. Southwestern Gambians who self-identify as Jola also engage in more hunting and gathering than their Mandinka counterparts of the late 20th and early 21st centuries.

The Manjaco originated in what is now Guinea-Bissau. They have been drawn to what is now The Gambia since the establishment of trade with Europeans to take advantage of associated market opportunities. Migration has accelerated since Guinea Bissau's war for independence in the 1970s. While there has been a great

3 As Mark (1992) has argued, the Jola cannot be considered as completely egalitarian, as some status differentiation occurred. Nevertheless, Jola social organization was much less vertical than that of the Mandinka, whose historical record of state-level societies and caste systems provides a marked contrast to the general lack of centralization and large political structures among the Jola. The Mandinka appear to have stimulated a slight centralizing trend in the late pre-colonial era, both through cultural diffusion and through slave-raiding that prompted some conglomeration as a defensive reaction (Baum, 1999).

deal of interaction and intermarriage between the Jola and the Mandinka, this is not the case with the Manjaco of the region. Manjaco settlements in southwestern Gambia are often clustered around Mandinka and Jola areas; their communities are much more insular than those of the other two groups.

British indirect rule left the management of most rural disputes to the Gambians, especially customary authorities recognized or appointed by the colonial regime (cf. Darboe, 1982). Many aspects of the colonial system have been reproduced by the post-independence regimes and Western-style courts have been limited to urban centers.[4] Local processes of mediation have consequently maintained a significant role in rural social life extending up to the time of this chapter was written.

Research Design and Methodology

The research design of this study was shaped by three propositions. The first is the previously discussed idea of culture as multidimensional. Culture was therefore not assumed to be reducible to ethno-linguistic identities, instead the relationship between such identities and shared values, norms, and habituated behaviors was tested. Furthermore, ethnographic data were used to identify additional participant characteristics of potential significance, such as religious affiliation, gender identity, home village, and age-set. These characteristics were added to the project codebook. Examining contextual factors, such as dispute type and the social status of the mediators and disputants, made it possible to control for other potential sources of variation in peacemaking activities. With these procedures in place, mediation activities were compared according to the particular identities of the mediation participants and their collective identities. Using individual, intra-group, and intergroup levels of analysis, the tests offered a thorough examination of social patterning in mediation styles.

The second proposition is that methodological triangulation enables a deeper investigation of complex social phenomena. Accordingly, both descriptive and empirical data were collected, and the analysis incorporated participatory, qualitative, and quantitative methods. The findings presented here are derived from three years of field research conducted in the southwestern Gambia between 1999 and 2005. The collected data include extensive ethnographic data and interviews, 129 semi-structured interviews with mediators, 21 panel sessions with expert peacemakers,

4 Decentralization and legal reform plans of the 1st decade of the 21st century call for the establishment of High Courts in rural areas.

and 132 observed cases of mediated disputes.[5] The descriptive data—ethnographic observations, interviews, and panel sessions—were used to identify categories and activities common to local mediations, to establish what constitutes normal procedures versus outlying divergences, and to control for inter-subjective bias. The panels were stratified according to ethnicity, age-set, gender, village of residence, and religion.

Third, the project design addressed problems of idealized representations of behavior and informant accuracy. Respondents' representations of social phenomena may be influenced by ideological factors or may serve utilitarian purposes. In a classic anthropological work, Malinowski (1922) argued for the use of empirical data. More recent studies have revealed significant problems with informant recall, underlining the potential for inaccuracy when answering questions based on memory (Bernard, et al., 1984). Mediation research has also highlighted the need for observed data. In a study by Kressel and Pruitt (1989), for example, mediators were given checklists of activities to fill out immediately after the conclusion of a session. When these lists were compared to empirical records of the mediations, significant discrepancies were found. Owing to such issues, conflict scholars have called for observations of what mediators actually do (e.g. Avruch, 1991, Bercovitch and Houston, 1996).

A purposive sampling strategy was therefore designed to maximize data quality and quantity. Active mediators were identified in the target communities.[6] The study initially concentrated on village officials and notables such as *alkalos* (village heads) and *nyansingbaas* (the women in charge of female age-grade ceremonies). Interviews with such high-profile individuals constituted one point of approach.

It quickly became apparent that many persons who did not hold a formal title or position were also prominent peacemakers. Ethnographic interviews generated lists of active mediators and discussions were held with many such individuals. Doing village-wide surveys and making connections with many different people mitigated the dangers of being limited to specific networks. In order to maximize the accuracy

5 "Expert peacemakers" signifies persons frequently sought out by disputants because of their experience and reputation as effective conflict interveners. Observed cases often involved multiple sessions dedicated to resolving the dispute in question; one dispute resulted in seventeen separate meetings, for instance.

6 Conflict management can be a highly sensitive subject. Extensive relationship building and language learning were essential for gaining the trust of potential project participants. The accuracy of the data was a key concern, and checks for accuracy were included in the processing techniques. One portion of the data supplied by a single informant was found to be suspect; consequently, all material associated with that person was discarded.

of collected information, data processing was done with great care. Teams of translators were used to reduce the possibility of interpreter bias, for example.

Micro-level mediations between individuals or small groups were the focus of this inquiry. Those cases concerned conflicts between family and clan members, spouses, neighbors, friends, and relative strangers. The disputes encompassed a variety of issues such as land disputes, crops damaged by domestic animals, marital and domestic conflicts, and personal insults or slights. The number of participants in each case was among the situational variables, with the overall number as well as the specific amount of mediators and of disputants all being controlled for.

The data were analyzed with qualitative and quantitative methods. Coding was done on 121 of the observed cases using The Ethnograph processing and analysis package. Cases of mediation were coded according to the activities that occurred throughout the mediation process. Each case was also tagged according to the characteristics of the participants, the dispute, and the mediation context. The tags represented potential independent variables and were derived from the literature, as well as the author's experience as a mediation practitioner and trainer, and the inductive data. We can distinguish between two categories of such variables, specifically the population characteristics of the participants and situational data. Key participant characteristics are listed in Davidheiser (2006); some examples of contextual variables that were controlled for include the type of dispute in question, the level of formality of the intervention effort, and the nature of the social relations between the participants. The goal was to identify and control for situational factors that may affect mediation behavior and thereby throw cultural influences into relief.

The cases were divided into different sets according to these tags, and cases were searched for themes, patterns, and areas of variation. This process produced matrices of mediation activities and potential independent variables. Data sets were imported into the statistical software package SPSS for further analysis. Most of the potential independent variables were nominal, so cross-tabulation was an appropriate tool for examining what activities occurred in different sets of cases. The cross-tabulation tables measured the frequency of specific mediation activities and highlighted their associations with various potential independent and control variables. The resulting relationships were analyzed for statistical significance using chi-squared and Fisher's Exact Tests. The multiple types and sources of data and elaborate research design enabled a fine-grained examination that illuminated in detail numerous trends, including modal convergences, less common manifestations, and seemingly idiosyncratic outliers. The methodological triangulation was invaluable as the descriptive data from interviews, focus groups, and panel sessions were vital to bolstering the findings from the observed data and comprehending the scope and nature of associations between the observed trends and the case and participant characteristics.

Study findings and Discussion

The analysis uncovered considerable variation in mediator styles and mediation activities. Each mediation was unique to some degree, but notable themes and patterns were also identified. Variations associated with the inductively generated categories were multiplex, occurring between different identity groups and within subsectors of specific groups. Less pronounced variation was discernible between individual mediators and also between cases when mediator identity was held constant.

Ethno-linguistic identities correlated with significant patterning in mediation preferences and behaviors, thereby seemingly substantiating the common view of ethnicity as the primary factor in cultural variation. Further stratifying the empirical data according to 1) gender, 2) age sets and 3) confessional affiliations revealed that ethnicity comprised only a portion of the overall picture, however. Out of numerous potential independent variables that were tested, the aforementioned three demonstrated the strongest relationships with the dependent variable of mediation styles, with gender showing the strongest association and confessional affiliations the weakest. There were complex interrelationships between these variables, but in the scale of relative significance, ethno-linguistic identities could be placed after gender. This paper should make clear, however, that such scales should not be considered as fixed phenomena that can be widely generalized to other settings and populations, but rather as an indication of the multiplex nature of socio-cultural patterning.

The descriptive data suggested that the first three attributes—ethno-linguistic, religious, and gender identities—correlated with variation not only in terms of actual behavior, but also with shared beliefs about conflict generation and mitigation. The variance in behavior related to age appeared to be associated more with expected social roles related to age than with attitudinal change brought about by processes such as globalization. In other words, the marked differences in the styles of younger and older mediators may stem less from modern generational divergences in shared values, mores, and beliefs than from normative views and conventions of the nature and behaviors of youths and elders. Several younger mediators postulated that as they aged their approaches would come to resemble those of their elderly colleagues. The many correlations between preferred styles of practice and mediator attributes and characteristics illustrate the complexity of socio-cultural perspectives. Narrowing the lens of this multilevel analysis made it possible to extend the investigation to the micro level, encompassing the more individualized domain connoted by the term "worldview."

The considerable intra-group variation highlighted the significance of individual experience and personality in the behavior of peacemakers. Comparing observed and interview data from specific individual mediators uncovered trends related to the experience and personality of mediators. For example, two mediators from the same family exhibited the most similarity in their preferred approaches, but there were noticeable divergences related to their personality types.

In addition, social action is highly situational, meaning that the influence of cultural perspectives should not be over-emphasized as human behavior is conditional. Individual mediators were observed employing disparate peacemaking styles in various cases. Key informants explained how they varied their approaches according to the nature of the dispute at hand. The following examples of trends in particular aspects of the mediation process may help to illustrate some of the aforementioned points.

Examples of found mediation

Significant variation was found in relation to the structuring of interventions (direct or indirect mediation) and two common features of the mediation process, namely, the collection of disputant narratives and testimony and the assignment of blame.

Indirect versus direct mediations

The use of caucuses with individual parties versus group meetings with all parties was one area of significant differentiation. Mediations ranged from pure shuttle diplomacy with no collective meetings of all parties to group meetings without any caucusing. In both the descriptive and empirical data, Manjacos relied more heavily on group meetings than Mandinkas or Jolas. Mediations consisting only of caucuses were extremely rare among the Manjaco, due to their emphasis on joint testimonials and discussions, judging, and ritualization.

The most common procedure was for mediators to caucus with the disputants first and then bring them together for a group meeting. In these mediations, the information gathering and exchange and negotiation took place during caucuses. The mediators shuttled back and forth between the disputants, sometimes carrying messages between them, and always encouraging them to settle. There may have been a single caucus with each party or many caucuses. In some of these cases the group meeting followed the model presented above with discussions of the dispute, disputant testimony, and assignment of blame.

Often the substantive negotiations were concluded during the caucusing, and the group meetings were essentially a matter of formalizing the agreements and reconciliation through ritualization or symbolic activities.[7] In such cases the mediators did most of the talking during the group meetings.

AGE	ACTUAL AND EXPECTED COUNTS	SHUTTLE DIPLOMACY		TOTAL
		Absent	Present	
MIXED (case included varied age groups)	Count	21	9	30
	Expected Count	20	10	30
ELDER (as defined locally, usually ca. 50 years and older)	Count	33	7	40
	Expected Count	27	13	40
YOUTH (as defined locally, roughly between 15 and 40 years of age)	Count	27	24	51
	Expected Count	34	17	51

Table 2: Shuttle diplomacy by age crosstabulation.

The mediators set the stage, giving a short discussion of the situation (without going into particulars) and the need for settlement. Sometimes the mediators restated judgments arrived at during the caucusing process. Other times they simply gave general advice to both disputants. The disputants often did not say much in such meetings, other than to perhaps make a formal statement about the reconciliation. They usually did not go into the details of the dispute. The group meeting often concluded with ritualization activities such as hand-shaking, the exchange of kola nuts, goods or money, prayer, and the sharing of food.

"Bridge" refers to mediators engaging in shuttle diplomacy by relaying messages between disputants in caucuses. The large percentile differences for each age-group illustrate how elders tended to engage in direct mediation and were much less interested in caucusing than younger mediators. The difference is likely partly attribut-

7. Ritualization activities included prayer, hand shaking, and sharing food or drink.

able to the higher status of older mediators and their greater expectations of their ability to move the disputants towards settlement and lower level of concern about disputant sensibilities.

ETHNICITY	ACTUAL AND EXPECTED COUNTS	DIRECT MEDIATION		TOTAL
		Absent	Present	
MIXED	Count	8	11	19
	Expected Count	6	13	19
JOLA	Count	6	27	33
	Expected Count	10	23	33
MANJACO	Count	2	22	24
	Expected Count	8	16	24
MANDINKA	Count	22	23	45
	Expected Count	14	31	45

Table 3: Ethnicity by direct mediation crosstabulation.

	Value	df	Asymp. Sig. (2-sided)
Pearson Chi-Square	16.004(a)	3	.001
Likelihood Ratio	17.311	3	.001
Linear-by-Linear Association	2.068	1	.150
N of Valid Cases	121		

Table 4: Chi-square tests.

Mediator collection of disputant narratives and testimony

The ethnographic (e.g. Gulliver, 1979) and prescriptive literatures (e.g. Folberg and Taylor, 1984) place great emphasis on disputant narratives, which are considered a vital component of the mediation process. Having the parties present their explanations is essential to the information gathering and exchange process that enables problem-solving. Disputant testimonies may also aid negotiation by supplying important but previously unavailable information and clarifying misunderstandings. Disputants presenting their perspectives and expressing their feelings is also a central aspect of the therapeutic aspect of mediation highlighted by some authors (see Gibbs, 1973, Robarchek, 1997).[8]

Gambian mediators included the collection of disputant narratives in their explanations of the process, and this activity was common in the empirical data as well. Some variation did occur in relation to this activity, however. In interviews and panel sessions some mediators stated that in some cases they instruct disputants not to relate the details of the dispute to them. There was some association with ethnicity here, as more women respondents than men mentioned this approach. This procedure occurred in the empirical cases as well and was associated with particular contextual variables.

One such variable was related to Gambian social structures and related cultural norms. In some Mandinka and Jola cases with disputants of markedly disparate social status, the lower ranking disputant did not give testimony in the presence of the senior disputant. In such cases, when there were no caucuses with the junior disputants, they often did not render their testimonies and express their feelings and viewpoints, at least until after the dispute had been formally resolved.[9]

This phenomenon was associated primarily with family disputes and was rare outside that context. There are strong, shared beliefs in The Gambia regarding the relationship between parents and children. In one mediation between a father and son, the mediator was informed about the dispute by the son's brother, but was not given much detail about the conflict. The mediator caucused with the father and then called the son in for a group meeting. The father repeated his explanation of the dispute in the group meeting, and the son spoke only briefly to beg for forgive-

---

8 Hearing the opposing parties' narratives may also aid in fostering recognition and generating empathy for the Other.

9 This supports the author's belief that mediation should be conceptualized in a more extended manner than is common. The mediation session with all parties present may be merely one phase of the process, and as this study suggests, it may not be the most significant part of some cases. Rather than depicting it as the core or even sole stage of the mediation process, more attention should be devoted to the activities occurring before and after that session.

ness and promise that he would never again quarrel with his father. The father accepted, and the reconciliation was celebrated with prayers of thanksgiving.

In other cases, the mediators said that they did not want to hear any explanations or details about the dispute in their introductory statements, in caucuses and/or group meetings, but the disputants elaborated anyway, sometimes at great length. This illustrates the significance of this activity. Disputant testimony is often the most important component of the information collection and exchange undertaken by mediators. It is also part of the "therapeutic" aspect of mediation (see Robarchek, 1997), as the disputants are able to express or ventilate their feelings and have them validated or at least heard.

Another pattern in the empirical data consisted of mediators limiting or attempting to halt disputant testimonials, usually because the mediators felt they were becoming repetitive or evoking negative emotions in a counterproductive fashion. Additionally, in cases where the substantive negotiations were completed during pre-meeting caucuses, it was common for the mediators to instruct the disputants to avoid discussing the causes of the conflict in group meetings.

There were, however, also instances in which there was no disputant testimony in either the caucuses or the group meetings, although these were rare. In such cases the mediators often already had heard many of the details of the dispute from other people. These mediations were associated with a particular kind of relationship between the participants—specifically when the mediators were of high social status, usually of higher status than the disputants. Ethnicity was also linked to these cases as they were most common among Mandinkas and almost absent among Manjacos, who strongly emphasized reviewing the details of a dispute. Dispute type also correlated with this pattern; these cases, most commonly marital disputes, tended to involve taboo or sensitive subjects. According to a well-known Mandinka saying, when a man and a woman fight in their house at night and someone goes to intervene, they should not ask about the cause of the problem. This pattern differs markedly from the models presented in the cross-cultural and the Western literature.

In general, the Mandinka typically favored a cautious, rather circumspect mediation approach. They often caucused with disputants and frequently avoided direct confrontations and negotiations. The Manjaco preferred the opposite approach. They overwhelmingly favored group meetings, direct negotiations, and explicit statements of which party was at fault. The Jola were more concerned with resolving specific issues than the other two groups. Their mediations were more likely to include negotiations and to produce agreements that addressed substantive issues.

Judging, evaluating, and assigning blame

The vast majority of US and Canadian literature and training materials depicts the third-party as neutral and instructs mediators to avoid evaluating disputes or at least to avoid expressing any evaluations that they may form. The assumption that mediators should be neutral facilitators who do things like use "objective criteria" to help "separate the people from the problem" (Fisher, et al., 1991) is deeply ingrained in Western mediation ideology (Cohen, 1996, Della Noce, et al., 2001). Despite the dominance of this viewpoint in the literature, evaluative approaches are more common than one might presume.[10]

In mainstream Gambian ideologies, mediators make judgments about cases. Mediators are often expected to "tell the truth" and "give the party their rights."[11] As these commonly used phrases imply, fairness is considered a vital quality of mediators. While observed behaviors varied, this was the modal approach when mediation was described. When questioned about this, respondents generally stated that explicit evaluation of cases was an integral part of the mediation and resolution process, often adding that if one does not tell the parties who is right and who is wrong then the conflict will never end. This pattern is congruent with descriptions of mediation from other African and non-industrialized societies (cf. Bourdieu, 1965, Cloke, 1990, Robarchek, 1997, King-Irani, 2000).

In response to further questioning, some mediators elaborated that not all mediations included this activity, as it could jeopardize settlement of the dispute if one of the parties rejected the judgment or became upset. In fact, many of the collected cases did not include judging or stating guilt. The variation was associated strongly with ethnicity. Manjaco mediators were more likely to insist that judging was necessary for dispute resolution than Jola or Mandinka respondents, and the observed cases reflected that pattern.

The table below depicts the number of cases in which the mediators assigned blame for the dispute during the course of the peacemaking. As was often the case, the contrast in distributions was highest for the Mandinka and Manjaco populations. The assignment of blame took place in 71% of the Manjaco cases and 35% of the Mandinka cases.

---

10 There are significant differences between mediation models and guidelines and the actual practices of mediators. For example, although the prescriptive literature is dominated by the facilitative paradigm, many practicing mediators have been trained as attorneys and bring an evaluative approach to the field.

11 These phrases are taken from interviews and were used frequently.

Ethnicity	Actual and Expected Counts	Assign Blame		Total
		Absent	Present	
Mixed	Count	9	10	19
	Expected Count	9	10	19
Jola	Count	14	19	33
	Expected Count	16	17	33
Manjaco	Count	7	17	24
	Expected Count	12	12	24
Mandinka	Count	29	16	45
	Expected Count	22	23	45

Table 5: Assign blame by ethnicity.

For the Mandinka and Jola groups, social status was a highly significant factor in terms of assigning blame. Mediators from these ethno-linguistic groups tended to avoid openly blaming the higher status party. The empirical and descriptive data are fairly congruent on this point. Although Mandinka and, to a lesser extent, Jola mediators did blame higher-status disputants in some cases, it occurred rarely. Manjaco cases in which the mediators blamed the higher-status disputants were much more common. Manjaco respondents tended to insist that judgments must be given according to the particulars of the situation; whereas Mandinka, and many Jola, mediators preferred to criticize high prestige individuals only privately when their opposing parties were not present. Ethnicity remained significant in this regard. There was virtually universal agreement within the Manjaco respondents that assignment of blame was essential and should be explicitly stated. Anticipated variation along gender lines did not occur consistently. Most female Mandinka and Jola respondents who addressed the topic said wives should not be told that they are right in disputes with their husbands.

The number of mediation participants and the forum in which it took place were also associated with whether the mediators expressed their opinions on disputant culpability. Across ethnic groups, large formal meetings in which disputants met together with multiple mediators, witnesses, and/or onlookers included the assigning blame activity. Most of the cases in which the mediators did not express judgments about the merits of each disputant's position were characterized by fewer participants and a more private setting.

Negotiation

"Negotiation" refers to purposive discussion of substantive issues, bargaining over settlement agreements, including such activities as making compromise offers and counterproposals, as well as problem-solving behavior of the mediators such as soliciting disputants' ideas for settlement proposals and discussing those plans. It is striking that, as illustrated in Table 6, the expected count for the Jola is almost half of the actual count, while the actual counts for the Mandinka and Manjaco are much lower than expected.

Ethnicity	Actual and Expected Counts	Negotiate		Total
		Absent	Present	
Mixed	Count	13	6	19
	Expected Count	14	5	19
Jola	Count	16	17	33
	Expected Count	24	9	33
Manjaco	Count	21	3	24
	Expected Count	17	7	24
Mandinka	Count	37	8	45
	Expected Count	32	13	45

Table 6: Ethnicity by negotiation crosstabulation.

Controlling for other potential variables did not eliminate the variation. Dispute type is particularly significant here, since disputes over material items or goods are more likely to involve negotiation than mediations of conflicts instigated by more abstract concerns such as face and honor. When the cases were divided by dispute type, however, we found that none of the four Mandinka material cases included negotiation of substantive issues. A test of statistical significance indicated a relationship between ethnicity and issue negotiation at a 99.8% level of certainty.

	Value	Df	Asymp. Sig. (2-sided)
Pearson Chi-Square	14.333	3	.002
Likelihood Ratio	14.099	3	.003
Linear-by-Linear Association	6.203	1	.013
N of Valid Cases	121		

Table 7: Negotiate by ethnicity chi-square tests.

The chi-square value of .002 indicates that there is a very high likelihood that there is a statistically significant relationship between ethno-linguistic identity and issue negotiation.

In terms of Riskin's widely used grids of mediation styles (Riskin 1996, 2003), Gambian mediators generally lean towards the evaluative/directive broad approach. In addition to assigning blame, Gambian mediators often offer proposals and plans for settlement, and they can be quite assertive in promoting their ideas. Although in some cases they focus only on the immediate concrete problem or issue (a "narrow" orientation in Riskin's terms), their definition and approach to the problem is generally broad with much concern for restoring harmony and the long-term relationship between the parties. In some cases, Gambian mediators also exhibited concern for the maintenance of community norms and values and applied them to the dispute, praising and criticizing the disputants in relation to their actions' conformity with societal conventions. That aspect of Gambian mediator orientations parallels descriptions of practices in other non-industrialized societies (see, for example, Cloke, 1990, Faure, 2000).

Two important caveats should be noted here. Several mediators participated intensively in the project and each of them provided a number of cases. Individual level variation in mediator style was quite apparent in the empirical data. Some variation was found between members of different clans—in particular two mediators from a clan in a position of religious leadership in a predominately Muslim village exhibited some commonalities in their mediation style. However, their approaches were not identical.

In fact, every mediator appeared to utilize a characteristic style. For example, some mediators would begin their meetings with elaborate introductions, setting the stage and defining the agenda, while others would quickly proceed to the issues at hand. Some mediators favored a facilitative approach over evaluative and directive methods, and they tended to help the disputants to explore options for settlement more than their colleagues who typically attempted to impose their own ideas on the disputants.

Situational dynamics added a further layer of complexity. Not only did preferred mediation styles diverge within each identity group, but the approaches of specific individuals also varied across cases. These findings are consistent with studies of US and Canadian mediator styles (e.g. Kressel, et al., 1994, Kressel and Pruitt, 1989, Silbey and Merry, 1986). No cross-cultural studies have been found that examine mediation styles at the individual level. This gap in the research record should be addressed.

It is important to note that the findings discussed above represent patterns or modal tendencies of specific social groups; all populations studied encompassed a range of styles and perspectives. The effects of cultural perspectives are highly specific and also situational; they are linked to the particular experience of the involved parties and the circumstances in question. Although patterned tendencies do exist, they are not absolute; contradictions and exceptions abound. Context, experience, and group and individual identities are mutually constitutive and exhibit multidimensional associations with conflict and mediation styles.

The study findings are congruent with contemporary anthropological approaches that propose that cultural analysis should focus on the individual rather than the group level (see Avruch, 1998, Handwerker, 2002). Societal attributes are unevenly distributed because individuals are active recipients of shared norms and values. It is within the individual that socialization takes place and transmitted conventions are re-interpreted. Individuals are the locus of multiple overlapping identities that blend with personal experiences in shaping cultural perspectives.

The range of variation within the Gambian data highlights the limitations of dichotomous approaches to cultural pluralism in conflict resolution. Cultural preferences in conflict resolution are not two-dimensional. Crafting a theory and an approach that adequately capture this complexity is one of the most significant tasks currently facing scholars and practitioners.

Conclusion

This study indicated that the range of factors involved in mediation and the complexity of their interrelatedness present an intricately woven tapestry. Some strands of this tapestry are knitted into discernible patterns. However, the level of movement is remarkable, which profoundly undermines the possibility of a singular model or static mediation process.

Some mediators carefully considered the particulars of a case and planned their interventions in advance, thereby demonstrating the salience of agency and the significance of context. At the same time, mediation practices could be described as "embedded." Social structures do have a discernible influence, but one must recognize that they are linked to macro- and micro-level influences and they vary according to the specific context and characteristics of each situation. The type of dispute in question, the nature of the social relations between the participants, the participants' personalities, and other structural dynamics all discernibly impacted mediators' behavior, thereby revealing a fascinating juxtaposition of agency and structure in mediation practice.

Cultural perspectives can extend far beyond modes of communication; they are implicated in the very interpretive and behavioral processes that generate disputes and facilitate reconciliation. Different persons and groups conceptualize conflict and mediation in dissimilar ways and this affects the nature of their practices. Although cross-cultural commonalities in mediation exist, they are neither absolute nor universal except at the most general level.[12]

The multivariate approach of the Gambian study and resultant detailed exploration of multiple facets of participant identity and activity have intriguing implications for the study of culture and social action. The research underlined the meaning-making aspect of conflict mediation, illustrating how mediation can illuminate the social geography of shared norms, values and behavioral expectations and provide glimpses of their boundaries. It also provides a powerful means for investigating the discursive negotiations underlying the continual adjustments of the boundaries and ongoing geographical shifting.

Further, the research conducted in The Gambia suggests strongly that cultural differences are not amenable to dichotomous schema or other reductionist explanations. To understand the complexities of human diversity requires a multivariate approach, exploration of potential interrelations between variables and observed phenomena, and the collection of multiple levels and types of data. Developing a robust body of mediation and conflict management research may provide a means to produce a more evolved social theory that can be applied to increase understandings of human relations and enhance the human condition.

12 Even at the general level of comparison the universal aspects are minimal, and seemingly limited to the ritualization that occurs in the initial and final phases of mediation. See Davidheiser, 2005 for more information.

Acknowledgements

Ba Nyakass Seidey and many anonymous Gambians provided assistance vital to the success of the research undergirding this paper. The study was funded by the United States Institute of Peace and the University of Florida. The text benefitted considerably from Allan A. Bonney and Consuelo Kelley's generous editorial assistance and Dominic Busch's content suggestions.

References

AUGSBURGER, D. W. (1992) *Conflict Mediation Across Cultures: Pathways and Patterns,* Louisville, KY, Westminster John Knox Press.

AVRUCH, K. (1991) Introduction. Culture and conflict resolution. IN AVRUCH, K., BLACK, P. W. & SCIMECCA, J. A. (Eds.) *Conflict Resolution. Cross-Cultural Perspectives.* (1-18), New York/Westport/London, Greenwood.

AVRUCH, K. (1998) *Culture and Conflict Resolution,* Washington, DC, United States Institute of Peace Press.

AVRUCH, K. (2003) Type I and type II errors in culturally sensitive conflict resolution practice. *Conflict Resolution Quarterly,* 20(3), 351-371.

AVRUCH, K., BLACK, P. W. & SCIMECCA, J. A. (Eds.) (1991) *Conflict Resolution. Cross-Cultural Perspectives,* New York, Greenwood Press.

BAUM, R. M. (1999) *Shrines of the Slave Trade: Diola Religion and Society in Precolonial Senegambia,* New York, Oxford University Press.

BERCOVITCH, J. (1996) Introduction: Thinking about mediation. IN BERCOVITCH, J. (Ed.) *Resolving International Conflicts: The Theory and Practice of Mediation.* (1-9), Boulder, CO, Lynne Rienner.

BERCOVITCH, J. (2001) Culture and international mediation. *International Negotiation,* 6(1), 3-23.

BERCOVITCH, J. & HOUSTON, A. (1996) The study of international mediation: Theoretical issues and empirical evidence. IN BERCOVITCH, J. (Ed.) *Resolving International Conflicts: The Theory and Practice of Mediation.* (11-35), Boulder, CO, Lynne Rienner.

BERNARD, H. R., KILLWORTH, P. D., KRONENFELD, D. & SAILER, L. D. (1984) The problem of informant accuracy: The validity of retrospective data. *Annual Review of Anthropology,* 13, 495-517.

BOURDIEU, P. (1965) The sentiment of honor in Kabyle society. IN PERISTIANY, J.G. (Ed.) *Honour and Shame: The Values of Mediterrannean Society.* London, Weidenfeld & Nicholson.

CLOKE, K. (1990) *Mediation: Revenge and the Magic of Foregiveness,* Santa Monica, CA, Center for Dispute Resolution.

COHEN, R. (1996) Cultural aspects of international mediation. IN BERCOVITCH, J. (Ed.) *Resolving International Conflicts: The Theory and Practice of Mediation.* (107-128), Boulder, CO, Lynne Rienner.

DARBOE, M. N. (1982) *The Interaction of Western and African Traditional Systems of Justice: The Problem of Integration. (A Case Study of The Gambia),* Philadelphia, PA, University of Pennsylvania: http://proquest.umi.com/pqdlink?did=748495671&Fmt=7&clientId=79356&RQT=309&VName=PQD [last accessed: 2008-09-26].

DAVIDHEISER, M. (2005) Culture and mediation: A contemporary processual analysis. *International Journal of Intercultural Relations*, 29, 713-738.

DAVIDHEISER, M. (2006) Conflict mediation and culture: Lessons from The Gambia. *Peace and Conflict Studies*, 13, 21-42.

DELLA NOCE, D. J., BUSH, R. A. B. & FOLGER, J. P. (2001) Myths and misconceptions about the transformative orientation. IN BUSH, R. A. B. & FOLGER, J. P. (Eds.) *Designing Mediation: Approaches to Training and Practice within a Transformative Framework.* (50-54), New York, Institute for the Study of Conflict Transformation.

DOOB, L. W. (1993) *Intervention: Guides and Perils,* New Haven, Yale University Press.

FAAL, D. (1999) *A History of The Gambia: AD 1000 to 1965,* Serekunda, The Gambia, Edward Francis Small Printing Press.

FAURE, G. O. (2000) Traditional conflict management in Africa and China. IN ZARTMAN, I. W. (Ed.) *Traditional Cures for Modern Conflicts: African Conflict "Medicine"* (153-168), Boulder, CO, Lynne Rienner.

FISHER, R., URY, W. & PATTON, B. (1991) *Getting to Yes: Negotiating Agreement Without Giving In,* Boston, Houghton Mifflin.

FOLBERG, J. & TAYLOR, A. (1984) *Mediation. A Comprehensive Guide to Resolving Conflicts Without Litigation,* San Francisco, Jossey Bass.

FREDERIKS, M. T. (2003) *We Have Toiled All Night: Christianity in The Gambia 1456—2000,* Zoetmeer, Uitgeverij Boekencentrum.

GALTUNG, J. (1997) Conflict life cycles in Occident and Orient. IN FRY, D. P. & BJÖRKQVIST, K. (Eds.) *Cultural Variation in Conflict Resolution: Alternatives to Violence.* (41-50), Mahwah, NJ, Lawrence Erlbaum Associates.

GIBBS, J. L. J. (1973) Two forms of dispute settlement among the Kpelle of West Africa. IN BLACK, D. & MILESKI, M. (Eds.) *The Social Organization of Law.* (368-378), New York, Seminar.

GOLDSTEIN, S. B. (1986) *Cultural Issues in Mediation: A Literature Review,* Manoa, HI, Matsunaga Institute for Peace, University of Hawai'i at Manoa: http://www.peaceinstitute.hawaii.edu/pages/resources/documents/wp_1986_01.pdf [last accessed: 2008-09-5].

GULLIVER, P. H. (1979) *Disputes and Negotiations: A Cross-Cultural Perspective,* New York, Academic Press.

HALL, E. T. (1959) *The Silent Language,* Garden City, N.Y., Doubleday.

HALL, E. T. (1976) *Beyond Culture,* New York, Random House.

HANDWERKER, W. P. (2002) The construct validity of cultures: Cultural diversity, culture theory, and a method for Ethnography. *American Anthropologist,* 104(1), 106-122.

HOFSTEDE, G. (1980) *Culture's Consequences: International Differences in Work-Related Values,* Beverly Hills, CA., Sage.

IRANI, G. E. (1999) Islamic mediation techniques for Middle East conflicts. *Middle East Review of International Affairs,* 3(2), http://meria.idc.ac.il/journal/1999/issue2/irani.pdf [25.09.2008].

KING-IRANI, L. E. (2000) Rituals of forgiveness and processes of empowerment in Lebanon. IN ZARTMAN, I. W. (Ed.) *Traditional Cures for Modern Conflicts: African Conflict "Medicine"* (129-140), Boulder, CO, Lynne Rienner.

KRESSEL, K. & PRUITT, D. G. (1989) Conclusion: A research perspective on the mediation of social conflict. IN KRESSEL, K. & PRUITT, D. G. (Eds.) *Mediation Research: The Process and Effectiveness of Third-Party Intervention.* (394-435), San Francisco, CA, Jossey Bass.

KRESSEL, K., FRONTERA, E. A., FORLENZA, S., BUTLER, F. & FISH, L. (1994) The settlement orientation vs. the problem-solving style in custody mediation. *Journal of Social Issues,* 50(1), 64-87.

KRIESBERG, L., T. NORTHRUP, and S. THORSON (1989) *Intractable Conflicts and Their Transformations,* New York, Syracuse University Press.

LEBARON, M. (1998) Mediation and multicultural reality. *Peace and Conflict Studies,* 5(1), http://www.gmu.edu/academic/pcs/lebaron.htm.

LEBARON, M. (2003) *Bridging Cultural Conflicts. A New Approach for a Changing World,* London, Jossey-Bass.

MALINOWSKI, B. (1922) *Argonauts of the Western Pacific,* London,, G. Routledge & Sons.

MARK, P. (1992) *The Wild Bull and the Sacred Forest: Form, Meaning, and Change in Senegambian Initiation Masks,* Cambridge, Cambridge University Press.

MENKEL-MEADOW, C. (2003) Correspondence and contradictions in international and domestic conflict resolution: Lessons from general theory and varied contexts. *Journal of Dispute Resolution,* 2, 319-352.

MERRY, S. E. (1987) Disputing without culture. *Harvard Law Review,* 100, 1057-2073.

MITCHELL, C. R. (1981) *The Structure of International Conflict,* New York, St. Martin's Press.

NADER, L. (1991) Harmony models and the construction of law. IN AVRUCH, K., BLACK, P. W. & SCIMECCA, J. A. (Eds.) *Conflict Resolution. Cross-Cultural Perspectives.* (41-59), New York/Westport/London, Greenwood.

NADER, Laura (1989) The ADR explosion: The implications of rhetoric in legal reform. *Windsor Yearbook of Access to Justice,* 8, 269-91.

RISKIN, L. (1996) Understanding mediators' orientations, strategies, and techniques: A grid for the perplexed. *Harvard Negotiation Law Review,* 1(7), 7-49.

RISKIN, L. (2003) Decision-making in mediation: The new old grid and the new new grid system. *Notre Dame Law Review,* 79, 1-53.

ROBARCHEK, C. A. (1997) A community of interests: Semai conflict resolution. IN FRY, D. P. & BJÖRKQVIST, K. (Eds.) *Cultural Variation in Conflict Resolution: Alternatives to Violence.* (51-58), Mahwah, NJ, Lawrence Erlbaum Associates.

SAGNIA, B. K. (1983) *Political and Social Organization of a Traditional Gambian Society,* Banjul, The Gambia, Gambia National Museum.

SILBEY, S. S. & MERRY, S. E. (1986) Mediator settlement strategies. *Law & Policy,* 8(1), 7-32.

SONKO-GODWIN, P. (1986) *Ethnic Groups of the Senegambian Region: Social and Political Structures,* Banjul, The Gambia, Gambia National Museum.

SONKO-GODWIN, P. (1997) *Social and Political Structures in the Precolonial Periods: Ethnic Groups of the Senegambia Region,* Banjul, The Gambia, Sunrise Publishers.

TING-TOOMEY, S. (1985) Toward a theory of conflict and culture. IN GUDYKUNST, W., STEWART, L. & TING-TOOMEY, S. (Eds.) *Communication, Culture and Organizational Processes.* (71-86), Beverly Hills, C.A., Sage.

WEHR, P. & LEDERACH, J. P. (1996) Mediating conflict in Central America. IN BERCOVITCH, J. (Ed.) *Resolving International Conflicts: The Theory and Practice of Mediation.* (55-74), Boulder, CO, Lynne Rienner.

WITTY, C. C. (1980) *Mediation and Society: Conflict Management in Lebanon,* New York, Academic Press.

Exporting Mediation Through Role Plays: Intercultural Considerations in Knowledge Transfer

Michelle LeBaron and Nadja Alexander

Laura and Marie, two newly-minted PhDs in conflict resolution, are engaged by a major international development agency to design training for a court-connected mediation project in Michadja, a fictitious country somewhere outside the west. Needless to say, they are thrilled. They arrive in Michadja—fresh, full of energy, fuelled with curiosity and bursting with cutting edge ideas. They want to be sure to deliver a training course that is engaging, clear and so compelling that their Michadjan hosts clamour for their return.

At the outset of the training, they invite a participant, Moses, to participate with them in a role play to demonstrate the dynamics of mediation. Moses had been identified by the hosts of the training as a "natural mediator"—someone people trust to solve problems. Several of his community members are participants in the training, all from a local indigenous group, along with other non-indigenous participants. Laura asks Moses to play her husband while Marie mediates a dispute about where the two will go on summer vacation. Moses is willing, and both trainers are pleased with his obstinate portrayal. They are elated at this animated start to the training, and ready to keep up the momentum after a break.

But during the break, it becomes clear that all is not well in Michadja. Several of Moses' fellow community members cluster around him, demanding to know whether things are off balance between him and his wife in real life. Faced with his denials, they express disappointed surprise that he chose to take on the identity—even make believe—of another's spouse. It was both disrespectful and inappropriate, they opine, and he realizes he had not thought carefully enough about community norms. Moses summarized the conversations to Marie and Laura, and the two trainers wondered what to do.

Apologizing early in a course is not necessarily a strong start, but apologize they did. They explained that they had not realized that a contrived role play depicting Moses as Laura's spouse would be offensive to community members, and indicated that they would attempt more sensitivity in the future. Participants' responses were muted, and a wait-and-see attitude permeated the training.

Far from being a figment of our fertile imaginations, this short vignette is drawn from a real life situation. Here, the trainers were fortunate enough to become aware of the cultural *faux pas* they had committed early on. They were hopeful they could rectify the situation and restore trust with the group. In other situations trainers in an unfamiliar cultural context may conduct an entire training program and remain blissfully unaware of the intercultural confusion they have left behind. How can this sort of thing happen? Aren't conflict resolution professionals supposed to be culturally fluent and able to put themselves in the shoes of the other?

Presently, we are witnessing an international mediation export explosion. Integral to this phenomenon is the rapid transfer of information and know-how to the 'third world' funded through 'first world' institutions as part of economic and legal reform.[1] In this context western mediation is frequently introduced to reforming countries by well-intentioned trainers as a culturally-inclusive and value-free process (on the value crisis and confusion in mediation see Della Noce, 2002)—which, we argue, it is not.

Mediation, like any relational process, reflects embedded values about disputing and what is useful to do about it. A wide range of ways of responding when differences surface, diverse communication strategies, and multiple intervention approaches are possible, depending on cultural norms and values. Training that proceeds from unmarked or unperceived cultural standpoints is not culture-free, but likely to transgress these often-hidden values.

In this section we explore the export of Western mediation training models to other cultures and, in particular, the use of role plays in workshops. Some of these training programs do not focus on intercultural mediations, that is mediations involving disputants from different cultures. Rather, they aim to train local participants to conduct local mediations as part of new local court-connected, community and private commercial mediation initiatives. However, these training programs are inherently intercultural given the interactions among local participants, foreign trainers and international aid agencies. It is in these different senses that we use the term "intercultural" throughout this section.

What are we trying to achieve in mediation training?

Let's explore why a whole range of experiential learning approaches may suit training goals in an intercultural context better than repeated uses of role plays. We be-

1 See, e.g., "ADR: A Practitioner's Perspective," which reports on five case studies of ADR reform in developing countries, available at http://www.usaid.gov/our_work/democracy_and_governance/publications/pdfs/pnacp335.pdf [last accessed 2009-08-08].
See also by way of example, the Report entitled "USAID Supports Alternative Dispute Resolution In Latin America and the Caribbean," (2004), available at http://www.usaid.gov/locations/latin_america_caribbean/democracy/adr/index.html [last accessed 2006-05-29].

gin with identifying some of the most common goals of mediation training, some specific and others more diffuse. These goals include:

- communicating a range of specific content modules, such as approaches to mediation theory and practice that translate to the participants' context;
- presenting and exploring the relative utility of various tactics and strategies;
- shifting competitive attitudes and approaches to more collaborative strategies;
- fostering skill development in communication and problem-solving;
- provoking critical reflection on mediation practices; and
- working from a range of theories to inform local mediation practice.

As trainers, we want participants not only to consider new ideas, but to change attitudes, beliefs and behaviors. We know that attitude and behavioral change do not arise only from hearing concepts from a "sage on stage," but from actual experiences that give participants embodied perspectives of the possibilities of collaborative problem-solving and mediation. So far, so good: we agree that getting people engaged is vital to effective mediation training. Not only does it keep their attention, it sets up the conditions under which durable change in attitude and behavior may occur.

Teaching specific concepts such as the relative benefits of collaboration over competition often involves a shift for participants accustomed to the competitive norms inherent in many social, organizational and political spaces. This shift is not only cognitive, but affective: for participants to change their strategies and attitudes in mediation, it is useful for them to come face to face with the limited fruits of competitive strategies. While the promise of "win-win" may have been oversold, we try to provide experiences in which participants learn that collaborative approaches to mediation can at least yield "mostly ok-mostly ok" solutions that support ongoing, interdependent relationships.

Beyond the level of these goals, there are deeper objectives at play. We depend on participants becoming at least a little more familiar with their inner terrains—to notice their often-engrained "scripts" that might lead to conflict escalation, and counter these with principled, creative strategies. What motivates someone to go through such a process of self-reflection and development? It can be hard work, after all, interrupting old, often-unconscious tracks of "common sense."

Enter the role play

Role plays, at first blush, are a good start. They are engaging and often entertaining ways of catching people in their old competitive habits. They involve elements of story-telling, play and drama which are said to work well in many indigenous and world cultures.

While known under different labels including simulations, practice sessions, and games, role play appears as the most widely used term. Essentially, it refers to a learning activity in which participants are asked to assume a role, the characteristics of which are usually provided to them in written form, and to play out a mediation or part of a mediation with others who also have assumed roles. In mediation training circles, role plays have become arguably the most popular form of experiential learning. But there are pitfalls in this terrain.

In a wide range of settings from Aboriginal communities in Canada to international gatherings in Europe, we have noticed that taking on others' identities is sometimes perceived as disrespectful or nonsensical. When a group has a strong ethic of non-interference, then "playing" someone else may feel inappropriate and invasive. While role playing does exist in social interactions in cultures around the world, it is generally a part of elaborately marked social rituals involving masks, music, drumming and other markers of "time outside of ordinary time" that clearly communicate the limited purposes of the role play. Without such markers, it is an approach that—for many—may be fraught with pitfalls and potential traps. Not only does it elicit cultural stereotypes (which may be all that are available to inform the playing of an unfamiliar identity), but it literally takes people "out of their skins" into a synthetic situation that may have little relevance to their lives, and limited transferability to the conduct of actual mediations.

Beyond cultural challenges are questions of neurophysiology and learning. What ingredients facilitate effective learning? Which elements will enable durable cognitive and affective shifts, internalization of new approaches and ongoing implementation of new strategies? From sports psychology and neuroscience comes the insight that mental rehearsal is useful in improving performance. Going through physical motions in imaginal ways, combined with the trial and error of practice, is an effective way to get better as an athlete. This is true even at an elite level, as the case of Laura Wilkinson shows. Wilkinson, a diving athlete from the United States, had suffered a serious injury in her preparation for the 2000 Olympics, which prevented her from training in the usual physical manner. During her recuperation, she used mental imagery to visualize her dives. At the 2000 Olympics, still in pain from her injury and to the surprise of the world, she won a gold medal. Significantly, athletes using this approach are not imagining themselves to be other people (Roure et al., 1998). They are imagining themselves doing their sport in optimized ways. Their objective is to improve their skill, so practicing physically and mentally with critical feedback makes perfect sense. And it works.

Why would this not be the case for mediation participants and especially for those whose worlds we cannot pretend to know? Is practicing authenticity and life-like applications not also important in principled mediation? Does the immediacy of a real situation evoke qualities of veracity in more compelling ways than something that can be discounted as a "game?" We argue that it does.

Often, the argument in favor of role plays is put something like this: Participants will get distracted by their emotions and attributions if they work with real situations from familiar contexts. Skill-building is best fostered by taking people away from the familiar to practice new tools. This reduces distraction and helps participants isolate techniques in ways that bring focus and discipline.

The key word in the previous paragraph is "isolate." Learning is contextual. Moreover, relational-identity theory tells us that we identify and portray ourselves differently in different contexts, and as a result our behavior varies (Shapiro, 2006). People need context to interpret and understand ideas, and learn to apply skills appropriately in a variety of real life situations. They need to be able to recognize and develop flexible strategies to deal with the emotional tension inherent in real mediations where something important is at stake, and they need to understand the impact of their own attitudes to risk in mediations. When context is artificial, knowledge and skills practiced may be similarly artificial, thus reducing the likelihood of successfully transferring skills to real situations. Many participants in mediation trainings report that they are better able to make the transfer from learning situations to real life when they have opportunities to respond in contexts that are as realistic as possible and that evoke authentic responses from them.

The staying power of role play—Til death do us part?

Given these concerns about role plays, why are they so ubiquitous? The answer has to do with ideas about the multiple benefits of this approach, as well as expediency and habit. It is pretty well accepted by mediation trainers that role plays are useful. They are thought to "spice up" a course, and they do bring color because they contain stories. These stories are often exaggerated to engage participants, evoking humor and vitality through clever characterizations and plot developments. Such elements are critical in a writing class. But they may be distracting and counterproductive in training if they take participants' attention away from conflict dynamics and the skills needed to mediate well.

Role plays are often lauded for the high levels of engagement they stimulate. Linking comprehension with motivation through role playing is said to yield deeper and broader learning (Jansiewicz, 2004). Yet, if colorful plots and theatrical nuances lead participants to demonstrate their improvisational flares—getting into the spirit of the activity by embellishing characters and chasing dramatic effect—we may not be as far ahead as we have hoped. With this caution in mind, we turn to the question of trainer preferences for role plays.

Trainers like role plays for a variety of reasons. Once devised, they provide a ready-made resource that can be used repeatedly in different settings. They are animating—a good change of pace from more didactic training. Role plays also contribute to positive evaluations, at least in western cultures; as participants enjoy themselves, a climate of motivation and interest infuses the learning environment (Movius, 2008).

It is true that role plays are more riveting than lectures from most faculty members or trainers. They invite and require participants to take an active part in learning. Activity by participants is certainly preferable to somnambulistic states. But there are many ways to actively engage participants. What if mediation trainers had dozens of types of experiential activities to draw upon in their work? Would changing modes communicate the importance of flexibility, creativity and intercultural sensitivity more fully than peppering training programs with variations on a singular role play format? We think it might. Even if role plays are kept in the standard toolkit of intercultural mediation trainers, varying experiential vehicles to address different elements of mediations would facilitate learning by those with diverse learning styles and ways of paying attention (Sogunro, 2004).

As mentioned earlier, there are also concerns about transferability of skills used by role players. It is widely believed that skills learned and demonstrated in role plays will be successfully applied in the "wider world." But will they? Let's take a look at the research on this question, most of which is drawn from the western cultural context of mediation exporting countries. There is evidence that role play is increasingly being used to train and assess a range of skills and behaviors such as communication, interviewing, counseling, negotiation and mediation skills (Van Hassalt, Romano and Vecchi, 2008, Movius, 2004). Moreover, there is a great deal of writing extolling the virtues of role plays in fields from political science to economics to dispute resolution (Armstrong, 1987, Sogunro, 2004). But much of this is anecdotal, or uses simple measures immediately following a role play without any subsequent structured reflection, follow up or observation in naturalistic environments.

The overall effectiveness of role plays to impart skills that are later transferred into real life settings has been questioned by a number of studies (Lewicki, 2000, Van Hassalt, Romano and Vecchi 2008, Movius 2004). A review of the literature on this subject by Dan Druckman and Noam Ebner (2008) concludes that the use of role play may heighten students' interest, motivation and positive attitudes toward a course. There is also some evidence that role plays may stimulate learning, resulting in longer retention of information than in settings where students are more passive. Apart from these aspects of learning, Druckman's and Ebner's (2008) review of relevant empirical studies indicated no significant difference in student learning based on the use of role plays compared with more conventional lecture-oriented teaching methods (Druckman and Ebner, 2008). It seems likely that the use of role play in teaching may not fulfill anecdotal expectations of enhancing learning of concepts or analytical skills, nor supporting real life skills transfer.

In light of this research, it is clear that role plays are not without challenges. Some specific difficulties associated with this mode include participants taking roles too far and exaggerating characters. Such dramatic excess is not only poor acting, it undermines the effectiveness of the experience for everyone else in that group. Role plays are artificial, and may also spawn the opposite problem: participants often do not experience much connection to roles, and may not play them authentically. They can also become boring for participants whose imaginations are not caught by contrived roles and as indicated earlier they can be offensive to certain cultures. In addition, written role plays may evoke luke-warm and even confused responses when conducted in cultural contexts with strong oral traditions.

If role plays aim to give training participants effective facsimiles of real life experiences and valuable opportunities to try strategies, this lack of connection may thwart the goal. We have seen participants on many occasions "go through the motions" of a role play, quite aware that they don't care one way or another about the outcome. As in real life, when we don't care about an outcome, there is little to stimulate our commitment or full involvement in an exchange.

What alternatives exist to role plays in mediation training?

Given these concerns, we believe role play use in diverse settings should be limited and complemented with other experiential activities. What alternatives exist? How do we make mediation learning more effective and transferable to real life situations? Many years ago when faced with this dilemma in mediation teaching, one of us was fortunate enough to encounter the world of adventure learning. Adventure learning is frequently used in leadership and teambuilding courses, yet it is relatively neglected in mediation training. But why? Like role playing, it offers participants the opportunity to participate in experiences followed by a period of reflection. But there is an important difference: the experiences offered by adventure learning are well beyond anything experienced during role plays. They are real.

Consider a group on an excursion who are given the simple task of mediating a menu for lunch. If participants do not mediate effectively, they eat poorly. Nothing is more effective than an empty stomach to generate real feelings of frustration, unfair treatment and overall grumpiness. This is great material for reflecting on one's own behavior in mediation and conflict, because the experience is upfront and personal. Guided reflection after the experience supports perspective and learning to catalyze change on cognitive, affective and kinesthetic levels.

Adventure learning activities do not have to be dangerous or exotic. They include outdoor experiences—both structured (e.g. ropes courses) and informal (hiking and other activities)—and other activities that can be done in or out of classrooms with minimal or no props. Where props are used, they can include ropes, buckets, wooden planks, old tires, newspapers, straws, balloons, plastic noodles and a limitless range of other materials.

Adventure learning need not be complex or time-consuming. These activities can fit easily into mediation training, whether in a two-hour session or a five-day course. Some activities, such as the trust circle, take between five and ten minutes to conduct and require no props. Others, such as the human knot, take up to 30 minutes, depending on participant numbers. More elaborate activities can take longer and involve fieldtrips or props. These and other possibilities are described in Priest and Rohnke (2000). While there may be no formal mediator role in these activities, participants can be asked to reflect on how they contributed to a meditative outcome, thus underlining the truism that much mediation is informal. Prospective mediators aware of informal mediation opportunities garner more practice and develop expertise sooner than those who imagine that mediation only occurs in formal settings.

The experiences of adventure learning do not come without risk. In fact, it is the element of perceived risk—frequently absent in role play—that heightens the realness of the experience (Hattie, Marsh, Neill and Richards, 1997). However, as in a David Lynch film, things in adventure settings are not always as they appear. Most participants are aware of physical risks such as slipping, falling or being dropped. While these risks are negligible in professionally prepared adventure learning environments, a cognitive focus on physical issues is useful. It raises levels of conscious alertness in the group and allows the subconscious, with its ways of knowing beyond the rational, to directly engage with deeper personal challenges. The same technique is used by the doctor who tells you to wiggle your toes and then quickly inserts a needle into your arm. The results can be surprisingly constructive and even pain free.

And what of the real life context? How will crossing an imaginary "wild river" with limited resources help you confront a tough corporate party in a mediation? That's where framing comes into play. Do the two ropes carefully placed on a grassy outdoor area (or alternatively in an indoor gymnasium) represent the boundaries of a wild river or are they a metaphor for the parameters of a complex team mediation? In one activity commonly referred to as minefield—the name of this activity may need to be changed to avoid uncomfortable or even painful associations in post-war regions—, you may literally be finding your way through a field of old car tires, balls, foam noodles and other junk, while metaphorically navigating a path through a series of mediation challenges. In another activity you are lifting your fellow participants through the holes in a larger than life size spider's web comprised of a series of intersecting ropes supported within a frame of metal poles; however at another level you are working your way through the layers of trust-building, issue identification, exploration of interests, option generation and implementation of solutions. Adventure learning activities should be conducted with sensitivity to cultural norms in relation to status and interaction between women and men, and participants from different age groups and ethnicities. In addition framing activities with sensitivity to local cultural experiences and conditions is important.

Back in Michadja, Marie and Laura have elicited from the participants a relevant and current conflict scenario. The two facilitators construct an adventure-based activity to mirror the conflict and take participants beyond the traditional educational parameters of the classroom. Outdoors, in the new environment, existing classroom power dynamics no longer apply and, a new range of skill-sets are in demand as participants negotiate their place in the "new social order." During post-activity debriefing, facilitators and participants become aware that a strong empathy has emerged across the fault lines of indigenous and non-indigenous participants.

Of course, adventure learning is just one form of experiential learning that can complement role plays. A huge range of creative possibilities loom—experiences involving drawing, miming, improvisation, movement, dance, free-writing, cooking, sound (including instruments)—all taking people out of their heads and into their bodies. These and other experiences that draw upon creative methodologies engage participants' visual and kinesthetic learning centers and their emotional histories. Using crayons to draw your own experience of conflict, and *sharing that drawing* can be a powerful experience for participants as they reveal themselves on affective and kinesthetic levels and respond to others' graphic interpretations and interventions. Story-telling activities also draw on the emotional brain.

Given the presence of art in every culture and the role of artists to disturb the status-quo, stimulate questions and offer alternative visions, it is a useful conduit for intercultural exchange. In a mediation training course, one of us took a group of international participants to a modern art museum in the United States. Through experiences of the art, they found themselves having complex and nuanced conversations about identity, cultural diversity as it relates to power and voice, and the role of history in conflict.

In another experience, participants from different cultures viewed Gerhard Richter's piece *Sanctuary*. This piece, with its multi-layered mélange of color and seamless yet distinct transitions catalyzed conversations about effecting transitions in mediation, and mediation processes as resilient spaces. Used to stimulate dialogue and reflection, art is a vehicle for penetrating both diffuse and specific aspects of mediation; it transports participants directly into the realm of somatic, emotional and spiritual inquiry.

Laura and Marie in Michadja, inspired by these examples, wanted to use art to invite discussions among participants about intercultural dimensions of mediation. Michadjan art, known for its symbolic colorful portrayals of life proved a fecund catalyst for conversations among the participants. Some of their insights included the importance of ritual in Michadjian culture as depicted in a right of passage piece; the counterpoint between simplicity and complexity contained in the art; the corresponding importance of mediating in ways that evidence both clarity and awareness of multiple layers; the significance of hidden features in the landscape which anchor old stories and highlight the importance of welcoming and making space for these stories in mediation processes.

The use of constellations, as derived from the work of Bert Hellinger (2007), offers participants a creative opportunity to develop a deep understanding of underlying issues and relationships from a systemic perspective. In constellation experiences, participants leave cognitive thinking behind as they create physical and emotional maps of conflict. Body sculpting activities also engage participants kinesthetically and emotionally, enhancing and deepening learning.

Rational analysis will only take negotiators so far, as scholarship discrediting the "rational actor" shows (Hanson and Yosifon, 2003-2004, Korobkin and Ulen, 2000). Creativity arises, in part, from changing modes of attention. Part of our task as educators has to be always extending awareness of ways of paying attention, giving negotiators flexible access to diverse resources within themselves and mediation processes. Using experiential learning in mediation training helps participants find a path where preaching meets practice and where they can be themselves, deepening awareness of their attitudes and behaviors, seeking to achieve their personal best.

Many of us can remember times in our lives when we did something so well, so excellently, so perfectly ... that it appeared effortless. Mihaly Csikszentmihalyi (2003) calls this state of being *flow*. It is a space of optimal performance and positive emotional experience that pushes our conscious envelope. Earlier we referred to the proven power of mental rehearsal to create and sustain peak performance and flow for athletes. In this context, "mental" refers to whole-brain engagement in imaginal activities. In educational settings, too, visual, auditory, affective, kinesthetic, olfactory and gustatory cues can be called upon in creating desired situations in the mind.

We have used this type of mental rehearsal technique with mediation trainees several days before they were to take part in a clinical assessment measuring their effectiveness in interviewing clients prior to mediation. Trainees were required to play themselves while demonstrating effective interviewing skills. In preparation, the students were asked to close their eyes and relax. Course leaders talked them through their preparation in groups of two, going over the interview environment, the client-centered process they were to use and how they would engage in a structured reflection with each other afterwards. Throughout the activity, the trainees were given time to use the power of their imaginations to rehearse the finer details of how they would set up the room, develop rapport with the client, work as a team and so on. While there was no control group with whom to scientifically compare performance outcomes, both trainees and course leaders considered this guided visualization to have enhanced their performance on the day.

The experiential activities described above share a number of features that differentiate them from basic role plays. These include:

- a move toward creativity and lateral thinking, and away from the primarily-cognitive workshop environment and its related assumptions about power and hierarchical relationships within the group,
- a challenge to participants to reveal themselves authentically,
- increased self-discovery through self-participation and -reflection,
- thicker contextual associations with learning that promote reproduction of effective behaviours in actual mediations;
- more meaningful learning as participants draw directly on their stories, associations, and experiences, and
- better mediation performance arising from engaging emotional and kinesthetic brain centers associated with deep shifts in skills, attitudes and behaviors.

Some readers may be thinking that it is all very well to talk about art, adventure and dance, but to use it in mediation training is a very different matter. How do trainers legitimize the use of non-mainstream learning experiences? How do we avoid making fools of ourselves? And what about participants? Are we not placing them in vulnerable situations? What if they just aren't artistic or adventurous? Even worse, what if we aren't? These are very real concerns. The next section offers some options to address them.

Moving role plays out of isolation: Advocating an integrated approach

The future of mediation training starts today. But that does not mean that we need to abandon role plays completely and start using only abstract or adventure-based exercises. It does mean that there are unlimited opportunities to begin to integrate other forms of experiential learning into mediation training. Start slowly. In your next training course, for example, you might leave out your first role play and substitute a story-telling or problem-solving activity. Notice how participants respond to the experience. Notice what they reveal about themselves, and how a range of experiential activities can foster a positive learning climate.

When you do use role plays, consider variations on your current practice. Health scientists tell us that exercise is much more effective if accompanied by stretching than if done on its own. In fact, it is even more effective if done regularly and in combination with a healthy diet and low stress, a lifestyle that features balance and meaningful activities. Similarly, emerging empirical research and anecdotal evidence suggests that role plays are most effective in increasing student learning when combined with immediate opportunities for reflection and feedback to "stretch" attention and promote synthesis (Williams, Farmer and Manwaring, 2008). Volkema (2007), for example, explains how he adds realism to his teaching by adding real financial risk to mediation role plays. Druckman and Ebner (2008) advocate engaging students in role play *design*. Their research suggests that getting students to write role plays rather than enacting them may achieve better learning outcomes with respect to (1) motivation and creativity in relation to the topic, (2) understanding negotiating concepts and (3) the relationship among these concepts, and (4) retaining information in the short and longer terms (Druckman and Ebner 2008). In this book Nelken, McAdoo and Manwaring take up in detail the idea of enlisting trainees in designing parts of a course (or even all of it) and strongly encourage this as a general teaching method.

When trainers come from abroad local participants may expect them to take a prescriptive approach and may initially feel uneasy offering input in relation to design and related issues. At the same time, the frames and approaches trainers bring may not fit well with the local context. By way of example in a conflict train the trainer program in Vanuatu trainers and participants agreed to change the frame of the training from "workshop"—a word which connoted knowledge transfer from a foreign expert to a local learner—to "storian"—a local word which centers around the ideas of story-telling, sharing and exchange. The effect of the changed frame on trainee behaviour encouraged greater confidence and participation in the design of ongoing activities and programs.

Not far away in the Solomon Islands a well-meaning team of Western trainers framed a workshop experience in terms of trainers and trainees working together towards a Solomon Islands model of mediation. Their intention was to create a culturally inclusive and collaborate learning experience. At the end of the five-day training program, a delegation of participants quietly approached the trainers to ask if they could delete the reference to the Solomon Islands in the title of the program. The surprised response from the trainers prompted a detailed explanation that participant identity was linked closely to their family, their tribe, and their customary traditional region. There relationship to the imposed post-colonial borders of a place called the Solomon Islands was ambivalent at best. As a result participation in designing a Solomon Islands model was lacking but interest in the design of programs to enhance contemporary local mediation skills and models was very high.

Maiese (2004) takes role play design beyond written form and encourages participants to utilize multiple modes of design including drama, mime, dance, drawing and dialogue. Such approaches may encourage a higher level of participation and understanding in cultures with strong ritual practices around these creative activities. In addition, combining role plays with observation learning—such as a video demonstration—has been shown to more successfully foster skills than the use of role plays alone (Nadler, Thompson and Van Boven, 2003).

All of these suggestions require heightened attention, focus and mindfulness on the part of the facilitator or trainer. Authenticity—the ability to be yourself—is vital for facilitators moving into previously unknown experiences. If you think an activity is insubstantial, then others will sense your attitude and follow suit. Transparency and signposting your way through activities and other aspects of the training will give participants the opportunity to have input and ask questions, thereby making your journey into new experiences a joint one rather than a solitary venture.

Curiosity is more helpful than certainty in both training and actual mediations. A spirit of enquiry and a healthy sense of humor will infuse participants with the same and encourage exploration rather than evaluation. The willingness to ask colleagues and others for help is empowering. Take small steps: knowing your own boundaries and having a sense of others is part of effective pedagogy.

Another important way to successful outcomes with a range of experiential activities—especially unusual ones—is to attend to how you frame them. Use words that are legitimate for your audience. For example, lawyers may not have positive associations with "playing a game", but may be quite willing to "engage in a learning activity or task." Village chiefs may respond well to an invitation to rehearse dealing with a simulated common conflict situation in their region but not specifically associated with their own village; nurses' curiosity might be piqued by being invited to explore a case. Staking activities on the truism that identities are not constant and consistent is another important element of framing. As Shapiro reminds us, identities shift across time and context (2006). Given the dynamism of mediation processes and identities, experiential learning can be usefully framed as a way to explore changing identities—participants' and counterparts'.

Interdisciplinary discourses including neuroscience and arts-based learning also smooth the way into unusual experiential activities. Participants may be asked to suspend judgment as they enter terrain that may be unfamiliar, given that the activity derives from neuro-scientific research and new insights into multiple intelligences. References may be made to the vast body of arts-based work that has been successfully applied in a wide range of social contexts (Goldbard, 2006). Given that mediation often involves achieving mutually acceptable outcomes across cultural and worldview differences, the utility of arts to engage mediators across differences and productively stimulate imagination and intuition can be emphasized (LeBaron and Honeyman, 2006). As educators push themselves to be inventive and try new strategies to foster learning, everyone benefits.

Dialogue and collaboration with community artists and others working in creative media can also be helpful in expanding training repertoires. Invite a mime artist to lead experiences related to non-verbal communication. Ask a visual artist to talk about what she learned about intercultural mediation from a collective mural project. This kind of engagement can generate useful and "out of the box" ideas, as a group of colleagues found when we staged an evening dialogue between community artists and conflict resolution practitioners (LeBaron and Honeyman, 2006).

Attard (2008) suggests that trainers and facilitators engage in their own reflective practice by keeping a journal themselves. His research indicates that self-reflection captured in journal narratives can help reveal the layers of complexity involved in teaching. He also normalizes the uncertainty that is often experienced when moving into new experiences, by arguing that uncertainty may be a constant companion for those engaged in life-long learning and development of their craft. Therefore, the advice for those feeling a little anxious about stepping into unknown teaching and learning experiences is (1) to be reassured by the certainty that we are all feeling uncertain and (2) to engage in some form of structured self-reflection as a basis for self-development.

Recommendations for how to approach role plays

Despite the dramatic implications of the title of section, we have good news: reports of the death of the role play have been exaggerated. Role plays will survive for a long time; they are so inculcated into the dominant culture of mediation training that even empirical studies impugning their value may take time to dislodge them. However, as a training method, role plays require some serious resuscitating and invigorating. We offer the following suggestions about ways to improve design and implementation of, and follow up with, role plays in mediation training courses:

1. Use elicitive ways to learn about the contours and language of conflict in local settings, and the role and identity preferences related to mediators.

2. Encourage improvisation in role playing rather than literal adherence to a script, so that participants draw on their own experience and behave as they would themselves, given the context. This will enhance the realism of the experience.
3. Precede role play activities with work on cultural fluency so that participants are attuned to the dangers of stereotyping.
4. Assign participants roles that do not involve playing ethno-cultural identities different from their own. Explore this aspect of cultural difference using alternative experiential activities.
5. Give participants the opportunity to create role plays for other participants to play, and then reverse the roles.
6. Design role plays that are as close to real life as possible, drawing on composites of actual scenarios or real issues so that the simulation has an air of authenticity. Consider using real situations that are close, but not identical, to contexts and situations experienced by participants in the wider world. Help participants avoid being swallowed up by emotional triggers related to these contexts by teaching them skills for managing such triggers.
7. Add reality to role plays, putting tangible resources—such as little gifts or sweets—at stake.
8. Design role plays that resist the temptation to dramatic excess—while the plot may sparkle, its utility may be diminished.
9. Design role plays with specific learning objectives, such as particular skills. All role plays are not equal, and they have different functions. Identify these during the design phase, and be prepared to articulate the objectives to participants in advance of using the role play.
10. Spend time preparing participants to role play. Model ways of overplaying and underplaying roles.
11. Allow participants to choose roles that have resonance for them.
12. Balance a spirit of play with an air of seriousness about the role play activity. Emphasize the particular learning objectives related to the role play in advance of its unfolding.
13. Provide coaching in situ for role players if appropriate (Van Hassalt, Romano and Vecchi, 2008).
14. Create space for structured and unstructured reflection.
15. Provide participants with meaningful, specific, constructive and culturally sensitive feedback.
16. Follow up with exploration of applications, and design follow-up learning activities to assist with integrating those concepts, skills and capacities that are difficult to implement.

17. Consider using demonstration role plays or fishbowl formats where trainers or actors depict roles that participants can analyze and respond to.

Implications for cross-cultural mediation trainers: Revisiting Moses and Laura's "Marriage"

We opened this reflective journey with the true story of Moses and Laura. Participants from Moses' indigenous community were upset by Moses' assumption of an intimate role with someone other than his wife. In many intercultural mediation training sessions given by Westerners to people outside the West, role plays are fraught with pitfalls and possible problems. Besides the potential that some people may not value—or even understand the purpose of—impersonating others, some groups have such a strong ethic of non-interference that role playing seems an unconscionable interference. It can seem contrived, disrespectful, inappropriately confronting, and not cognizant of status and hierarchies in a given context. For all of these reasons, we argue that role plays should be used with caution, and supplemented with a wide range of experiential activities. This approach—implemented with cultural fluency and sensitivity—is more likely to yield effective intercultural collaborations when Western trainers work in non-Western settings.

References

ARMSTRONG, J.S. (1987) Forecasting methods for conflict situations. IN WRIGHT, G., PAYTON (Eds.) *Judgemental Forecasting*. Chichester, UK: Wiley.

ATTARD, K. (2008). Uncertainty for the reflective practitioner: a blessing in disguise. *Reflective Practice,* 9(3), 307-317.

CSIKSZENTMIHALY, M. (2003) *Good Business: Flow, Leadership and the Making of Meaning*, New York, Viking.

DELLA NOCE, D. (2002) Mediation Theory and Policy: The Legacy of the Pound Conference. *Journal on Dispute Resolution,* 545.

DRUCKMAN, D. and EBNER N. (2008) On stage or behind the scenes? Relative learning benefits of simulation role play and design. *Simulation and Gaming* 39(4), 465-497.

GOLDBARD, A. (2006) New Creative Community: The Art of Cultural Development, Oakland, CA, New Village Press.

HANSON, J.D. and YOSIFON, D. (2003-2004) The situation: An introduction to the situational character, critical realism, power economics, and deep capture. *University of Pennsylvania Law Review,* 152, 129.

HATTIE, J., MARSH, H.W., NEILL, J.T. and RICHARDS, G.E. (1997) Adventure education and outward bound: Out-of-class experiences that make a lasting difference. *Review of Educational Research,* 67(1), 43-87.

HELLINGER, B. (2007) *Das klassische Familienstellen. Die fünf Standardwerke: Die Quelle braucht nicht nach dem Weg zu fragen: Ein Nachlesebuch*, Heidelberg, Germany, Carl-Auer Verlag.

JANSIEWICZ, D. (2004) E=MC2: Teaching with simulations". *Paper presented at the annual meeting of the APSA Teaching and Learning Conference, NA, Washington, DC,* Feb 19, 2004.

KOROBKIN, R.B. and ULEN, T.S. (2000) Law and Behavioral Science: Removing the Rationality Assumption form Law and Economics. *California Law Review* 88(4), 1053-1147.

LEBARON, M. and HONEYMAN, C. (2006) Using the creative arts. IN SCHNEIDER, A.K., HONEYMAN, C. (Eds.) *The Negotiator's Fieldbook: The Desk Reference for the Experienced Negotiator,* Washington D.C, American Bar Association.

LEWICKI, R.J. (2000). Teaching negotiation and dispute resolution in colleges of business: The state of the practice and challenges for the future. IN WHEELER, M. (Ed.) *Teaching Negotiation: Ideas and Innovations,* Cambridge MA, PON Books.

MAIESE, M. (2004) Elicitive Training. *Beyond Intractability,* www.beyondintractability.org, date accessed: January 30, 2009.

MOVIUS, H., (2008) The effectiveness of negotiation training. *Negotiation Journal,* 24(4), 509-531.

NADLER, J., THOMPSON, L. and VAN BOVEN, L. (2003) Learning negotiation skills: Four models of knowledge creation and transfer. *Management Science,* 49(4), 529-540.

PRIEST, S., and ROHNKE, K. (2000) *101 Of The Best Corporate Team-building Activities We Know,* Dubuque, Iowa, Kendall/Hunt Publishing

ROMANO, G. and VECCHI, M. (2008) Role playing: Applications in hostage and crisis negotiation skills training. *Behavior Modification,* 32(2), 248-263.

ROURE, R. COLLET, C., DESCHAUMES-MOLINARO, C., DITTMAR, A., RADA, H., DELHOMME, G. and VERNET-MAURY, E. (1998) Autonomic nervous system responses correlate with mental rehearsal in volleyball training. *Journal of Applied Physiology,* 78(2), 99-108.

SHAPIRO, D.L. (2006) Identity: More than meets the 'I'. IN SCHNEIDER, A.K., HONEYMAN, C. (Eds.) *The Negotiator's Fieldbook: The Desk Reference for the Experienced Negotiator,* Washington D.C, American Bar Association.

SOGUNRO, O. A. (2004) Efficacy of role-playing pedagogy in training leaders: some reflections. *Journal of Management Development,* 23(4): 355-371.

VAN HASSELT, V.B., ROMANO, S.J., VECCHI, G.M. (2008) Role playing: Applications in hostage and crisis negotiation skills training. *Behavior Modification,* 32 (2), 248-263.

VOLKEMA, R.J. (2007) Negotiating for money: Adding a dose of reality to classroom negotiations. *Negotiation Journal,* 23(4), 473-485.

WIKIPEDIA (2008) *Simulation.* http://www.en.wikipedia.org/wiki/Simulation, Date accessed: January 30, 2009.

WILLIAMS, G.R., FARMER, L.C. and MANWARING, M. (2008) New technology meets an old teaching challenge: Using digital video recordings, annotation software, and deliberate practice techniques to improve student negotiation skills. *Negotiation Journal,* 24(1), 1-87.

Cross-Cultural Business Mediation. The Model of Identity-based Managerial Mediation in International Management

Claude-Hélène Mayer

Introduction

Changing global trends and migration flows in international co-operations as well as joint ventures have changed the way business is conducted and organisations are managed. With globalisation causing organisations to grow in complexity and resulting in managers having to co-operate internationally, the experience of 'cultural transition situations' (Boness, 2002, Dadder, 1987) and cross-cultural business interactions is increasing (Trompenaars and Hampden-Turner, 1997). These diverse cross-cultural impacts influence managers in their daily work routine and, at the same time, impact on their managerial and individual identity constructions (Mayer, 2008b). The (re-)construction of identities in managers with diverse backgrounds can lead to identity-based conflict, thereby evoking strong intra- and interpersonal distress, distraction from work, reduction of effectiveness, productivity and creativity, as well as difficulties in decision-making and interpersonal contact in organizations (Cowan, 1995: 24). Conflicts in the workplace impact on the health and well-being of the parties involved (Friedman et al., 2000, Zapf, 1999) and have been described as stressors (Selye, 1957, Vester, 1997, Zimbardo, 1995) that may lead to an increase in health problems (El-Sheikh and Harger, 2001, Kiecolt-Glaser et al., 1993; Kiecolt-Glaser et al., 1997; Michie and Williams, 2003).

These potential negative impacts caused by managerial conflicts on organisations need to be transformed into constructive impacts to promote international business and co-operation (Mayer, 2008). Thereby, the concept of identity that responds to the question 'Who am I?' (Lutgen-Sandvik, 2008: 98) plays a major role in constructing and managing conflicts in an organizational setting. Identity work (Alvesson and Willmott, 2002, Beech, 2008, Watson, 2008) in cross-cultural conflicts and conflict management settings can contribute positively to conflict management processes and mediation across cultures.

Mediation means assistance to and intervention with two or more interacting parties (Kressel and Pruitt, 1989) and is one of the oldest and globally most-used forms of conflict resolution (Wall et al., 2001). Internationally, mediation as a tool for conflict management is used in various fields, such as in international relations

(Bercovitch, 1996), labour-management negotiations (Mumpower and Rohrbaugh, 1996), community disputes, legal disputes and school conflicts (Mayer and Boness, 2004). Mediation is often conducted in settings comprising cross-cultural influences and is then usually described as cross-cultural, cross-cultural or cross-cultural mediation (Mayer and Boness, 2004).

The purpose of this article is to contribute to the theoretical discourse on mediation across cultures and to present the model of Identity-based Managerial Mediation (IMM) by embedding it into selected theoretical discourses on identity and conflict in managerial and organizational settings. More specifically, the aim of this paper is to introduce the new Identity-based Managerial Mediation (IMM) model embedded in relevant theoretical approaches. Furthermore, the impact of IMM on managerial identity work, particularly in cross-cultural business organisations, will be introduced. This theoretical discourse imparts new perspectives on identity-based conflict management in the cross-cultural managerial field, specifically regarding the IMM model as a new tool for cross-cultural business mediation and identity-based conflict management. It provides new stimuli for the scientific debate on identity-based conflict management in organisations, in addition to being of practical importance to organisational conflict managers, business consultants and trainers. It is, therefore, argued that the IMM model may serve as a basic tool for cross-cultural conflict management in organizations, thereby managing identity-based conflicts in cross-cultural management settings (Lederach 1996, Miall, 2004, Reimann, 2004).

Relevant background theories on managing cross-cultural identities and conflicts in business-related organisations are integrated within the model description. Recent literature on mediation across cultures will be introduced and the IMM model will be profiled with regard to the transformation of conflictual cultural aspects and identities. Finally, a conclusion will be drawn and recommendations will be provided.

Managerial mediation across cultures

Conflict research is currently often embedded in constructivist theories which view conflicts as a reality construct created by mutual inter-relationships between the individual and the environment (Aggestan, 1999; Applefield, Huber, and Moallem, 2000; Demmers, 2006; Lederach, 2000; Wallensteen and Sollenberg, 1995).

A wide range of research on conflict and its management has been developed worldwide (Coleman, 2003, Miall, 2004, Miall et al., 2000, Schmidt and Trittmann, 2002), specifically regarding the organizational and management field (Francis, 2003, Kumar and van Dissel, 1996, Lipsky et al., 2004, Pondy, 1967,

Putnam and Poole, 1987, Rahim, 2001, 2002, Wall and Callister 1995, Zapf, 1999).

Organisational conflict and its pervasive nature can be observed in any organisation (Schermerhorn et al., 1997) as organisations are inherently competitive and "riddled by conflict" (Pondy, 1992: 257). It occurs easily in an organisation as a result of changing identity concepts and increasing cross-cultural complexities, strengthening autonomy, self-management, individual responsibilities, as well as the replacement of traditional and collective values and identity aspects (Mayer, 2008a).

Conflict is a concept that "encompasses a wide range of interaction sequences: a social conflict arises when two or more persons or groups manifest the belief that they have incompatible objectives" (Kriesberg, 2003: 2). Conflict can, therefore, be defined as "a feeling, a disagreement, a real or perceived incompatibility of interests, inconsistent worldviews, or a set of behaviours" (Mayer, 2000: 3) and is a "conflict is a psycho-social process" (Northrup, 1989: 54) which includes social interactions and individual perceptions and is shaped by individual and cultural meanings (Augsburger, 1992, Avruch, 1998, Lederach, 2000). These meanings are constructed by "perceptions, interpretations, expressions and intentions" (Lederach, 1996: 9) and can lead to conflict. Thus, "conflict situations are those unique episodes when we explicitly recognize the existence of multiple realities and negotiate the creation of a common meaning" (Lederach, 1988: 39). This means that, in conflict situations, people experience the relativity of realities and identity aspects while simultaneously negotiating and creating their shared meaning.

Conflict management is the art of appropriate intervention to achieve settlements and designing appropriate institutions to guide inevitable conflict into appropriate channels (Nye, 2005). It is "the positive and constructive handling of difference and divergence. Rather than advocating methods for removing conflict, [it] addresses the more realistic question of managing conflict: how to deal with it in a constructive way, how to bring opposing sides together in a cooperative process, how to design a practical, achievable, cooperative system for the constructive management of difference" (Bloomfield and Reilly, 1998: 18). It does not necessary imply the avoidance, reduction or termination of conflict. Moreover, it assists in designing effective strategies to "minimize the dysfunctions of conflict and enhancing the constructive functions of conflict in order to enhance learning and effectiveness in an organization." (Rahim, 2002: 208).

Conflict management involves the diagnosis and analysis of organisational conflict, as well as effective intervention techniques and methods, and evokes new solutions for conflict management in organisations (Wils et al., 2006: 9) and is still often viewed as a challenge for organisations (Bradshaw, 2006: 20). Well-established concepts in the scientific debate on conflict management in organisations (Bradshaw, 2006, Rahim 2001, 2002) include negotiation (Castro and Nielsen, 2001, Crump and Zartmann, 2003, Montoya-Weiss et al., 2001, Ury, 2000), facilitation (Hill, 2005, Wayne et al., 2007) and mediation (Augsburger, 1992, Busch, 2005, 2006, Mayer, 2005, 2008a, Mayer and Boness, 2004).

Mediation has become a popular tool of conflict management in organizational management settings (Dana, 2001, Galade and Ivery, 2003, Lauzen and Dozier, 1994, Maedche et al., 2003, Simons et al., 1999). According to literature, conflict mediation often seems to be used in the public (Bingham, 2004) and health sectors (Sarangi and Roberts, 1999), but less in the managerial business arena. However, mediation is often closely connected to concepts of workplace justice in the organizational field (van Gamberg and Teicher, 2006).

Many authors have attempted to define mediation with regard to cultural aspects and different terms are, therefore, used: Myers and Filner (1994, 1997) and Augsburger (1992) use the term "mediation across cultures"; Shah-Kazemi (2000) views it as "cross-cultural mediation", Cohen (1996) addresses "international mediation" and "cross-cultural aspects"; several authors (Cole, 1995, Jones, 2002) refer to "culture mediation"; Busch (2005, 2006), Liebe and Gilbert (1996), Haumersen and Liebe (1999), as well as Mayer and Boness (2004, 2005), define it as "intercultural mediation"; whilst Mayer (2008a) terms it "trans-cultural mediation". In this article, it is referred to as "cross-cultural mediation", due to its intention and implication to bridge and transcend cultural differences across cultures.

With regard to environmental influences, culture seems to be one of the strongest and most varied factors impacting on mediation. The best-documented effects of culture are those referring to Eastern versus Western influences (Gire and Carment, 1993). Eastern mediation, in contrast to Western mediation (Abu-Nimer, 1996), relies heavily on harmony techniques (Baine and Swatzky, 1991). Differences in mediation styles occur, for example, when employing psychological and professional skills on the one hand, or methodological and technical approaches on the other hand. These methodological and technical approaches impact on the decision to use non-violent communication techniques, systemic approaches or specific question techniques or, alternatively, content- or process-based approaches in mediation (Glasl, 2003, Kessen, 2003, Kessen and Troja, 2002, Riskin, 2003). According to Shah-Kazemi (2000: 318), there is a need for "guiding principles" in cross-cultural mediation to share the notion cross-cultural perspectives in conflict management.

Two basic concepts of mediation are often applied in Western mediation settings:

The “Harvard concept”, commonly used in management contexts (Fisher and Ury, 1991), is a mediative approach which focuses on negotiation techniques and win-win-solutions and which is solution-oriented and ration-biased. The Harvard style of mediation is used in business-related fields of management due to its approach being based on negotiation techniques and focusing on win-win-solutions. These two aspects fit well into Western-based organizational and management systems.

“Transformative mediation”, on the other hand (Bush and Folger, 1994, Dukes, 1996, Schwerin, 1995), leans on psychology and therapeutical approaches and is in Western contexts often used in, for example, family mediation. In this article, the focus lies on the concept of transformative mediation aspects in Western organizational contexts. This process is defined as a mediation process that particularly considers psycho-social learning and identity-work and which aims to change conflictual and destructive behaviour through relationship-building (Gabel, 2003) and identity-based processes (Mayer, 2008a). Empowerment and recognition of managerial needs are seen as key factors in conflict management, as well as trust-building and mutual understanding of the other’s reality constructs. Transformative mediation allows practitioners to more intentionally and consistently tap into the intrinsic transformative and healing potential of mediation due to its “dialogue-driven” humanistic approach and its nondirective style of mediation which is grounded in compassion, strength and humanity (Umbreit, 1997).

Ways of defining mediation across cultures

Generally, there are three common ways of defining cross-cultural mediation in recent literature (Mayer, 2006). These ways can be described as follows:

Firstly, a Western mediation model may be applied to the mediation process, even though the western model has been criticised due to its advantaging western cultural groups over others (Beattie, 1997) with regard to power imbalances and mediation methodologies. The conflicting parties bear different cultural backgrounds, culture-specific value-orientations, communication styles and perceptions. Culture-specific differences are often highlighted—not the similarities which may be even more important—and attempted to be understood by the involved parties. In this mediative approach, the cross-cultural aspect of mediation is introduced by means of highlighting cultural values and identities, whilst the individuals involved are often reduced to their national, regional or ethnic affiliations. Simultaneously, culture might be used in strategic ways and culturalisation processes happen.

Secondly, cross-cultural mediation can take place by using non-western, e.g. a Chinese mediation model in the business mediation between a French and Chinese manager in Latin-America. The Chinese mediation approach, in this instance, has been chosen with regard for the cultural background of one of the conflict parties and, probably, the mediator who should be experienced in using this specific mediation model. In this model of cross-cultural mediation, however, both conflict partners and the model of mediation is reduced to cultural, ethnic or national identity aspects and mediation styles.

Both the first and second approaches stereotype cultural, ethnic or national belonging and easily reduce the identity of a person to the cultural identity only. In addition, these mediation models only apply in certain organizational settings and do not work in organizational settings which are influenced by various cultural aspects.

The third approach, namely that of the "Culture-Synergetic Model of Cross-cultural Mediation" (CSTM), was first introduced by Mayer (2005). This variant of cross-cultural mediation is influenced by different aspects of organizational and cultural contexts. Here, aspects of culture-specific mediation practices are drawn together to adjust the process of cross-cultural mediation in the organizational setting according to culture-specific needs (Mayer, 2006) of the managers and the organization. Empowerment and recognition, trust and understanding are key concepts in this approach which tries to build cross-cultural bridges. The development of the managerial identity through identity work is, thus, defined as one of the core competencies for the development of managerial cross-cultural competencies. Cross-cultural mediation in CSTM becomes a process of individual and cultural synthesis (Mayer, 2006) based on the development of managerial identities. The Identity-based Managerial Mediation (IMM) model, as depicted in Figure 1, becomes a key concept of CSTM as it provides building blocks of cross-cultural conflict management in a managerial organizational setting.

Identity and managing conflicts

Multiple factors impact on conflict and its management and identity is one of the major factors (Burton, 1990a, 1990b, Buttner, 2001, Lederach, 2000, Reimann, 2004). Burton (1990a) highlights the influence of the individual on conflict and pays special attention to unfulfilled needs and their influences on conflict processes. Discovering the "real person" (Burton, 1990: 147), as well as the values and identity aspects, is extremely important. To address (cross-cultural) conflicts adequately, aspects of values, needs, identities and their inter-relationships need to be analysed and addressed (Burton, 1988: 71); the "transformation of relationships" (Burton, 1990a: 2) needs to be induced; and major organisational restructuring processes need to be implemented.

Cultural and social values that are embedded in cultures impact on the mediation process in business organizations; on the way mediation is conducted; and on the values and norms guiding the individuals involved (Wall et al., 2001: 271). Therefore, the influences of cultural values and norms, the meanings behind these concepts, the emotions involved and the implications thereof for behaviour increase the complexity in cross-cultural mediation. The complexity in cross-cultural mediations is increasing, particularly with regard to the discussion of culture-specific value and identity concepts.

Neutrality is of high importance in conflict management processes referring to "power imbalances and the creation of symmetry" (Cooks and Hale, 1994: 64) within or between organizations (Carnevale and Pruitt, 1992) in Western contexts. Mediation and its techniques form part of cross-cultural conflict management strategies in organizational contexts (Bagshaw, 1998, Harvey and Evans, 1994, Leung et al., 2002).

The long-term aim of transforming and managing conflicts as validating and building on human beings and their resources on different levels (Lederach, 2000: 52) include the:

1. personal level (emotional, perceptual and spiritual aspects of conflict);
2. relational level (expressive, communicative and interactive aspects of conflict);
3. structural level (human needs, access to resources, and institutional decision-making patterns); and
4. cultural level (the way culture affects the development and handling of conflict).

Referring to the personal level, conflict and its management are bound not only to external, but also to internal realities (Gaziano, Jensen-Campbell, and Hair, 1996): How a person manages conflict is related to inner values, feelings, resources and prioritising identity aspects. Constructively managed conflict simultaneously (re-)contributes positively to job satisfaction, well-being and stress reduction (De Dreu et al., 2004: 15; Friedman et al., 2000: 32).

Identity concepts have been redefined (Sökefeld, 2001) as embracing possibilities of emergence, plurality, discontinuity, polyphony and the social embeddings of identity processes (Simpson and Carroll, 2008: 31). Management scientists (Beech, 2008, Sennett, 1998, Sveningsson and Alvesson, 2003, Watson, 1994, 2008) promote the idea of identity construction as an inter-related process of internal and external realities that is based on post-modern constructivist theories (e.g. Kriesberg, 2003a) which often define identity on the notion of "Pluralisierung des Selbst" (pluralisation of the self) and, consequently, on the assumption of a so-called "healthy" form of multiple identity (Keupp, 1988, 1994, 1997, Kraus, 1996) that is described by Keupp (1988) as a "Patchwork Identität" (patchwork identity). Identity becomes, besides its multiplicity, an "interactional accomplishment"

(Cerulo, 1997: 387) and a (re-) construction of discursive practice (Musson and Duberley, 2006), particularly in constructivist approaches (Ainsworth and Hardy, 2004; Humphreys and Brown, 2002).

The multiple identity turns into an adequate counterpart to present organizational ambiguity. Its contribution is to reflect a shared organisational identity as an "attracting resource" (Brown, 2001) essential to organisational success (Collins and Porrass, 1996) and one which might enhance "proactivity" (Gioia and Thomas, 1996: 396). Identity is a major tool in managing critical incidents and conflicts in organizations (Oliver and Roos, 2003) and serves as a major force to activate, prioritise and deploy core capabilities and resources in the organization (Glynn, 2000: 295).

Multiple identities include various interests, roles, attitudes and value orientations which the individual has to integrate and which assume varying degrees of importance, depending on the situation and the context (Layes, 2003). This assumption of multi-layered (organizational) identity constructs has gained weight in management studies during the past years (Albert et al., 2000, Ashforth and Mael, 1989, Pratt and Rafaeli, 1997) and identity has become a well-explored and prominent domain (Albert and Whetten, 1985, Gioia et al., 2002; Hatch and Schulz, 2002, Rothman, 1997, Special, 2000, Whetten and Godfrey, 1998), but not yet with regard to managerial management contexts and health (Michie and Williams, 2003, Lutgen-Sandvik, 2008).

Identity work and conflict management

Identity work can support constructive processes in future organizational development and conflict management. The term "identity work" has been used in "an informal manner, unattributed and without formal definition" (Watson, 2008: 127). According to Pullen (2006: 25), identity work is "complex and unpredictable". Alvesson and Willmott (2004), however, assert that identity work includes "the interpretative activity involved in reproducing and transforming self-identity". It simultaneously induces and reworks self-identity and prompts and informs self-regulation. Sveningsson and Alvesson (2003: 1165) define identity work as being "engaged in forming, repairing, maintaining, strengthening or revising the constructions that are productive of a sense of coherence and distinctiveness". This means that a set of active processes serve to construct a sense of identity. Here, identity work is socially and discursively determined, even though the focus is on the individual and intra-personal processes. Sveningsson and Alvesson (2003: 1165) point out that individuals "strive to shape their personal identities in organizations and are being shaped by discursive forces". Watson (2008: 128) emphasises that identity work needs the internal process on the one hand, but would gain more power, on the other hand, if the concept of external identity aspects was incorporated "alongside with shaping of the 'internal' aspects of personal identity". Satir, Banmen and Gerber (2007) emphasise "parts party", a special kind of identity work which refers to the confrontation and integration of internal and external identity aspects.

Various authors (Coupland, 2001, Fineman, 1997, Thomas and Linstead, 2002) have illustrated how interactions impact on managerial identities. According to Beech (2008: 52), identity work comprises how individuals categorize themselves; how they are categorized by others; and how "images and representations (physical, symbolic, verbal, textual and behavioural) become imbued with meaning and are taken as being part of one's identity". Identity is, therefore, also a melange of different identity projects (Beech and Huxham, 2003). According to Alvesson and Willmott (2002), two aspects impact on self-identity; namely the identity regulation which is the discursive practice of identity definition, as well as identity work which is viewed as the interpretative activities involved in reproducing self-identity.

In fairly stable conditions identity work is reasonably automatic and instinctual (Giddens, 1991); it is "effortless" and "unselfconscious" at the same time (Alvesson and Willmott, 2002: 626). For the purposes of this paper it is assumed that the self-identity of managers is multi-faceted and that identity reproduction and identity work happen through self-reflection, narration, the experience of difference and sameness and the inner construction of social and cultural belonging. Identity work occurs automatically in conflictual situations when managers clarify their interests, roles, feelings and needs and reflect their own position in the conflict, whilst at the same time redefining aspects of the self. This process can happen either consciously or unconsciously, depending on the degree of self-reflection.

Identity-based Managerial Mediation (IMM) in management

The Identity-based Managerial Mediation (IMM) model stands in the epistemological tradition of constructivism (Berger and Luckmann, 2000) and is embedded in post-modern, systemic approaches that define reality as a construct of individuals and their social interactions (Watzlawick, 1998).

IMM is an identity-based conflict management tool that includes aspects of conflict transformation and "transformative mediation" (Bush and Folger, 1994), person-centred theories (Rogers, 1998), systemic approaches (Satir, 2004) and non-violent communication (Rosenberg, 2001). At the same time, IMM is a process of psycho-organisational experiences and socio-managerial learning that supports the change of managerial attitudes, behaviours, and stereotypic interpretations. IMM is part of CSTM, as explained above, specifically with regard to the managerial contexts in cross-cultural and organizational mediation processes.

The core aspect in IMM is to manage conflicts across managerial levels by using an identity-based approach which particularly considers managerial identity aspects. In the following, the various important aspects and their interrelationship in IMM will be explained in detail.

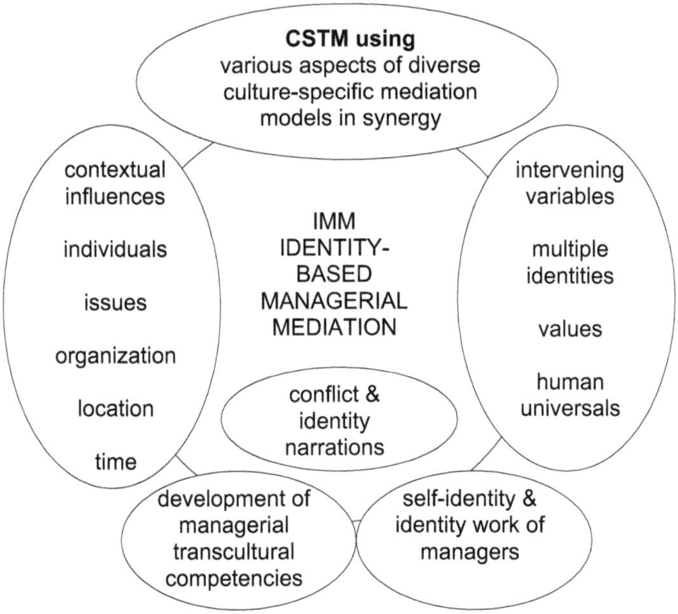

Figure 1: The Identity-based Managerial Mediation (IMM) model. Source: author's own construction.

Conflict and identity narrations

The base of IMM lies in the conflict- and identity narrations of the conflict partners. By narrating the conflict experiences and the perceptions, the conflict parties include narrations on their values and identities which are highly important in IMM across cultural lines. Whilst narrating conflicts and identities during the mediation process, conflict parties are encouraged to both develop and improve their managerial intercultural competencies and their self-identity through identity work.

The conflict and identity narrations are highly interrelated with the development of managerial cross-cultural competencies and the aspects of self-identity and identity work in managers. They are also connected to the contextual influences in the mediation process as well as with the intervening variables. Finally, the build the base for the decision of the mediator and the conflict parties with regard to the culture-specific mediation model that is used in the process of mediation.

Development of managerial cross-cultural competencies

Cross-cultural managerial competencies are important in the IMM model. Recent literature on cross-cultural competence and conflict mediation (Bolten, 2003, Mayer, 2006, Mayer and Boness, 2004, Müller and Gelbrich, 2001, Ting-Toomey and Kurogi, 1998, Xin et al., 2001) clearly indicates that these two topics have gained major importance in the social and managerial sciences during the past decade.

Cross-cultural competence includes empathy, tolerance, culture-specific knowledge and emotional intelligence (Müller and Gelbrich, 2001) and is, therefore, particularly bound to aspects of identity and identity work. Bolten (2003) highlights strategic, individual, social and language competencies as being important parts of cross-cultural competence. These aspects of cross-cultural competence should be developed with regard to self-identity in managers throughout the cross-cultural mediation process.

Self-identity and identity work

Self-identity and identity-work provide one of the key aspects to manage cross-cultural conflicts in managerial contexts. Managerial inter-cultural competencies are developed throughout the identity-based mediation process by exchanging culture-specific, value-related and identity-based information with regard to attitudes, behaviour and emotions of the conflict parties. These cultural and identity-based developments take place through narrating and reflecting on conflicts and self-identity with the support of a mediator who mediates between external and internal conflict issues, values and identities.

In IMM, the notion of identity is based on the concept of pluralization of self (Keupp, 1994, Kraus, 1996) and the concept of "patchwork identity" (Keupp, 1988, Keupp et al., 2002) which is constructed through a process of interactive storytelling that at the same time defines in-group and out-group members (Sims, 2005a). With regard to this narrative-based definition, identity work is a combination of telling stories of the self, of others and of the self in the stories of others. The process of identity work can become dominating and dysfunctional in managerial and organizational contexts (Sims, 2005b). The post-modern identity concepts are seen as an adequate counterpart to the currently existing managerial and organizational ambiguity. In this notion, the self is seen as a dynamic multiplicity of positions and aspects formed through dialogical relationships which occur simultaneously (Hermans, 2001). These dialogical relationships are in resonance with narrations of self and others which usually occur in managerial mediation sessions.

"Managing the inside of managers" and the "meaning given tensions" are the spectra along which people can place themselves, and be placed by others (Beech, 2008:68). IMM can, therefore, have an effect on "managing the inside" of a managerial identity, on the one hand, and creating meaning through inter-personal relationships and communication, on the other hand. Beech (2008: 55) points out there are "various types of stimuli which could initiate dialogue" and, therefore, identity work; IMM is thus seen as a model that stimulates identity work through listening to, (re-)narrating and eventually (re-)defining conflicts and conflictual narrations and, therefore, parts of identities. Through the third-party-setting, narrations on managerial conflicts provide the initiating stimulus for identity work and the (re-)creation of meaning. Conflict narrations allow the creation of the meaning to the self and the other, either through agreement (Bakhtin, 1981) or disagreement (Wittgenstein, 1958) which are inter-related with the values as intervening variables in IMM. Thus, the work with negations of self-concept, self-esteem and individual resources (Keupp, 2001) are an important part of IMM. Other aspects of identity work include self-awareness and the conscious (re-)construction of multiple identity aspects (Mayer, 2007), such as managerial, cultural or position-bound aspects. Identity aspects are shaped and priorities and orientations are newly defined through conflict experiences and a conscious attempt to manage these. Priorities of different identity aspects might change throughout the identity-work process and aspects of culturalisation, stereotyping or prejudices might change due to gaining deeper understanding of meanings behind conflicts in IMM. IMM aims at discussing and reflecting identity aspects by:

5. activating individual resources (releasing energies, relaxation and recovering strategies, self concept, self esteem);
6. reflecting social aspects (individual and organisational belonging, social managerial status, prestige, class);
7. becoming aware of cultural aspects and resources (cultural value orientations and priorities, leadership styles, power concepts, rhetoric, languages, cultural mental schemes); and

8. discovering universal aspects and resources (needs, concepts of humanity).

Working with identity parts implies the discussion of these four aspects which affect "organisational practices and success" (Kanungo, 2006). Identity work in third-party-conflict management provides managers new stimuli on how to manage conflicts effectively across cultural lines, as well as how to use these processes to develop managerial identities. This further allows for the development of competencies which impact on future conflicts, and the management thereof, in organizational managerial settings.

The IMM model aims at intensifying identity work in conflict management processes through both listening to, and re-narrating narratives of self and others in conflictual situations, as well as implementing conscious identity work. This process of identity work in the IMM model can support the empowerment of the parties involved (Mayer, 2008b) and can impart managerial self-identity, specifically by addressing the personal development and cross-cultural competence.

Contextual influences

In IMM it is also of importance to consider contextual influences with regard to the individuals (mediators, conflict parties and for example colleagues, superiors or subordinates) involved, the conflict issues, the organization (including the organizational culture, the guiding principles of the organization and the organizational vision). In parallel, time and location in which the conflict and the mediation process take place need consideration in IMM processes to address the conflict issues adequately.

The mediator plays a significant role in transforming conflicts (Bercovitch, 1996). In guiding the IMM in a management setting, the mediator needs organizational and managerial expertise and knowledge on organizational management, leadership concepts, organizational identity and human resource management. The mediator's role in IMM processes is to be impartial and fair, tolerant, sovereign and sufficiently competent to guide the process and the mangers through times of change. According to Cohen (1996: 111), the mediator in cross-cultural contexts assumes different roles by being the interpreter, the decoder and the person who explains the parties' culturally encoded messages and enables them to communicate intelligibly. The mediator protects the face of adversaries (Cohen, 1996: 115) and, simultaneously, serves as the co-ordinator (Cohen, 1996: 118) on the base of a "respectful and empathetic understanding" (Rogers, 1998: 277) and a identity-based self-reflective attitude (McLeod, 1981).

Intervening variables

Variables of multiple identity aspects in managers, value-orientations and the basic assumptions of human universals further impact on the mediation process and are, therefore, taken into account. IMM aims at discovering underlying multiple identity aspects and values by referring to cultural and individual orientations, images of the self and the other, communication styles and conflict management processes (Mayer, 2008a). Multiple identity aspects can become intervening variables in conflict management processes and are often inter-connected with values. Values, in IMM, comprise one major aspect of multiple identities and conflicts which need to be evaluated (Mayer and Boness, 2006) to forward the mediation process. According to Taylor (2002), individuals know their value priorities. Through (re-)narration of conflict stories, value priorities become negotiable and re-definable and "the coherence of identity, the feelings of authenticity, meaningfulness and self-acknowledgement are constructed" (Keupp, 2004: 10).

In parallel to multiple identity aspects and values, human universals, such as the general human ability of building relationships and communicating and addressing needs, are used in IMM to build a common ground of human understanding which goes beyond values and identities. Human universals can constitute the base for a common understanding based on human needs in IMM.

Culture-specific transcultural mediation (CSTM)

IMM uses the CSTM which is based on a spontaneously-constructed cross-cultural mediation process of picking out and re-bonding single aspects of culture-specific mediation elements; referring to the setting of mediation; the mediation techniques used; the definition of the role of mediator and conflicting parties; the rules of mediation; and the set-up of communication (Mayer and Boness, 2004). In cross-cultural organizational contexts it cannot be presumed that terms and mediation concepts, such as neutrality, impartiality or confidentiality, are equally understood across cultures or even that they exist in the different cultural contexts.

Identity-based managerial mediation is based on the dynamic inter-relationship of conflict- and identity narrations, cross-cultural competency developments, self-identity and identity work components as well as contextual influences and intervening variables. All of these aspects impact on the chose and construction of culture-specific aspects of mediation models which become inherent in IMM.

Conclusion

The purpose of this article was to introduce the IMM which is embedded in relevant theoretical approaches of cross-cultural conflict management, managerial identity work and managerial mediation in organizations and contribute to the theoretical debate on cross-cultural identity work in managers through managerial mediation.

The potential for cross-cultural conflict grows with the increase in globalization and cross-cultural interactions in management organizations. To manage such conflicts between managers within, or between organizations, cross-cultural mediation practices can be used to transform destructive conflicts into constructive conflicts, particularly with reference to managers of different cultural backgrounds.

In conclusion, the Identity-based Managerial Mediation (IMM) model particularly refers to identity and identity work in mediation due to the assumption that conflict experiences are highly connected to identity issues and value-orientations. IMM is, therefore, viewed as a model for developing managerial identities, whilst simultaneously managing conflicts in organizational settings and impacting on the development of cross-cultural competencies and identity aspects in managers. Through the reflection of self and others, as well as the flow of conflict and identity narrations in IMM, culture-specific identity aspects particularly can be discussed and (re-)constructed in third-party intervention. The mediator in the IMM processes aims at implementing reflections and narrations with regard to conflict and identity, thereby processing managerial identity work which contributes positively to both managerial competencies and the construction of a strong organizational identity. By mediating between the conflicting parties, mediators improve managerial skills in conflict management across cultures and build managerial competencies in culture-, diversity and conflict management on the basis of identity work in organizational settings.

With regard to the afore-mentioned conclusions, IMM could play a major role in facing future challenges created by an increased potential for conflict resulting from diversity within and between organizations. The ability to cope with inner diversity and multiple identity aspects within organizations and individuals will further prepare managers to face the complexity of organizational diversity and the multiplicity of identities, thereby improving conflict management skills, identity work and self-reflection in managers.

References

ABU-NIMER, M. (1996) 'Conflict resolution approaches: Western and Middle Eastern lessons and possibilities'. *American Journal of Economics and Sociology*, 55, 35-52.

AGGESTAN, K. (1999) *Reframing and Resolving Conflict. Israeli-Palestinian Negotiations 1988-1998*, Lund, Lund University Press.

AINSWORTH, S. AND HARDY, C. (2004) 'Discourse and Identities', IN GRANT, D., HARDY, C., OSWICK, C. and PUTNAM, L. (Eds.), *The Sage Handbook of Organizational Discourse*, 153-173, London, Sage.

ALBERT, S., ASHFORTH, B. and DUTTON, J. (2000) 'Organisational identity and identification. Charting new waters and building new bridges'. *Academy of Management Review*, 25, 13-17.

ALBERT, S. and WHETTEN, D.A. (1985) 'Organizational identity', IN CUMMINGS, L.L. and STAW, M.M. (Eds.), *Research in organizational behaviour*, 263–295. Greenwich, CT, JAI Press.

ALVESSON, M. and WILLMOTT, H. (2002) 'Identity Regulation as Organizational Control: Producing the Appropriate Individual'. *Journal of Management Studies*, 39(5), 619–644.

ALVESSON, M. and WILLMOTT, H. (2004) 'Identity Regulation as Organizational Control Producing the Appropriate Individual' IN HATCH, M.J. and SCHULZ, M. (Eds.), *Organisational identity. A Reader. Oxford Management Readers,* (436-468). Oxford, Oxford University Press.

APPLEFIELD, J.M., HUBER, R. and MOALLEM, M. (2000) 'Constructivism in Theory and Practice: Toward a Better Understanding'. *The High School Journal*, 84(2), 35-53.

ASHFORTH, B. and MAEL, F. (1989) 'Social identity theory and the organization'. *Academy of Management Review*, 14, 20-39.

AUGSBURGER, D.W. (1992) *Conflict Mediation between Cultures. Pathways and Patterns*, Louisville, John Knox Press.

AVRUCH, K. (1998) *Culture and Conflict Resolution*, Washington D.C., USIP Press.

BAGSHAW, M. (1998) 'Conflict management and mediation: key leadership skills'. *Industrial and Commercial Training*, 30(6), 206-208.

Baine, D. and Swatzky, D. (1991) 'Mediation methods as an adjunct to counselling couples', *International Journal for the Advancement of Counseling*, 14, 273-84.

BAKHTIN, M., (Ed.) (1981) *The Dialogic Imagination: Four Essays by M.M. Bakhtin, M. Holquist*, Austin, University of Texas Press.

BEATTIE, S. (1997) 'Is mediation a real alternative to law? Pitfalls for Aboriginal Participants.'. *Australian Dispute Resolution Journal*, 8(1), 57-69.

BEECH, N. (2008) 'On the Nature of Dialog Identity work', *Organization*, 15(1), 51-74.

BEECH, N. and HUXHAM, C. (2003) 'Cycles of Identity Formation in Interorganizational Collaborations'. *International Studies of Management and Organization*, 33(3), 28-52.

BERCOVITCH, J. (1996) 'Understanding mediation's role in preventive diplomacy'. *Negotiation Journal*, 12, 241-258.

BERGER, P. L. and LUCKMANN, T. (2000) *Die gesellschaftliche Konstruktion der Wirklichkeit. Eine Theorie der Wissenssoziologie*, 17th ed, Frankfurt: Fischer Verlag.

BINGHAM, L.B. (2004) 'Mediation at Work: Transforming Workplace Conflict at the United States Postal Service'. IN BREUL, J.D. and GARDNER, N.W. (Eds.), *Human Capital,*Washington, IBM Center for The Business of Government.

BLOOMFIELD, D. and REILLY, B. (1998) 'The Changing Nature of Conflict and Conflict Management'. IN HARRIS, P. AND REILLY, B. (Eds.), *Democracy and Deep-rooted conflict,* Stockholm, Institute for Democracy and Electoral Assistance (IDEA).

BOLTEN, J., (ed.) (2003) *Interkulturelle Kompetenz,* 2nd ed. Thüringen, Landeszentrale für politische Bildung.

BONESS, C. (2002) *Kritische Situationen in Begegnungen zwischen Tansaniern und Europäern. Eine Felduntersuchung im Secondary School System Tansanias,* Frankfurt, Peter Lang.

BRADSHAW, G.J. (2006) *Course Outline: Managing Conflict in Organizations.* Internal Document. St Louis, University of Missouri Department of Sociology

BROWN, A. (2001) 'Organization studies and identity. Towards a research agenda'. *Human Relations,* 54(1), 113-121.

BURTON, J.W. (1988) *Conflict Resolution as a Political System,* Fairfax, George Mason Press.

BURTON, J. W. (1990a) *Conflict: Human Needs Theory,* London, Macmillian.

BURTON, J.W. (1990b) *Conflict: Resolution and Provention,* New York, St. Martin's Press

BUSCH, D. (2005) *Interkulturelle Mediation. Eine theoretische Grundlegung triadischer Konfliktbearbeitung in interkulturell bedingten Kontexten,* Frankfurt/Main, Peter Lang.

BUSCH, D. (Ed.) (2006) *Interkulturelle Mediation in der Grenzregion,* Frankfurt/Main, Peter Lang.

BUSH, R.A.B. and FOLGER, J.P. (1994) *The Promise of Mediation. Responding to Conflict through Empowerment and Recognition,* San Francisco, Jossey-Bass.

BUTTNER, E.H. (2001) 'Examining Female Entrepreneurs' Management Style: An Application of a Relational Frame'. *Journal of Business Ethics,* 29(3), 253-269.

CARNEVALE, P.J. and PRUITT, D.G. (1992) 'Negotiation and Mediation'. *Annual Review of Psychology,* 43, 531-582.

CASTRO, A.P. and NIELSEN, E. (2001) 'Indigenous people and co-management implications for conflict management'. *Environmental Science and Policy,* 4(4-5), 229-239.

CERULO, K. (1997) 'Identity Construction: New Issues, New Directions'. *Annual Review of Sociology,* 23, 385-409.

COHEN, R. (1996) 'Cultural aspects in international mediation'. IN BERCOVITCH, J. (Ed.) *Resolving International Conflicts. The Theory and Practice of Mediation,* 107-129, Boulder, Lynne Rienner.

COLE, M. (1995) 'Culture and Cognitive Development: From Cross-Cultural Research to Creating Systems of Cultural Mediation'. *Culture and Psychology,* 1(1), 25-54.

COLEMAN, P.T. (2003) 'Characteristics of Protracted, Intractable Conflict: Toward the Development of a Metaframework'. *Peace and Conflict: Journal of Peace Psychology,* 9(1), 1-37.

COLLINS, J. and PORRAS, J. (1996) *Built to last,* Chatham, Random House.

COOKS, L.M. and HALE, C.L. (1994) 'The Construction of Ethics in Mediation'. *Mediation Quarterly,* 12(1), 55-84.

COUPLAND, C. (2001) 'Accounting for Change: A Discourse Analysis of Graduate Trainees' Talk of Adjustment'. *Journal of Management Studies*, 38(8), 1103-19.

COWAN, D. (1995) *Taking Charge of Organizational Conflict: A Guide to Managing Anger and Confrontation*, Spring Valley, Inner Choice Publishing.

CRUMP, L. and ZARTMANN, I.W. (2003) 'Multilateral negotiation and the management of complexity'. *International negotiation*, 8(1), 1-5.

DADDER, R. (1987) *Interkulturelle Orientierung: Analyse ausgewählter Interkultureller Orientierungsprogramme*, Saarbrücken, Verlag Breidenbach.

DANA, D. (2001) *Conflict Resolution: Mediation Tools for Everyday Worklife*, New York, McGraw-Hill.

DE DREU, C.K.W., VAN DIERENDONCK, D. and DIJKSTRA, M.T.M. (2004) 'Conflict at Work and Individual Well-Being'. *International Journal of Conflict Management*, 15(1), 6-26.

DEMMERS, J. (2006) 'Conflict research: lancunas, mantras and pitfalls'. *ISYP Journal on Science and World Affairs*, 2(2), 99-102.

DODSON, M. (1996) 'Power and cultural difference in native title mediation.'. *Aboriginal Law Bulletin*, 3(84), 8-11.

DUKES, E. F. (1996) *Resolving Public Conflict. Transforming Community and Governance*, Manchester, Manchester University Press.

EL-SHEIKH, M. and HARGER, J.A. (2001) 'Appraisals of Marital Conflict and Children's Adjustment, Health, and Physiological Reactivity'. *Developmental Psychology*, 37(11), 875-885.

FINEMAN, S. (1997) 'Constructing the Green Manager'. *British Journal of Management*, 8, 31-38.

FISHER, R. and URY, W. (1991) *Getting to Yes. Negotiating Agreement without Giving in*, Boston, Houghton Mifflin Company.

FISHER, R., URY, W. and PATTON, B.M. (1993) *Das Harvard-Konzept: Sachgerecht verhandeln—erfolgreich verhandeln*, Frankfurt. Campus Verlag

FRANCIS, D. (2003) 'People, peace and power: Conflict transformation in action'. *Peace Review*, 15(2), 241-243.

FRIEDMAN, R.A., TIDD, S.T., CURRALL, S.C. and TSAI, J.C. (2000) 'What goes around comes around: the impact of personal conflict styles on work conflict and stress'. *The International Journal of Conflict Management*, 11(1), 32-55.

GABEL, S. (2003) 'Mediation and Psychotherapy: Two Sides of the Same Coin?' *Negotiation Journal*, 19(4), 315-328.

GALADE, G.A. and IVERY, M. (2003) 'The impact of human resource management and work climate on organizational performance'. *Personnel Psychology*, 56(2), 383-404.

GAZIANO, W.G., JENSEN-CAMPBELL, L.A. and HAIR, E. (1996) 'Perceiving interpersonal conflict and reacting to it: The case of agreeableness'. *Journal of Personality and Social Psychology*, 70(4), 820-835.

GIDDENS, A. (1991) *Modernity and Self-Identity*, Stanford, CA, Stanford University Press.

GIOIA, D., SCHULTZ, M. and CORLEY, K. (2002) 'On celebrating the organisation identity metaphor: A rejoinder to Cornelissen'. *British Journal of Management*, 13, 269-275.

GIOIA, D.A. and THOMAS, J.B. (1996) 'Identity, image and issue interpretation: Sensemaking during strategic change in academia'. *Administrative Science Quarterly*, 41, 370–403.

GIRE, J.T. and CARMENT, D.W. (1993) 'Dealing with disputes—the influence of individualism-collectivism'. *Journal of Social Psychology*, 133, 81-95.

GLASL, F. (2003) 'Das Anwendungsspektrum unterschiedlicher Mediationsformen: Ein kontingenztheoretisches Modell'. IN MEHTA, G. and RÜCKERT, K. (Eds.) *Mediation und Demokratie. Neue Wege des Konfliktmanagements in größeren Systemen*, 102-119, Heidelberg, Carl-Auer-Systeme.

GLYNN, M. (2000) 'When cymbals become symbols: Conflict over organizational identity within a symphony orchestra'. *Organization science*, 11(3), 285-298.

HARVEY, M. and EVANS, R.E. (1994) 'Family Business and Multiple Levels of Conflit'. *Family Business Review*, 7(4), 331-348.

HATCH, M. and SCHULZ, M. (2002) 'The dynamics of organizational identity', *Human Relations*, 55(8), 989-1018.

HAUMERSEN, P. and LIEBE, F. (1999) *Multikulti: Konflikte konstruktiv. Trainingshandbuch. Mediation in der interkulturellen Arbeit*, Mühlheim an der Ruhr, Verlag an der Ruhr.

HERMANS, H. (2001) 'The Dialogical Self: Toward a Theory of Personal and Cultural Positioning'. *Culture and Psychology*, 7(3), 243–81.

HILL, E.J. (2005) 'Work-Family Facilitation and conflict, working fathers and mothers, work family, stressors and support'. *Journal of Family Issue*, 26(6), 793-819.

HUMPHREYS, M. and BROWN, A. (2002) 'Narratives of Organizational Identity and Identification: A Case Study of Hegemony and Resistance'. *Organization Studies*, 23, 421–47.

JONES, C. (2002) *Aboriginal Boundaries: The Mediation and Settlement of Aboriginal Boundary Disputes in a Native Titel Context, Occasional Papers Series, No. 2*, Perth, The Research Unit of the National Native Title Tribunal.

KANUNGO, R. P. (2006) 'Cross Culture and Business Practices: Are they Coterminous or Cross-verging?' *Cross Culture Management: An International Journal*, 13(1), 23-31.

KESSEN, S. (2003) 'Fragen in der Mediation. Familiendynamik'. *Interdisziplinäre Zeitschrift für systemorientierte Praxis und Forschung*, 28(3), 356-375.

KESSEN, S. and TROJA, M. (2002) 'Die Phasen und Schritte der Mediation als Kommunikationsprozess'. IN HAFT, F. and SCHLIEFFEN, K. V. (Eds.), *Handbuch Mediation*, 393-420, München, Beck Verlag.

KEUPP, H. (1988) 'Auf dem Weg zur Patchwork-Identität'. *Verhaltenstherapie and Psychosoziale Praxis, Mitteilungen der dgvt*, 4, 425-438.

KEUPP, H. (1994) 'Ambivalenzen postmoderner Identität'. IN BECK, U. and BECK-GERSHEIM, E. (Eds.) *Riskante Freiheiten. Individualisierung in modernen Gesellschaften*, 336-350, Frankfurt, Suhrkamp.

KEUPP, H. (2001) *Fragmente oder Einheit? Wie Identität heute geschaffen wird*, http://www.ipp-muenchen.de/texte/fragmente_oder_einheit.pdf [last accessed 01-08-2009].

LANDESHAUPTSTADT MÜNCHEN. STELLE FÜR INTERKULTURELLE ZUSAMMENARBEIT (Eds.) *Dokumentation der Fachtagung: Baustelle Identität. Zu Sanierungsarbeiten an einem beschädigten Konstrukt,* München, Stelle für Interkulturelle Zusammenarbeit, 7-15.

KEUPP, H. (2004). *Sich selber finden—Identitätskonstruktionen heute und welche Ressourcen in Familie und Gesellschaft sie benötigen.* http://www.ippmuenchen.de/texte/sich_selber_finden.pdf [last accessed 30-05-2007].

KEUPP, H., AHBE, T., GMÜR, W., HÖFER, R., KRAUS, W., MITZSCHERLICH, B. and STRAUS, F. (2002) *Identitätskonstruktionen. Das Patchwork der Identitäten in der Spätmoderne,* Hamburg, Rowohlt.

KIECOLT-GLASER, J.K., GLASER, R., CACIOPPO, J.T., MACCALLUM, R.C., SNYDER-SMITH, M., KIM, C. *and* MALARKEY, W.B. (1997) 'Marital conflict in older adults: endocrinological and immunological correlates'. *Psychosomatic Medicine,* 59(4), 339-349.

KIECOLT-GLASER, J.K., MALARKEY, W.B., CHEE, M., NEWTON, T., CACIOPPO, J.T., MAO, H. and GLASER, R. (1993) 'Negative behavior during marital conflict is associated with immunological down-regulation'. *Psychosomatic Medicine,* 55(5), 395-409.

KRAUS, W. (1996) *Das erzählte Selbst. Die narrative Konstruktion von Identität in der Spätmoderne,* Pfaffenweiler, Centaurius.

KRESSEL, K. and PRUITT, D.G. (1989) *Mediation research,* San Francisco, Jossey-Bass.

KRIESBERG, L. (2003a) *Constructive Conflicts: From Escalation to Resolution,* 2nd ed, New York, Rowman and Littlefield.

KRIESBERG, L. (2003b). *Factors Shaping the Course of Intractable Conflict.* Beyond Intractability. http://www.beyondintractability.org/m/factors_shaping_intractable_conflict.jsp [last accessed 22-10-2007].

KUMAR, K. and VAN DISSEL, H. (1996) 'Sustainable collaboration: Managing conflict and cooperation in Interorganizational Systems'. *MIS Quarterly,* 20(3), 279-300.

LAUZEN, M.M. and DOZIER, D.M. (1994) 'Issues Management Mediation of Linkages Between Environmental Complexity and Management of the Public relations Function'. *Journal of Public Relations Research,* 6(3), 163-184.

LAYES, G. (2003) 'Interkulturelles Identitätsmanagement'. IN THOMAS, A., KINAST, E.-U. and SCHROLL-MACHL, S. (Eds.) *Handbuch interkultureller Kommunikation und Kooperation. Band 1: Grundlagen und Praxisfelder.* 117-126, Göttingen, V and R.

LEDERACH, J.P. (1988) *Of Nets, Nails and Problems: A Folk Vision of Conflict in Central America.* Unpublished Doctoral thesis, Colorado, United States of America, University of Colorado.

LEDERACH, J.P. (1996) *Preparing for Peace. Conflict Transformation across Cultures,* New York, Syracuse University Press.

LEDERACH J.P. (2000) 'The cultural dimension', IN MENNONITE CONCILIATION SERVICE (Eds.) *Mediation and Facilitation Training Manual, 4th ed,* Pennsylvania, Akron.

LEDERACH, J.P. (2003) *The Little Book of Conflict Transformation,* Intercouse, Good Books.

LEUNG, K., TREMAIN KOCH, P. and LU, L. (2002) 'A Dualistic Model of Harmony and its Implications for Conflict Management in Asia'. *Asia Pacific Journal of Management,* 19, 201–220.

LIEBE, F. and GILBERT, N. (1996) 'Interkulturelle Mediation—eine schwierige Vermittlung. Eine empirische Annäherung zur Bedeutung von kulturellen Unterschieden'. IN BERGHOF FORSCHUNGSZENTRUM FÜR KONSTRUKTIVE KONFLIKTBEARBEITUNG (Eds.), *Berghof Report No. 2,* Berlin, Berghof Forschungszentrum.

LIPSKY, D.B., SEEBER, R.L. and FINCHER, R.D. (2004) 'Emerging Systems for Managing Workplace Conflict: Lessons from American Corporations for Managers and Dispute Resolution Professionals'. *Industrial and Labor relations Review,* Article 82, 57(4), 614-617.

LUTGEN-SANDVIK, P. (2008) 'Intensive remedial Identity Work: Responses to Workplace Bullying Trauma and Stigmatisation'. *Organization,* 15(1), 97-119.

MAEDCHE, A., MOTIK, B., STOJANOVIC, L., STUDER, R. and VOLZ, R. (2003) 'Ontologies for enterprise knowledge management'. *Intelligent Systems,* 18(2), 26-33.

MAYER, B. (2000). *The dynamics of conflict management: A practitioner's guide,* San Franscisco, Jossey-Bass.

MAYER, C.-H. (2005) Interkulturelle Mediation im Spannungsfeld westlicher und afrikanischer Perspektiven. IN BUSCH, D. and SCHRÖDER, H. (Eds.) *Perspektiven interkultureller Mediation. Grundlagentexte zur kommunikationswissenschaftlichen Analyse triadischer Verständigung.* 245-267, Frankfurt am Main, Peter Lang.

MAYER, C.-H. (2006) *Trainingshandbuch interkulturelle Mediation und Konfliktlösung. Didaktische Materialien zum Kompetenzerwerb,* Münster, Waxmann.

MAYER, C.-H. (2007) Ressourcen interkultureller Identitäten'. IN KRAUSE, C., LEHMANN, N., LORENZ, F. and PETZOLD, T. (Eds.), *verbunden gesunden—Zugehörigkeitsgefühl und Salutogenese,* 251-262, Heckenbeck/Bad Gandersheim, Verlag Gesunde Entwicklung.

MAYER, C.-H. (2008a) 'Identity and health in transcultural mediation. The model of Culture-Synergetic Transcultural Mediation and its impacts'. *Journal of Intercultural Communication,* in press.

MAYER, C.-H. (2008b) *Managing conflict across cultures, values and identities. A case study in the South African automotive industry,* unpublished PhD thesis, Rhodes University, South Africa.

MAYER, C.-H. and BONESS, C. (2004) *Interkulturelle Mediation und Konfliktbearbeitung. Bausteine deutsch-afrikanischer Wirklichkeiten,* Münster, Waxmann.

MAYER, C.-H. and BONESS, C. (2005) *Intercultural Mediation and Conflict Resolution,* Stuttgart, Ibidem.

MAYER, C.-H. and BONESS, C. (2006) 'Mediative Prozesse zur Konstruktion fließender Grenzen. Studien aus den kulturellen Grenzgebieten Südafrikas'. IN SCHROEDER, H. and BUSCH, D. (Eds.) *Interkulturelle Mediation in der Grenzregion. Studien zur interkulturellen Mediation, Band 2,* Frankfurt, Peter Lang.

MCLEOD, B. (1981) 'The Mediating Person and Cultural Identity'. IN BOCHNER, S. (Ed.), *The Mediating Person: Bridges Between Cultures,* 37-52, Cambridge, Schenkman.

MIALL, H. (2004) 'Conflict Transformation: A Multi-Dimensional Task'. IN BLOOMFELD, D., FISCHER, M. and SCHMELZLE, B. (Eds.) *Berghof Handbook for Conflict Transformation.,* Berlin, Berghof Forschungszentrum.

MIALL, H., RAMSBOTHAM, O. and WOODHOUSE, T. (2000) *Contemporary Conflict Resolution: The Prevention, Management and Transformation of Deadly Conflicts,* Oxfordk Polity Press.

MICHIE, S. and WILLIAMS, S. (2003) 'Reducing work related psychological ill health and sickness absence: a systematic literature review'. *Occupational and Environmental Medicine,* 60, 3-9.

MONTOYA-WEISS, M.M., MASSEY, A.P. and SONG, M. (2001) 'Getting it together: temporal coordination and conflict management in global virtual teams'. *Academy of Management Journal,* 44(6), 1251-1262.

MÜLLER, S. and GELBRICH, K. (2001) 'Interkulturelle Kompetenz als neuartige Anforderung an Entsandte: Status Quo und Perspektiven der Forschung'. *Schmalenbacher Zeitschrift für betriebswissenschaftliche Forschung,* 53(5), 246-272.

MUMPOWER, J.L. and ROHRBAUGH, J. (1996) Negotiation and design: Supporting resource allocation decisions through analytical mediation'. *Group Decision and Negotiation,* 5, 385-409.

MUSSON, G. and DUBERLEY, J. (2006) 'Change, Change or Be Exchanged: The Discourse of Participation and the Manufacture of Identity'. *Journal of Management Studies,* 44(1), 143–64.

MYERS, S. and FILNER, B. (Eds.) (1994) *Mediation Across Cultures. A Handbook about Conflict and Culture.* San Diego, San Diego Mediation Centre.

MYERS, S. and FILNER, B (1997) *Conflict Resolution across Cultures: From Talking it out to Third Party Mediation,* Amherst, Amherst Educational Publishing.

NORTHRUP, T.A. (1989) 'The Dynamic of Identity in Personal and Social Conflict'. IN KRIESBERG, L., NORTHRUP, T.A. and THORSON, S.J. (Eds.) *Timing the De-escalation of International Conflict,* Syracuse, Syracuse University.

NYE, J.S. (2005) *Understanding International Conflicts. An Introduction to Theory and History,* 5th ed, New York, Longman.

OLIVER, D. AND ROOS, J. (2003) 'Dealing with the unexpected: Critical incidents in the LEGO Mindstorms team'. *Human Relations,* 56(9), 1055-1080.

PONDY, L.R. (1967) 'Organizational Conflict: Concepts and Models', *Administrative Science Quarterly,* 12(2), 296-320.

PONDY, L.R. (1992) 'Reflections on organizational conflict'. *Journal of Organizational Behaviour,* 13(2), 257-261.

PRATT, M. and RAFAELI, A. (1997) 'Organizational dress as a symbol of multilayered social identities'. *Academy of Management Journal,* 40(4), 862-898.

PULLEN, A. (2006) *Managing Identity,* Basingstoke, Palgrave Macmillan.

PUTNAM, L. and POOLE, M. (1987) 'Conflict and Negotiation'. IN JABLIN, F.M., PUTNAM, L.L., ROBERTS, K.H. and PORTER, L.W. (Eds.) *Handbook of Organizational Communication: An Interdisciplinary Perspective,* Newbury Park, Sage.

RAHIM, M.A. (2001) *Managing Conflict in Organizations,* 3rd ed, Westport, Quorum Books.

RAHIM, M.A. (2002) 'Toward a Theory of Managing Organizational Conflict'. *The International Journal of Conflict Management,* 13(3), 206-235.

REIMANN, C. (2004) 'Assessing the state-of-the-art in conflict transformation'- IN BLOOMFELD, D., FISCHER, M. and SCHMELZLE, B. (Eds.) *Berghof Handbook for Conflict Transformation.* Berlin, Berghof Forschungszentrum.

RISKIN, L.L. (2003) 'Who Decides What? Rethinking the Grid of Mediator Orientations' *Dispute Resolution Magazine*, 9(2), 22-25.

ROGERS, C. (1998) *Entwicklung der Persönlichkeit. Psychotherapie aus Sicht eines Therapeuten. Konzepte der Humanwissenschaften,* 12th ed, Stuttgart, Klett-Cotta.

ROSENBERG, M. (2001) *Gewaltfreie Kommunikation. Aufrichtig und einfühlsam miteinander sprechen. Neue Wege in der Mediation und im Umgang mit Konflikten*, Paderborn, Junfermann.

ROTHMAN, J. (1997) *Resolving Identity-based conflict: In Nations, Organizations and Communities*, San Francisco, Jossey-Bass.

SARANGI, S. and ROBERTS, C. (Eds.) (1999) *Talk, Work, and Institutional Order: Discourse in Medical, Mediation and Management Settings*. Berlin, Mouton de Gruyter.

SATIR, V., BANMEN, J. and GERBER, J. (2007) *Das Satir-Modell. Familientherapie und ihre Erweiterung*, Paderborn, Junfermann Verlag.

SCHERMERHORN, J.R., HUNT, J.G. and OSBORNE, R.N. (1997) 'Conflict and Negotiation'. IN SCHERMERHORN, J.R., HUNT, J.G. and OSBORN, R.N. (Eds.) *Organizational Behavior,* 378-396, New York. John Wiley and Sons.

SCHMIDT, H. and TRITTMANN, U. (Eds.) (2002) *Kultur und Konflikt—Dialog mit Johan Galtung*. Münster, Agenda-Verlag.

SCHWERIN, E. (1995) *Mediation, Citizen Empowerment, and Transformational Politics*, London, Westport.

SELYE, H. (1957) *Stress beherrscht unser Leben*, Freiburg, Rombach and Co.

SENNETT, R. (1998) *The corrosion of character*, New York, Norton.

SHAH-KAZEMI, S. N. (2000) 'Cross-cultural mediation: A critical view of the dynamics of culture in family disputes'. *International Journal of Law, Policy and the Family*, 14, 302-325.

SIMONS, T., HOPE PELLED, L. and SMITH, K.A. (1999) 'Making Use of Difference: Diversity, Debate, and Decision Comprehensiveness in Top Management Teams'. *Academy of Management Journal*, 42(6), 662-673.

SIMPSON, B. and CARROLL, B. (2008) 'Re-viewing 'Role' in Processes of Identity Construction', *Organization*, 15(1), 29-50.

SIMS, D. (2005a) 'Living a Story and Storying a Life: A Narrative Understanding of Distributed Self'. IN PULLEN, A. and LINSTEAD, S. (Eds.) *Organization and Identity*, 86-104, London, Routledge.

SIMS, D. (2005b) 'You Bastard: A Narrative Exploration of the Experience of Indignation within Organizations'. *Organization Studies*, 26(11), 1625–40.

SÖKEFELD, M. (2001) 'Der Lehr- und Forschungsschwerpunkt 'Ethnizität und interethnische Beziehungen' am Hamburger Institut'. *Ethnoscripts*, 3(1), 1-9.

SVENINGSSON, S. and ALVESSON, M. (2003) 'Managing managerial identities: Organizational fragmentation, discourse and identity struggle'. *Human Relations,* 56(10), 1163-1193.

TAYLOR, C. (2002) *Wieviel Gemeinschaft braucht die Demokratie? Aufsätze zur politischen Philosophie*, Frankfurt. Suhrkamp.

THOMAS, R. AND LINSTEAD, A. (2002) 'Losing the Plot? Middle Managers and Identity'. *Organization*, 9(1), 71–93.

TING-TOOMEY, S. and KUROGI, A. (1998) ' Facework competence in intercultural conflict: an updated face-negotiation theory'. *International Journal of Intercultural relations*, 22(2), 187-225.

TROMPENAARS, F. and HAMPDEN-TURNER, C. (1997) *Riding the waves of culture. Understanding Diversity in Global Business,* 2nd ed, London, Nicholas Brealey Publishing Ltd.

UMBREIT, M.S. (1997) Humanistic mediation: A transformative journey of peacemaking. *Conflict Resolution Quarterly*, 14(3), 201-213.

URY, W. (2000) *The Third Side. How we fight and how we can stop*, New York, Penguin Books.

VAN GAMBERG, B. and TEICHER, J. (2006) 'Managing neutrality and impartiality in workplace conflict resolution: the dilemma of the HR manager'. *Asia Pacific Journal of Human Resources,* 44(2), 197-210.

VESTER, F. (1997) *Phänomen Stress. Wo liegt sein Ursprung, warum ist er lebenswichtig, wodurch ist er entartet*, Stuttgart, Deutsche Verlags-Anstalt.

WALL, J.A. and CALLISTER, R.R. (1995) 'Conflict and its management'. *Journal of Management*, 21(3), 515-558.

WALL, J.A., STARK, J.B. and STANDIFER, R.L. (2001) 'Mediation. A current review and theory development'. *Journal of Conflict Resolution*, 45(3), 370-391.

WALLENSTEEN, D.P. and SOLLENBERG, M. (1995) 'After the Cold War: Emerging patterns of armed conflict 1989-94'. *Journal of Peace Research,* 32(3), 345-360.

WATSON, T.J. (1994) *In search of management*, London, Routledge.

WATSON, T.J. (2008) 'Managing Identity: Identity Work, Personal Predicaments and Structural Circumstances'. *Organization*, 15(1), 121–143.

WATZLAWICK, P. (1998) 'Wirklichkeitsanpassung oder angepasste Wirklichkeit? Konstruktivismus und Psychotherapie'. IN FOERSTER, H. V., GLASERSFELD, E. V., HEJL, P.M., SCHMIDT and S.J., WATZLAWICK, P. (Eds.) *Einführung in den Konstruktivismus*, 89-108), München, Piper.

WAYNE, J.H., GRZYWACZ, J.G., CARLSON, D.S. and KACMAR, K.M. (2007) 'Work-family facilitation: A theoretical explanation and mode of primary antecendents and consequences'. *Human Resource Management Review,* 17(1), 63-76.

WHETTEN, D. and GODFREY, P. (Eds.) (1998) *Identity in organizations*. London, Sage.

WILS, O., HOPP, U., ROPERS, N., VIMALARAJAH, L. and ZUNZER, W. (2006) *Systemische Konflikttransformation. Konzepte und Anwendungsgebiete*, Berlin, Berghof Forschungszentrum Berlin.

WITTGENSTEIN, L. (1958) *Philosophical Investigations*, 2nd ed, Oxford, Basil Blackwell.

XIN, Y., WEILER, B. and HAM, S. (2001) 'Intercultural communication and mediation: A framework for analysing the intercultural competence of Chinese tour guides'. *Journal of Vacation and Marketing*, 8(1), 75-87.

ZAPF, D. (1999) 'Organisational, work group related and personal causes of mobbing/bullying at work'. *International Journal of Manpower,* 20(1/2), 70-85.

ZIMBARDO, P.G. (1995) *Psychologie*, Berlin, Springer Verlag.

Mediated Doctor-Patient Interaction. An Italian Case Study

Viola Barbieri and Federico Farini[1]

Introduction: state of the art

Intercultural Mediation (IM) is of growing interest for Italian Public services, whose users now include an increasing number of migrants. The evidence of such interest is given by a significant number of recent studies on IM. Current Italian research has been dealing with topics connected with education, psychology and sociology (for example: Aluffi Pentini, 2004, Andolfi, 2003, Belpiede, 2002, Ceccatelli Gurrieri, 2003, Favaro and Fumagalli, 2004, Fiorucci, 2000, Johnson and Nigris, 2000). These studies provide a comprehensive description of IM's procedures and purposes for public services, and are aimed to clarify the qualifications and ethics of professional mediators.

Nevertheless, Italian research on IM is actually lacking an empirical method. For the purposes of the present paper, we have analysed a number of works centred on lists of principles that the mediator is supposed to comply with, which, however, neither provide the mediator with any explanation on how to reach the presumed goals of communication, nor present any practical working input to study the mediation flow associated to the various social contexts.

Specifically, what all the above-mentioned studies have in common is the final objective to be attained by IM, namely the construction of "bridges" between cultures through the promotion of intercultural dialogue. However, with few exceptions (Baraldi, 2006 a/b/c; Baraldi 2008; Gavioli and Baraldi, 2005), no clear methodical proposal has so far been made to verify the introduction of dialogue in IM procedures.

The present work aims precisely at suggesting possible methods for IM observation, focusing on the analysis of communication processes involving a cultural mediator, with particular reference to IM in healthcare services.

At present, IM is considered one of the pivotal strategies of multicultural society (Colombo, 2002), employed to cope with difficulties connected with transnational migration otherness (Melotti, 2004, Zanfrini, 2004). IM is a practice primarily

1 Both authors have contributed to all sections of this paper. However, Viola Barbieri is mainly responsible for sections 1, 2, 3, and 4, and Federico Farini is mainly responsible for sections 5, 6, and 7.

used by institutions to encourage foreign groups to access public facilities, especially those related to healthcare, social integration, education, justice and job assistance.

At the beginning of the nineties, Italian scientific literature started to analyse IM experiences from different perspectives: pedagogical, strictly related to intercultural education (Fiorucci, 2000, Favaro, 2001, Nigris, 2000), sociological and anthropological (Castiglioni, 1997), and sociological (Belpiede, 1997, Ceccatelli Gurrieri, 2003). From these analyses, we can draw some definitions of IM applied to different social contexts (Belpiede, 1997), narrations of mediators' biographies (Aluffi Pentini, 2004, Ceccatelli Gurrieri, 2003) and prescriptions on basic ethics and qualifications that a mediator should be provided with to produce an effective IM (Belpiede, 1997, Favaro and Fumagalli, 2004). The Italian literature on IM qualifies it as a pivotal strategy to favour the promotion of a multicultural citizenship in multinational societies (Kymlicka, 1995). As pointed out by Jabbar: "The presence of a cultural mediator is an essential executive moment, but most of all a valuable scheduling resource for all commissions promoting integration policies, such as educational or housing ones" (2000: 88).

Many have tried to clearly define IM, especially using metaphors and synonyms, such as "Finding a common view, coming to an agreement, favouring compromise. It's the creation of bridges and networks" (Ceccatelli Gurrieri, 2003: 15) or "It' a way of getting closer, facilitating contact, including, favouring interaction and exchange" (Favaro, 2001: 10). According to Johnson and Nigris (2000: 373-374), IM demand occurs in the following cases:

a) People belonging to different linguistic and cultural groups are involved in mutual communication activities.

b) The interaction between these people takes place in institutional contexts lacking a balance of powers between the parties involved.

It is necessary to specify that Italian public services have shown a preference to work with mediators from the guest-migrant community, rather than the host-Italian community.

Even if the functions of IM are various (Favaro, 2004: 32-33) the fundamental dimensions of IM meanings are almost universally recognized: the kind of IM that literature describes consists in facilitating communication and understanding between people belonging to different cultures, eliminating misunderstandings between the migrant and the social agent that are caused mostly by different cultural codes and values. In sum, the ultimate purpose of IM is to allow every party involved in the communication to access the other party's "cultural imagination" (Fiorucci, 2003).

The above-mentioned definitions refer to two vitally important functions of IM. On the one hand literature insists on defining IM as a communicative action capable of "building bridges", i.e. connecting individuals belonging to different cultures. On the other hand, IM is described as an action aimed to reduce asymmetries of role and authority characterising the institutions of the mainstream cultural background. From this perspective the Italian literature (see in particular: Favaro, 1997/2004) observes that the mediator can have two contrasting functions: s/he can reconcile, seek an agreement, and facilitate the harmony between the two parties, or s/he intercedes, and intervenes in favor of one part.

According to the first perspective, the mediator as reconciler is viewed as a "referee", as a link between the parties. The mediator knows both parties and places her/himself betwee the two. In the second definition, the mediator is a sort of "advocate" who defends the interests of one of the parties involved in the communication. The mediator is a partial speaker, clearly oriented toward a position representing the culture s/he belongs to.

According to the first perspective, the mediator-referee connecting the parties involved should give voice to the questions, needs, and thoughts of the service user while at the same time clarifying the needs and functions of the institutional service. The aim is to improve communication, preventing misunderstandings, establishing an agreement through the explanation of users' requests and agents' requirements. The mediator therefore connects the parties in two directions: from the user to the service provider and from the service provider to the user. Differently from the mediator-referre, the mediator-advocate defends the interests of the service user, who is considered the weakest and most vulnerable party, due to her/his inability to independently formulate questions and obtain relevant replies. The mediator-advocate establishes a privileged relationship with its culture of origin and tends to develop a complicity with the user coming from her/his same country.

In some cases we can clearly distinguish the two functions of the mediator and her/his position, while in others, the "connecting" function between the two parties involved goes hand in hand with the one of "defender" of one of the two. This is one of the cases in which the mediator's position can be ambiguous, thus revealing the limits of the mediator's role within the institution.

As to the difference between the two kinds of mediators, we can further differentiate IM practices as either actions aimed to defend the rights of those users experiencing discriminations and having difficulties in making the others recognize their needs (advocacy), or actions aimed to support users so that they can better use the information they have been provided with, and use the most effective strategies to solve problems—thus reaching a high level of independence in defending their position (empowerment).

According to the studies mentioned above, empowerment comes before advocacy: Belpiede (2002: 39) asserts that the mediator should first of all maintain an impartial position, not preferring any of the parties; nevertheless, considering the disparity of the roles played by provider and user, the mediator should as well be close to the migrant, as a reconciler who supports the user's bargaining capacities, thus favouring empowerment.

The debate on the mediator's actions suggests that should the mediator belong to the minority cultural group, then a disfunction could occur in the intercultural relationship. This reflects the concerns about the position of the mediator as defender of the users' interests. From our point of view, however, the concept of mediation as empowerment and at the same time the concerns about mediation as advocacy in favour of the minority group are not supported by practical examples showing either the effectiveness of the first kind of mediation or the harmfulness of the second kind.

A methodology for IM research

The above-mentioned Italian debate on IM's functions and goals is the result of studies conducted in various fields. From a methodological point of view, although these studies originated from different scientific backgrounds, they have been based on data, such as reports on mediators' biographies and experiences that in our opinion are only partially useful to observe IM processes.

The reported information appears strongly categorized and often far from showing the actual dynamics of IM practices. As previously explained, the attempts to find an empirical approach to systematically observe IM forms in various contexts are very few (Apfelbaum, 2007, Baraldi, 2006a/2006b, Baraldi and Gavioli, 2007, Merlini and Favaron, 2007). For this reason, it would be better to propose a brand new theoretical and methodical background, developed around different approaches, particularly linguistic and sociological, in order to obtain a working definition of IM. To do that, as explained in section 1, the observation of communication processes involving provider of an institution, migrants and a cultural mediator plays a crucial role.

In order to help analysing IM-promoted communication forms between the participants in interaction, it may be helpful to consider some recent linguistic studies on dialogue interpreting (Davidson, 2000/2001/2002, Bolden, 2000, Mason, 1999/2001, Wadensjö, 1998), which propose a brand new approach about the role of the interpreter in intercultural exchanges, using conversation analysis. These studies focus on the interpreter in multicultural contexts, and provide precious instruments to observe the role of the intercultural mediator in Italian contexts.

Dialogue interpreting studies originated from empirical analyses inspired by applied linguistics, and developed around collections and transcriptions of mediated conversations. They clarify that IM can be seen as a special kind of interaction defined as "interpreter-mediated" (Wadensjö, 1998).

Against this backdrop, IM is a communication form used in interactions between speakers of different languages, presenting different cultural orientations, particularly interactions between migrants belonging to ethnic minorities and providers working for legal institutions, public administration bodies, healthcare services, information and support centres, etc.

Specifically, IM is considered as a triadic interaction (Mason, 1999/2001, Wadensjö, 1998) involving two primary participants (service provider and service user) and a third one (the mediator), who has to allow the user to access the service by translating from the user's language to the agent's language, making both aware of each other's differences, and who also allowing the provider to provide the user with the service requested.

The interpreter's actions, therefore, are fundamental for the result of the interaction: the interpreter, being the only participant who can be fully aware of the linguistic elements of the interaction, has a strong influence on the communicative processes. According to Wadensjö (1998: 15) the most important function of the interpreter-mediator is not simply the faithful translation of what the participants say, but has to do with the promotion of a shared knowledge and with coordination. The interpreter-mediator is the only participant of the interaction able to understand everything that the others say, therefore the interpreter can define the context of the encounter, draw attention on the production of shared topics, and manage misunderstanding. According to Davidson (2000/2002), in healthcare settings, the interpreter can act as a gatekeeper, i.e. a pre-filter that evaluates the importance of the patient's contributions before translating them. In other words, the interpreter is not a "linguistic parrot", but an independent agent, responsible of an unbalanced flow of information and medical evaluations. In fact, the interpreter is involved in a preliminary diagnostic process. In this respect, we can see the mediator as an active participant and evaluate the effects that her/his action determines on the orientation of the communication. To simplify, in intercultural terms we can hypothesise that through translation and coordination activities the mediator builds intercultural communications, promoting the active participation of the people involved in the interaction, while at the same time gatekeeping, i.e. acting as a filter in the information flow and promoting a separation of perspectives. Indeed, translation, differently from gatekeeping, should guarantee participants' guarantees theaccess to the information that is one of the basic requirements of dialogue.

In order to demonstrate the empirical value of the methodological premises mentioned so far, the next sections will introduce some sequences of mediated conversations that have been tape-recorded and transcribed.

The analysis of this conversations will be the basis of the observation of communication in IM. Specifically, the next few sections will focus on the analysis of the mediator's actions promoting dialogues, allowing participants' expression and influence on perspective separation. The analysis is not aimed to be exact and to show the systematic functioning of IM actions, but is nevertheless a valuable instrument to show which kind of communicative processes can emerge from the mediator's actions.

Case analysis

The following collection of data is the result of a project called "Interlinguistic and intercultural communication: analysis of translation as a form of mediation for the bilingual dialogue between foreign citizens and institutions", promoted by the University of Modena and Reggio Emilia. In particular we will analyse:

a) forms of communication promoted by IM;

b) linguistic aspects of IM communication and consequences (be they explicit or not) characterizing the relationship between the participants involved in the communication.

Our analysis is based on 55 conversations in Arabic and Italian in two public healthcare services in Emilia Romagna: the *Centro per la salute delle famiglie straniere* (Healthcare support centre for foreign families) in Reggio Emilia and the *Consultorio* (Local centre for low-cost health and social services) in Vignola (Modena). All conversations have been tape-recorded and transcribed according to conversation analytical conventions, reporting in italic the bits in Arabic. The conversations involve at least one Italian provider of the institution (doctors, gynaecologists, obstetricians) (D), an Arabic-speaking mediator (M) and an Arabic-speaking patient (P). These analysis of the recorded conversations concentrate on the communicative processes emerging when a mediator is present, and can be intended as an evaluation of IM processes in the contexts under examination. An English translation of the Italian original is also provided.

Medical encounters in intercultural settings: a socially organized activity

Patients visit doctors for a variety of medical issues, including acute problems (e.g. injuries, infections, etc.), chronic diseases (e.g. high blood pressure, depression, etc.), and general physical examinations. The object of our analysis consists of medical encounters in Italian general hospitals with the presence of an interlinguistic intercultural mediator (IIM).

Although medical interviews represent a basic resource for doctors to formulate diagnosis and treatment (Mishler, 1984), very frequently migrant patients encounter severe difficulties in presenting their case history, concerns and worry. In the course of this article, it will be possible to see that such difficulties are not always overcome through the intervention of IIM. Beyond the institutional purposes of interlinguistic intercultural mediation, we will discuss in which ways doctors' and IIM's actions may promote or discourage patients' participation in medical encounters

Previous research suggests that medical encounters are an institutionalized project of phased activities (i.e., opening, problem presentation, information gathering, diagnosis, treatment, closing), to which doctors and patients orient (Robinson, 2003, Robinson & Heritage, 2005). Research has showed that medical encounters have internal social and interactional organizations (Robinson, 1998; Stivers, 2002), but few studies account for medical encounters in intercultural settings involving an IIM, at least in the Italian context (Baraldi, 2006a, Amato and Gavioli, 2008, Baraldi and Gavioli, 2008).

In this article, we analyze in which ways specific actions-in-interaction by doctors and mediators may empower or inhibit migrant patients' participation in medical encounters. Specifically, we highlight the relevance of a specific conversational resource, namely formulation, showing how this may be either inclusive, promoting patient's active participation, or exclusive, cutting out the patient from relevant pieces of healthcare information. Our research shows that the relevance of the patient's voice in medical encounters largely depends on the forms formulation used by the mediator. According to Heritage (1985: 100), formulation is an interactional moves "summarising, glossing, or developing the gist of an informant's earlier statement". Formulations project a direction for subsequent turns by inviting responses insofar as they "advance the prior report by finding a point in the prior utterance and thus shifting its focus, redeveloping its gist, making something explicit that was previously implicit in the prior utterance, or by making inference about its presuppositions or implications" (Heritage, 1985: 104).

The inhibition of patients' active participation in medical encounters

Doctors' proxies and adversative responses

Doctors' actions that reduce patients' participation in medical encounters are forms of proxies and adversative responses produced in Italian. We use the term proxy to refer to a course of action-in-interaction whereby healthcare providers request the mediator to explain routine medical procedures to the patient. By doing this, doctors avoid directly addressing patients, excluding them from active participation in the interaction, and inhibiting them from asking questions or expressing concerns.

In excerpt CO20 below, the doctor asks the mediator to explain to the patient the sequence of ultrasounds examinations she has to undergo during her pregnancy. The mediator aligns with the doctor's request (turns 216 and 218), starting a dyadic sequence involving the patient but not the doctor.

By giving a proxy to the mediator, asking her to play the role of medical expert firsthand, the doctor brings about a dyadic mono-linguistic sequence between the mediator, who explains medical procedures, and the patient, who accepts the mediator's explanations, marking her understanding through either backchannels such as "Ah" and "Yes" (turns 220, 222, 224, and 226). The doctor's self-exclusion, enhanced by the mediator's alignment, has relevant consequences on doctor-patient relationship. In excerpt CO20 it is the mediator, not the doctor, who gives recommendation to the patients. In the frame of a dyadic form of interaction, in order to addres questions to the doctor, the patient should involve the doctor in the encounter, possibly threatening her negative face (Brown & Levinson, 1987), without the support of the mediator.

CO20

215 D: Allora adesso le dobbiamo spiegare le tre ecografie (..) allora la prima la facciamo il primo trimestre la seconda è la più importante però si vedono solo le cose fisiche=
Now we have to explain her the three ultrasounds (..) so the first one will be the first quarter the second one is the most important but you see just physical stuff=

216 M: Sì
Yes

217 D: =La terza che vediamo quanto è cresciuto
=*The third one we see how he grows*

218 M: Ok

219 M: بتقلك هلىء احنة خلال الحمل (..) في ايطاليا بنعمل تلات تلفزات (..) التلفزة
نقول zالاولى اللي بتنعمل
في الشهر الثاني الشهر الثالت تقريبا اللي تثبت انو موجود الحمل والطفل
داخل الرحم وكلشي مزيان (.)
التلفزة الثانية اللي بتنعمل تقريبا في الشهر الخامس او بين الرابع
والخامس هاذي تبين انو الطفل كامل
الاعضاء

She's telling you with regard to the pregnancy (..) in Italy we make three ultrasounds (..) the first around the second or third month we may say we check pregnancy and if the foetus is in the right position and if everything's fine (.) the second one will be around the fifth—between the fourth and the fifth to see the baby is ok in all of his body parts

220 P: اه

Ah

221 M: ايديه ورجليه والراس والبطن والمعدة

Feet (.) hands and whatever

222 P: اه

Ah

223 M: يعني كل حاجة موجودة في الجسم

If everything's in its own place

224 P: ايوة

Yes

225 M: والتلفزة الاخرى اللي على الشهر نقول بين السابع واخر السابع واول الثامن تقريباالكتر حد

The third one will be (.) between the (.) beginning of the seventh and the eight at the latest-

226 P: اه

Yes

Reduced renditions and the role of mediator as responder

Besides doctor's proxies, also mediator's actions may inhibit patient's active participation in the medical encounter. In our data, the mediator may inhibit patient's participation either 1) acting as the principal patient's interlocutor, substituting the doctor or, 2) producing reduced renditions or zero renditions of patient's and doctor's turns of talk, leaving out some of their contents from the translation.

Excerpt CS13 is a noticeable instance of zero rendition. The patient, who suffers from insomnia, begins turn 51 with a pre-sequence ("I will tell"), which informs his interlocutors that in the next turn of talk he will start a story, that is a multi-turn unit (Schegloff, 1980). After a pre-sequence the next relevant action is to either accept or refuse the role of story recipient. In excerpt CS13, the mediator encourages the patient's narration through a short turn working as a continuer ("Eh", cf. Schegloff, 1982), indicating that she has understood that the patient is starting a narration in the next turn, and accepting to play the role of story recipient in the following turns.

In turn 53, the patient is in the sequential position where starting a narration about his health problem is a relevant action. The narration takes the form of troubles-talk (Jefferson & Lee, 1981; Jefferson, 1988), emphasising the troubles that insomnia produces in his everyday life, rather than providing the healthcare provider with doctorable symptoms (Heritage, 2008), i.e. medically relevant pieces of information.

At the first transition relevant point, when the patient has produced a first meaninguful turn of talk *("I can't sleep I go back and forth to the balcony")* has been said, the mediator as a story-recipient is expected to take the turn of talk. In fact different options are available for her: she may translate the prior turn to the doctor, she may solicit the continuation of troubles-talk by providing another continuer, she may request clarifications to the patient, she may treat the troubles-talk humorously, and so on. However, she drops the narration producing a zero-rendition (Wadensjö, 1998) turn, i.e. not translating the first part of the trouble-talk. The subsequent course of action shows that the zero rendition is not relevant. Specifically, the long stretch of silence after the transition relevant point (3.0 seconds) shows that the patient holds his right to continue the trouble-talk, as he is leaving room for a mediator's contribution of some kind. After some seconds of silence, the doctor progresses in the interaction, entering the next phase of the medical encounter, i.e. the treatment phases. The patient is now expected to listen to doctor's instructions- He may ask clarifications but the opportunity to express his own personal feelings about his disease, has gone.

CS13

42 D: Ascolta vuoi che ti diamo qualcosina per riposare alla notte (.)
Sempre (.) indipendentemente dal lavoro e non lavoro?
Listen do you want we give you something to sleep at night (.)
Either if you have to work or not?

43 M: بتقولك (.) تحب نديك حاجة , نديك دوة حاجة تنام بيها بالليل , تعبان مش
تعبان (.) تنومك بالليل والة ؟
He says (.) do you want we give you something to sleep at night? Tired or not helps you at night or-?

44 D: una compressina?
a little tablet?

45 M: -عشان تنام بالليل حاجة [
[something to sleep at night or-

46 D((to the nurse)): [Dammi del
[Gimmie some

47 P: يا ريت
I wish

48 M: Sì (.) sì (.) magari dice
Yes (.) yes (.) I wish, he said

49 D: Eh?
Eh?

50 M: I wish
magari

51 P: -اقول
I will tell—

52 M: ـــاه
Eh -

53 P: ـــالحاجة دي عملالي زهق في حياتي , لما مبنام اروح للبالكونة وارجع
I can't sleep I go back and forth to the balcony - (3.0)

54 D: Allora lui viene mercoledì pomeriggio alle 2/2.30 che gli facciamo il prelievo (…) poi per l'Aids così abbiamo fatto tutto, eh?
So he comes Wednesday afternoon at 2/2.30 and we take the blood sample (…) then everything will be done about Hiv, eh?

Another class of actions which weaken the patient's voice, limiting her/his capability to create a direct connection with the doctor, are those related to the mediator playing the role of responder, giving directly to the patient the information s/he requested to the doctor, and avoiding the involvement of the doctor in the interaction.

For instance, in excerpt CS5 the patient produces two questions (turns 24 and 26) asking about the possibility to obtain the drugs recommended by the doctor directly in the doctor's office. Instead of translating the patient's questions to the doctor, the mediator responds directly, thus hindering patient-doctor communication.

CS5

22 D: Allora signora (.) possiamo provare a dare (..) del Fastum gel in pomata (.) che però se lo deve comprare perché non ce l'abbiamo (.) due volte al giorno
So madam (.) we can try (..) Fastum gel ointment (.) but she has to buy it herself because we don't have it (.) twice a day

23 M: فهمتني"الفارماجيا" تعمليها, لما تشتريها من "بوماتا"بتعطيك).(
She gives you (.) ointment you put it (.) buy it at the pharmacy

24 P: ما بتعطينيها؟
Does she give it to me?

25 M: خاطر مش موجودة عندهم هنا فهمتني
They do not have it

26 P: ما بدها تعطينيها؟
Doesn't she want to give it to me?

27 M: معندهمش, معندهمش مش مشكل ايه..)تبتسم(كيف لو عندهم بيعطوك همة بنفسهم
يعني)..(مش غالي
غالية فمتيهو مفيهوش حاجة
That's not the issue ((smiling)) they don't have it (..) really don't have it

The mediator's formulation (turn 23) is a reduced rendition of the doctor's contribution in the prior turn, which leaves out the information regarding the drug not being available at the doctor's office. The mediator's reduced rendition ("she gives you the ointment") creates the conditions for a misunderstanding between the mediator herself, who uses "give" as a synonym of "prescribe", and the patient, who understands the verb in its literal sense.

Consequently to her interpretation of the verb "give", the patient is uncertain about the doctor's intentions. Is the doctor about to give her the drug? Does she have to buy it at the pharmacy? In order to solve this problem of understanding, she initiates a repair sequence in turn 24 ("Does she give it me?"). The repair sequence is completed by the mediator, who responds to the patient without translating the request to the doctor ("They do not have it", turn 25). Acting as responder, the mediator keeps the two parties distant, making the creation of a common ground between the doctor and the patient very unlikelydoctor. In this way, the risk of patient's disaffiliation becomes concrete. The patient's reiteration of the question in a different format (turn 26) is an evidence of dissatisfaction with the mediator's response. Again, the mediator does not translate the question to the doctor but provides a direct response (turn 27) and, again, s/he increases the distance between the two parties.

The promotion of active participation in the medical encounter

Our data make it possible to appreciate that doctors' and mediators' actions may also encourage patients' self-expression, giving voice to their concerns, doubts, needs and requests, thus promoting their active involvement in the medical encounter.

According to our data, doctors' actions promoting patients' active participation are not very common, essentially because their need for linguistic mediation limits their opportunity to communicate directly with the patients. In some instances, however, doctors may encourage patients' active participation in the medical encounter addressing them directly.

Our data provide evidence that mediators' promotional actions are more common than doctors'. Mediators may promote patients' active participation through different interactional practices, depending on the nature of the interaction, i.e. either dyadic (patient-mediator) or triadic (patient-mediator-doctor). Within dyadic interactions, promotional intentions are mainly realized through backchannelling (Schegloff, 1982, Schriffin, 1999), when the mediator uses short conversational markers or echoing to manifest attentiveness and involvement in patients' contributions.

The main difference between dyadic and triadic interactions consists in the way in which the doctor re-enters doctorinteraction, which in its turn depends on the mediator's actions. The conversational resources whereby mediators may involve doctors in patients's troubles, making them aware of patients' emotional stances, are affective formulations of patients' contribution. By producing affective formulations, mediators introduce to doctors both patients' current symptoms (Robinson and Heritage, 2005), and patients' emotions, doubts and concerns. Affective formulations highlight both informative and emotional contents of patients' turns. In this way, doctors are made aware of patients' concerns, and patients assume a local identity that goes beyond the generalized social role of the sick.

Feedback and formulations re-including the doctor in the interaction

In dyadic sequences, the mediator may promote patient's self-expression through conversational resources such as feedback tokens, continuers and echoing, expressing attentiveness and understanding of prior patient's turns. In excerpt CO1, the mediator expresses her attentiveness and understanding through feedback tokens ("Ah", "mmh", "Ah I understand you"). In turns 122, the mediator encourages the patient to express her concerns, making her participation relevant to the medical encounter, as a person with specific needs and worries rather than a generic sick required to play the role of current symptoms provider. The reiteration of affective and promotional actions encourages the patient to express her doubts about the therapy, promoting her partecipation in the medical encounter. Being empowered as an active participant, the patient is confident enough to finally advance a request for clarification (turn 123).

CO1

113 P: النمرة بتاع المحمول بتاعك بتكتبيلياها
Your phone number, can you write it for me?
114 M: اه
Eh
115 P: وعطوني شي حاجة ورقة مشان الفحص

(I had to say) I received the paper ((the invitation)) for an examination -

116 M: اه (.) اه
Ah (.) ah

117 P: كل ثلاث سنوات ادوز فحص للرحم
I pass the examination for the uterus every three years

118 M: اه
Mmh

119 P: جتني الورقة وما بغيت نمشي لان لازم نفهمهم اني عملت العملية
I received the paper and I don't want to go, because I would have to explain I put the coil

120 M: اه (.) فهمت عليكي
A:h (.) I understand you

121 P: كنت استنى اسال
I was waiting to ask it

122 M: خفتي انك تيجي وتكوني-
You were afraid to come and being -

123 P: الاحسن انو يعطوني ورقة اه انو يقلبوني ويحركو المكينة والة شي حاجة (..) فمن ويقولو اني عملت
العملية (.) بس انو يعني يقلبوني
Yes that they examine me and move the coil or whatever (..) so it's better if you give me a paper saying I made the operation (.) so they examine me (.) because they examine the uterus

In triadic conversations where patients' active participation in the medical encounter is promoted, doctors are made aware of patients' emotions through mediator's formulations. Mediator's formulations consist of translations which follow patient-mediator dyadic sequences, adapting their contents for the benefit of doctors. Through formulations, mediators build, expand, and recreate the meanings of prior dyadic sequences according to presuppositions and orientations for which they are responsible. Formulations are not word-for-word translations of contributions in prior dyadic sequences, but they rely on mediators' discursive initiative and willingness to create a common emotional ground between patients and doctors. In this way the mediator acts as a coordinator of the medical encounter.

Specifically, formulations are conversational resources available to the mediator in order to: a) provide a translation which highlights some contents of prior sequences of turns; b) make what is thought to be implicit or not clear in the prior urns of talk explicit; c) propose inferences about presuppositions or implications of participants' contributions (Baraldi & Gavioli, 2008). Formulations are "informational" when they elicit explanations from doctors, which patients are somehow inhibited from requesting, and are "affective" when they bring in patients' emotions, doubts and concerns into the medical encounter.

Excerpt CO23 below offers an instance of informational formulation. In the course of the examination of a pregnant woman, it comes out that the foetus is not yet in the appropriate cephalic position. In turn 59 the doctor reassures the patient about this issue, and in turn 60, the mediator offers reassurance and further suggestions to the patient. The doctor is re-involved in the interaction in turn 63, through an informational formulation which is introduced by the mediator to obtain therapeutic recommendations for the patient's benefit. In CO23, the informational formulation is an initiative motivated by the mediator's interpretation of the patient's stance as refraining from uttering a request for recommendations.

59	D:	((sorridendo)) Ma dai che si gira! *((smiling)) come on, he will turn!*
60	M:	ـــتحركي وتمشي وان شاء الله *Exercise and take long walks and God willing -*
61	P:	ـــوان تحركت ومشيت *If I exercise and take long walks-*
62	M:	بيساعد *It would help -*
63	M:	C'è qualche cosa particolare che aiuta a girare? (..) camminare (..) fare delle – *Is there something that helps to turn (..) walking (..) do some -*
64	D:	No *No*
65	M:	Della ginnastica particolare delle cose? *Exercises of some kind whatever?*
66	D:	No (.) he will turn by himself *No (.) si gira da solo*
67	M:	بتقلك هاي شغلة ما فينا نقول انك تعملي مشي او تتحركي او تلعبي رياضة بيعي هوة من راسو هاي ط بدو يدور بدور ما بدو يدور بيظلو قاعد هيك *He says that in this case we cannot say it is useful (.) walking or exercising or making specific movements, it will happen spontaneously, he will turn by himself or will stay like this*

Affective formulations are discursive initiatives taken by the mediator to give voice to patients' emotions, which in most cases manifest themselves as worries and concerns. In excerpt CO1 below, the patient reports a delay in her menstrual period, but mitigates the relevance of this information by assuming she will get her period within the following few days. The mediator's formulation in turn 65 ("she's a bit worried") is affective because, while making current symptoms available to the doctor, highlights the patient's emotional stance, which could have gone unnoticed by the doctor in prior turns.

CO1

55 M: *(...) When you had your period last?*
56 P: جتني تلاتعش من شهر عشرة
It was the thirteen in the month of october
57 M: تلاتعش عشرة؟
Thirteen october?
58 P: اي
Yes
59 M: L'ultima mestruazione è il 13 (..) ottobre
The latest menstrual period is the thirteen (..) october
60 D: Mmh
Mmh
61 M: Ora siamo al 13 novembre
Now it's November thirteen
62 P: شهر لليومكانت تهبط علي كل شهر نيشة (.) الدم ما هبط صار
It comes each month exactly, now it's a month that it's not coming (.) a month today
63 M: اه
Mmh
64 P: استنى تلات ايام والة اربع ايام بش مش عارفة اذا تجي
I will wait three days or four, maybe it will come
65 M(to D):Ah (.) può darsi che tra 4 o 5 giorni al massimo (.) arriva (..) però (..) lei è un po'preoccupata
Ah (.) maybe in four or five days at latest (.) it will come (..) however (..) she's a bit worried

By affectively formulating the patient's emotions, the mediator brings to the fore patient's emotions, which have remained implicit up to that moment, making them a topic for communication and a concern for the doctor.

The affective formulation offers the doctor the ability to tune in with the emotional status of the patient, reassuring her in case she needs it. Affective formulations are inclusive because, while highlighting the emotions of the patient, they involve the doctor in the making of local affective relations.

Conclusions

Moving from the assuption that Italian studies on intercultural mediation, though producing a fair amount of information on this practice, have not yet designed a methodology for the evaluation of mediation practices, this paper aimed at proposing and applying a new methodological approach for an empirical observation of IM.

Most studies on mediation in the healthcare system have pointed out that migrants, consequently to their status of newcomers in a foreign country often experiencing severe economic conditions, may find themselves in a disadvantaged position with regard to access to healthcare services. From this perspective, the main goal of mediation is to facilitate access to and use of public services, as a premise to the integration of migrants in the new society.

From our point of view, the functions of IM can be empirically looked at starting from the observation of the communication forms that take place in public services. In this article we have highlighted the way in which different classes of actions-in-interaction by doctors and mediators may promote or inhibit migrant patients' participation in medical encounters.

Specifically, dyads between mediators and patients may be useful for mediators to explore patients' health conditions and emotional status. In order to re-involve doctors in the interaction, when relevant health and emotional statuses emerge in the course of dyadic sequences, it is necessary for mediators to make use of a specific conversational resource, namely formulation. Formulations may be inclusive, when they bring to the fore patients' voices, promoting patients' active participation in the medical encounter. On the contrary, zero or reduced renditions may exclude the patient from relevant pieces of healthcare information. Thus, the possibility that patients' voices become relevant in medical encounters largely depends on mediators' actions. By translating patients' turns of talk, including in the formulations their interpretation of implicit contents, primarily emotions, mediators may improve attentiveness and emotional ties between patients and doctors, taking the medical encounter well beyond a mere exchange between standardized role performances. Through an emotion-sensitive translation, interlingustic and intercultural mediation makes it possible for doctors to access doctorthe many facets of patients' specificity, at both personal and cultural level.

References

ALUFFI PENTINI, A. (Ed.) (2004) *La mediazione interculturale. Dalla biografia alla professione.* Milano, Angeli.

AMATO, A. & GAVIOLI, L. (2008) Il ruolo dell'interprete-mediatore nella comunicazione istituzionale medico-paziente: un'analisi dei contributi traduttivi. IN BOSISIO, C., CAMBIAGHI, B., PIEMONTESE, M.E. & SANTULLI, E F. (Eds.) *Atti del 7° Congresso dell'Associazione Italiana di Linguistica Applicata. Aspetti linguistici della comunicazione pubblica e istituzionale,* 293-319.

ANDOLFI, M. (Ed.) (2003) *La mediazione culturale. Tra l'estraneo e il familiare*. Milano, Angeli.

APFELBAUM, B. (2007) Conversational dynamics as an instructional resource in interpreter-mediated technical settings. IN WADENSJÖ, C., ENGLUND, B., DIMITROVA, A.L. & NILSSON (Eds.) *The Critical Link 4, 53-64.* Amsterdam, John Benjamins.

BARALDI, C. (2006a) L'accettazione della diversità nella mediazione interlinguistica ed interculturale. IN BANFI, E., GAVIOLI, L., GUARDIANO, C. & VEDOVELLI, E M. (Eds.) *La mediazione interlinguistica e interculturale, atti del V congresso di studi dell'associazione italiana di linguistica applicata.*

BARALDI, C. (2006b) Diversity and adaptation in intercultural mediation. IN BUSCH, D. (Ed.) *Interkulturelle Mediation. Eine theoretische Grundlegung triadischer Konfliktbearbeitung in interkulturell bedingten Kontexten.* Frankfurt, Peter Lang.

BARALDI, C. (2006c) Comunicazione interculturale e analisi sociologica: come e perché? *Studi di sociologia, Università Cattolica del Sacro Cuore Milano,* XLIV (2), 241-265.

BARALDI, C., AND GAVIOLI, L. (2007) Dialogue interpreting as intercultural mediation. An analysis in healthcare multicultural settings. IN GREIN, M. & WEIGAND, E. (Eds) *Dialogue and Culture,* 155-175. Amsterdam: John Benjamins.

BARALDI, C. GAVIOLI, L. (2008) Cultural presuppositions and re-contextualisation of medical systems in interpreter-mediated interactions. *Curare. Journal of Medical Anthropology.* 31 (2-3), 193-203.

BELPIEDE, A. (Ed.) (2002) Mediazione culturale. *Esperienze e percorsi formativi.* Torino, UTET.

BOLDEN, G. B. (2000) Toward understanding practices of medical interpreting: interpreters' involvement in history taking. *Discourse Studies*, 4,2, 387-419.

BROWN, P., LEVINSON, S. (1987) *Politeness: Some Universals in Language Usage*, Cambridge, Cambridge University Press.

CASTIGLIONI, M. (1997), *La mediazione linguistico-culturale. Principi, strategie, esperienze*, Milano, Angeli.

CECCATELLI GURRIERI, C. (2003) *Mediare culture. Nuove professioni tra comunicazione e interven,.* Roma, Carocci.

COLOMBO, E. (2002) *Le società multicultural,.* Roma, Carocci.

DAVIDSON, B. (2000) The interpreter as institutional gatekeeper: the social-linguistic role of interpreters in Spanish-English medical discourse. *Journal of Sociolinguistics*, 4(3), 379-405.

DAVIDSON, B. (2001) Questions in cross-linguistic medical encounters: the role of the hospital interpreter. *Anthropological Quarterly*, 74(4), 170-178.

DAVIDSON, B. (2002) A model for the construction of conversational common ground in interpreted discourse. *Journal of Pragmatics*, (34), 1273-1300.

FAVARO, G. (2001) *I mediatori linguistici e culturali nella scuola*, Bologna, EMI.

FAVARO, G. & FUMAGALLI, M. (2004) *Capirsi diversi.* Roma, Carocci.

FIORUCCI, M. (2000) *La mediazione cultural.* Roma, Armando.

HERITAGE, J. (1985) Analysing News Interviews: Aspects of the Production of Talk for an Overhearing Audience. IN VAN DIJK, T. (Ed.) *Handbook of Discourse Analysis, Vol. 3. Discourse and Dialogue,* 95-117,. London, Academic Press.

HERITAGE, J. (2008) *Negotiating the legitimacy of medical problems: A multi-phase concern for patients and physicians.* http://www.sscnet.ucla.edu/soc/faculty/heritage/publications/MEDICAL_LEGITIMACY.pdf

JEFFERSON, G. (1988) On the sequential organization of troubles talk in ordinary conversation. *Social Problems,* 35, 418-41.

JEFFERSON, G. & LEE, J.R.E. (1981) The rejection of advice: managing the problematic convergence of a "TroublesTelling" and a "Service Encounter". *Journal of Pragmatics,* 5, 399-422.

JOHNSON, P. & NIGRIS, E. (2000) *Le figure della mediazione culturale in contesti educativi.* IN: NIGRIS, E. (Ed.) *Educazione interculturale.* Milano, Bruno Mondatori.

KYMLICKA, W. (1995) *La cittadinanza multiculturale.* Bologna, Il Mulino.

MASON, I. (Ed.) (1999) *Dialogue Interpreting. The Translator special issue,* 5(2).

MASON, I. (Ed.) (2001) *Triadic exchanges. Studies in dialogue interpreting,* Manchester, St. Jerome.

MELOTTI, U. (2004) *Migrazioni internazionali,* Bruno Mondatori, Milano.

MERLINI, R., FAVARON, R. (2007). Examining the "voice of interpreting" in speech pathology. IN PÖCHHACKER, F. & SHLESINGER, M. (Eds.), *Healthcare Interpreting,*101-137. Amsterdam, John Benjamins.

MISHLER, E. G. (1984) *The discourse of medicine: dialectics of medical interviews,* Norwood, Ablex.

MOERMAN, M. (1987) *Talking Culture. Ethnography and Conversation Analysis,* Philadelphia, University of Pennsylvania Press

ROBINSON, J.D. (1998) Getting down to business: talk, gaze, and body orientation during openings of doctor–patient consultations. *Human Communication Research,* 25(1), 97–123.

ROBINSON, J.D. (2003) An interactional structure of medical activities during acute visits and its implications for patients' participation. *Health Communication,* 15, 27–57.

ROBINSON, J.D. & HERITAGE, J. (2005). The structure of patients'presenting concerns: the completion relevance of current symptoms. *Social Science & Medicine,* 61, 481–493.

STIVERS, T. (2002) "Symptoms only" and "Candidate diagnoses": Presenting the problem in pediatric encounters. *Health Communication,* 14(3), 299-338.

SCHEGLOFF, E.A. (1982) Discourse as an Interactional Achievement: Some Uses of "uh huh" and Other Things That Come Between Sentences in Georgetown University. IN TANNEN, D. (Ed.) *Roundtable on Languages and Linguistics l98l. Analyzing Discourse: Text and Talk,* 71-93. Washington DC, Georgetown University Press.

SCHEGLOFF, E.A. (1980) Preliminaries to Preliminaries: "Can I ask you a question". *Sociological Inquiry,* 50(3-4), 104-152.

SCHIFFRIN, D. (1999). "Oh" as a Marker of Information Management. IN JAWORSKI, A. & COUPLAND, N. (Eds.) *The Discourse Reader,* 275–288. London-New York, Routledge.
WADENSJÖ, C. (1998) *Interpreting as interaction*, London, Longman.
ZANFRINI L. (2004) *Sociologia delle migrazioni*, Roma/Bari, Laterza.

National Unity and Cultural Diversity in Conflict Resolution: Capacity Building for Sustainable Peace and Reconciliation in Namibia

Angela Mickley

This article examines the intercultural adaptability and growth potential of a German capacity building project in Namibia conducted between 2003 and 2007 and describes first impressions and exemplary instances from different workshops.

The leading question of how a model of Conflict Resolution and Mediation competence and operative availability could be initiated in a country and implemented sustainably into the socio-political systems developed out of a long-standing dilemma in political science and peace politics. Macro-political peace making is slowly beginning to use the systemic and holistic approaches from social and psychological sciences to resolve crisis and conflict. The necessity to include attitude, behavior and cultural context of people and groups in evolving conflicts, is recognized within approaches on a micro- and meso-level of society, but not on the macro-political level of decision-making. This has led to peace agreements failing as substantial top level initiatives were not communicated to and supported from the relevant actors in the conflicting societies.

Outside the present complexities of German-Namibian relations with the memory of colonial atrocities and the disputed focus of development aid in an unresolved balance, the possibility and scope of an intercultural mediation expert initiative in a country in political and social transformation with recently acquired independence was the focus of the planned action research.

The project process, contents and focus were developed in several steps with Namibian partners, who had previously identified the need for training and capacity building and voiced interest in participating and shaping it.

The aims identified were multiple and in an initial phase of carving out a precise profile, it made sense to first clarify and address the different needs and interests of the social, cultural and political groups and institutions involved and then proceed into defining their common aims.

The people contacted in the initial research were key actors from the Namibian economic, religious and political sector, the first interviews were conducted in February and March 2003 in Windhoek, further talks and app. 20 Conflict Resolution and Mediation workshops in 2004-2007.

The interviews combined open, narrative and guided elements and focused on biographical and political aspects within the last few decades of suppression, resistance and eventual change to independence and autonomy. They always started with introductions of the people present and their professional position, explanations of the personal and academic interest in Namibia and perspectives and experiences with conflict and methods of resolution.

Very often it was possible to relate to personal experiences in Namibian history or more recent events of the interview-partner and compare these to Germany's history of separation and recent re-unification with a plethora of few constructive and a multitude of destructive examples of managing a fundamental socio-political change in a country.

After these preliminaries the counterparts discussed their country's situation very openly and pointed to some of the acute deficits and problems in society and politics, while at the same time reflecting on successful remedies that had been applied already or could be envisioned.

The dynamic and direction of the talk often took the shape of an inward moving spiral, in that they touched quite a few issues of only relative importance before progressing to difficult or controversial subjects.

The following gives a shortened version of the groups' interests and ideas which became clearer in the course of the discussions:

Previously disadvantaged members of the population / Young managers of different Namibian cultures in economic companies:

- gain additional competence in negotiation skills, ethics and value systems, political concepts and activities, decision-making processes,
- wider vocational basis to their usual "on the job" training in the factory, further education in various areas to make up for knowledge and competence deficits from exile or independence struggle.

Commercial farmers:

- saw an urgent need to widen competence in negotiation and advocacy to improve cooperation with trade unions when trying to establish consensual and sustainable co-management systems with agricultural workers who are seen as potential landowners in the country's future.

Members and clergy of church community:

- identified the need to develop competence in facilitating open fora and dialogue meetings with victims of apartheid and SWAPO internal violence before independence and
- initiate voluntary conflict resolution (victim-offender-mediation) and reconciliation processes with surviving victims and perpetrators to deal with growing pressure from survivors and victims' families.

Judiciary/Ombudsman's Office:

The Ombudsman's Office had been created as an independent institution directly answerable to the President, following the Scandinavian model of providing citizens with an institutionalized address for their complaints against the state or its agents. This seemed a necessary precaution for unrest after the political change to an independent Namibia. It was one of several measures of the newly elected majority government aiming at providing visible channels of communication for the expected complaints.

The Ombudsman was particularly interested in enabling the Office's Directors and Investigators to fill the gap between standard judicial help and adequate social measures of restitution or reconciliation. Mediation he saw as providing this.

- Train directors and investigators of the Office in mediation to provide them with additional competence "between their legal and their human compassionate abilities."
- Provide members of Special Field Forces, mainly recruited from combatants in the independence struggle, with basic communication-, deescalation-, gender- and police- training to give their frequently controversial interventions a civil, i.e. non-violent character, and thereby reduce the Ombudsman's Office's load of citizens' complaints against state institutions. This wish was seen as not only a necessary improvement of the behaviour of official agents of the administration, but also in connection with the general policy of gaining acceptance for the institutions of the new independent state in all cultures of the country.
- The Ombudswoman Bience Gawanas[1] in 2003 had thought it particularly important for state agents to show an entirely different behaviour towards the citizens than the agents of the suppressive South African Apartheid administration. She regarded it as an essential contribution to the growth of general civic conscience the new state was trying to develop and the sustainable stability and security of the new social and political system.

With these identified interests for capacity building and the initial exchange about possible methods that were seen as potentially helpful in the Namibian setting, a tentative project outline was sketched with the following steps:

1. Develop a capacity building concept together with Namibian partners in inter-active processes with target groups of:
    - different cultures,
    - identified conflict issues,
    - traumatic experiences,
    - years of exile,
    - need for reconciliation

1 Head of Social Commission in the African Union/ Addis Abbeba since 2004.

2. Involve key actors and decide on operative steps: Identify deficits and issues in individual, social and political areas in open interviews with key actors from cultural, economic and political life in Namibia, through highlighting personal observation and reflection, adding criteria from other countries in transformation, e.g. East-West Germany after re-unification, questions touched experiences, oberservations, problems deriving from colonial and apartheid times, exile, independence struggle and racial discrimination in South-West Africa.

3. Proceed from a) narrow identification of deficits and problem issues to b) possible ways of improving living conditions, c) build competence clusters in the country, to c) a wider approach of creative, cultural design of Namibian society.

4. Identify entry points and people in key positions to start design of training elements.

Within the project, the following theses guided the operative steps and follow-ups of workshops:

1. Assuming, from comparable phenomena, a similarity in conflict genesis and escalation between different cultures and political systems, it should be possible to use successful methods from other parts of the world in a democratic Namibia pursuing unity and diversity as national policies.

2. A basic requirement for the implementation of innovative methods is a critical openness towards external experts, on the experts' side it is an awareness of the country's needs and traditional structures and a personal and professional interest in the non-violent resolution of economic, political, cultural differences and conflicts. Given these factors, it should be possible to develop operational procedures for implementing Conflict Resolution competence in interactive cooperation of national key actors with foreign experts.

3. Using the authority of key actors on the macro-level of society, who have experienced the training and have tested the effectiveness of this approach, can then initiate a deliberate top-down growth in conflict resolution competence and sustainable transformation of a society.

Such a training of leaders and top-level civil servants can be the start of a pre-emptive capacity-building, i.e. the UN or other civil agencies receive the request and organise an external training intervention. A positive collateral effect of this training is creating the basis of a regional network. This seems preferable to waiting for an emergency situation which could generate a UN military mission.2

---

2 UNDP Conference on Zimbabwe Capacity Building Program, Windhoek, July 2005. Comparisons with Kenya, Zimbabwe and other countries and warnings of similar escalations that might develop into crisis have been cited frequently from political, academic and journalistic sources in Southern Africa.

The cultural, economic and political / judicial fields of Namibian society provide different settings for generating or experiencing structural or personal conflicts. In the next paragraph we will look at a typical situation in which key actors in a community learn, apply and reflect a mediative approach.

Triadic addressing of conflict (resolving) in community settings

Ex-combatants from SWAPO independence struggle take part in a three-day Mediation training with a mixed group of community workers, trauma experts, psychologists, secretary, volunteers (two Namibian, one German) in a Windhoek township.

The NGO team had expressed interest in widening their professional repertoire to include conflict analysis, resolution and mediation for all the staff and trauma or psychological experts to use as they see fit in their work with the community. As the information about helpful methods, processes and therapies is not generally available, they face a continuous difficulty in bringing together client and cure.

This touches a problem post-colonial Africa faces even more than Europe, i.e. the ability to make an informed decision in matters personal, social or political when individual knowledge of potential options is limited. The experts here face both a professional and a personal problem in knowing what might help the particular situation, but not feeling authorized to tell the potential client what to do. In the context of this Windhoek township with its many ex-combatants this can appear as or result in keeping necessary information from people who haven't had much chance of receiving formal education, having space for personal development and shaping participation in their society. This the NGO came to see as a danger in their professional reticence.

To support people in developing autonomous methods for dealing with problems in their life and surroundings, Mediation can provide the essential element by helping the conflict partners keep control of the contents of their solution while being guided through the process by an expert.

Alternatively, as information on and experience in methods and therapies is not generally available professionals could feel responsibility to provide these, without urging people into accepting a particular treatment.

An essential element of this NGO's concept is helping as much as necessary, but keeping a self-help option open parallel to the external support given and letting people in the community know that they are present and can be approached when needed. The NGO in their professional attitude deliberately refrains from trying to convince people to accept measures the professionals offer. They rather wait for potential clients to identify and voice their demand and then use the help given to address the particular deficit in the social or individual setting.

The incident described below put this attitude to the test of social reality in the township and opened a controversial debate on the basic attitude towards clients with a background of disadvantagement.

The political system has been changed, but the people haven't had much time to change their ingrained attitudes of resignation, submission or resistance. As political and social influences and challenges have for decades been hazardous and hostile to the majority population, resisting these has become a survival reflex. Now it is extremely difficult to turn around in perception, mind and emotion towards a creative shaping of their lives in natural or social environments.

Here we find a difference between the people who had to stay in the country and those who had to or managed to go into exile, indifferent of culture, status or sex. Most people in exile received formal education, experienced a variety of value systems and met people from very different parts of the world and backgrounds, e.g. East Germany, Soviet Union, Britain, USA, Scandinavia, African countries.

To feed the macro-political change into all layers of the social and economic system and the many individuals who have grown up with a totally different set of enforced discriminating values, requires a multi-level approach of formal and further educational systems.

Professional responsibility: Integrating mediation into traditional problem-solving procedures

Five months after the mediation training we conducted a follow up with most members of the group. This topic was brought up und debated with regard to the professional options possible while at the same time showing respect to the couple's individual and mutual decision-making process.

Shooting in a domestic violence incident occurred when the husband, an ex-combatant, lost his temper during a verbal and physical fight with his wife, and shot his gun into the roof of the shack. Neighbours called the police, who arrived quickly, arrested the man, removed the gun and advised him to use counselling and mediation to improve his personal behaviour in a dispute situation.

Surprisingly for everybody, the man accepted this, approached the local counseling office and arranged an appointment with the trauma therapist of the NGO. When after a first meeting the couple failed to turn up for the second one, the team discussed how to respond and concluded that outside another attempt at finding an appointment, anything further would be pushing the clients towards agreeing to a process they obviously had decided not to continue.

In trying to first identify existing criteria and then develop new ones for evaluating the past process we included elements like professional ethics, traditional African and tribal justice considerations and practices, other African and Western cultural values relevant in Namibia, and, of course, modern constitutional frameworks the independent Namibian state had adopted after 1990.

Here the different team members contributed their diverse backgrounds and assumptions to clarify the situation in question and develop wider options in dealing with it constructively and sustainably.

Their aims were the following

1. to help the couple find an understanding of the violent incident,
2. to foster / come to an agreement that enabled them to face their marital future with hope instead of fear,
3. to provide them with communication methods and practical use of their empathic abilities for having appropriate conflict styles at hand in a mutual problem situation they faced,
4. to accompany them in a process of considering their relationship and its role in their indivdual lives,
5. to enable them to look past their husband-wife-children circle into the wider family and community and peruse questions of present and future aspects of living there and then, in a country with its own specific possibilities, limitations and challenges
6. to organize help for future difficulties in themselves, wider family and community, trying to build a support network of instant and long-term assistance for early or low level stages of escalating conflict. The support part of this procedure is known from an Australian method close to mediation called Family Group Counseling.
7. to understand, on a biographical level, the learning steps they had already taken and identify the ones waiting to be taken „in their own good time" to use an Irish colloquialism, i.e., when they felt ready and able to face the particular problem in their own behaviour, attitude or context.

This included more and wider aspects of therapeutic consulting than just solving the immediate conflict or violent outbreak. It can be described as a taylor-made interactive process to help develop new options for problems the clients identify. On the intervening side this requires seeing a competence in the clients, activating and constructively using it to address the acute problem.

The various professions—psychologist, trauma therapist, social worker—and cultural traditions—Oshivambo, Nama, Afrikaans, German, South African English—in the team were often used as a complimentary resource for creative ways of helping in and outside the NGO framework. This took the form of comparing the experiences of members in similar cases, eliciting effective or successful elements and attributing them to the case in question with regard to abilities and wishes of the people concerned.

The specific conflict resolution aspects included referring to the gender- and age-related social position in the family or organisational hierarchy and the way a particular person was used as advice resource by members of the community or family. The team discussed and eventually concluded that they had a professional responsibility to make the process of mediation known to the couple and not to wait for them to take a decision.

Family case—Integrating Mediation with traditional approaches

In the following case mediation was used as an additional element in a traditional consensual process to work with a problem not covered by the hitherto available system of elders and family hierarchy. It did not go as far as coming into either traditional or new constitutional law, but was regarded as sufficiently severe within the wider family to consider other, non-traditional methods.

A member of a traditional family and community with a strong rural base and a few urban relatives experienced growing problems with his role as second or third brother in the sibling and family hierarchy. The advice younger brothers and cousins asked of him, he was happy to give, but noticed a frequent collision with his family's sense of hierarchical propriety. He was advised to adhere to the routine of father and elder brothers giving advice, not any of the younger siblings. This put him in a difficult position as his young relatives were very interested in city life and gadgets and loved using him as a link to flashy, fascinating urban life.

He tried to comply with these polarized demands and not offend his elders or disappoint the younger family, but find a way of doing justice to both.

Keeping Traditional Cultures alive—the Military

Mediation as a possible support for keeping the diverse cultures of the country alive became an unexpected issue while working with Namibian military leaders.

The ever-present issue of cultural diversity and the quality of the educational system arose to a heated debate in a University of Namibia seminar with military[3] when participants discussed their experiences in United Nations Peace Missions in African armed conflicts. On reconnaissance missions with mixed groups in Ethiopia/Eritrea they had noticed the advantage of using culturally accepted communication with locals, while being confronted with walls of silence when the non-African commanding officers attempted to force information giving.

---

3 while teaching in the Master of Arts in Strategy and Security Studies at the University of Namibia.

Unity and diversity being the proclaimed policy directive of the ruling party SWAPO and the Namibian Government, the academic and political discourse on defining these concepts often faces controversial attributions. In a country with different and often polarized cultures, the main aim of social actions is preserving the tribal cultures within a multi-cultural context and thereby to create sound cultural systems in an age of uncertainty. The idea to proclaim a new national language seemed a little hasty considering the history of suppression of the languages of the many tribes in the country. The traditional attitude of solidarity with the members of one's own tribe and culture seems to stand in the way of the aim of national unity with only English as the lingua franca.

The impression that it is an either-or decision for or against the traditional languages, reduces the Namibians' access to their inherited culture and thereby perpetuates suppressive elements of the colonial and apartheid powers. One essential indicator of a real change in official policy is seen to be the freedom to use one's own language in a respectful environment.

Access to knowledge and the ability to understand and evaluate its worth is at the core of all skills concerning critical thinking and decision-making, both collaborative and individual. Simple access to knowledge is a problem in developing countries, which lack a comprehensive system of education for both men and women (cf. Trotta Tuomi, 2004: 127).

They compared the Namibian language education in schools and universities after independence with other countries and criticized the mono-lingual focus on English while local and tribal languages were left out of the curriculum and not integrated as an appreciated basis of Namibian cultures.

When experimenting with the integral methods of the mediation process, like reframing, voicing the grievances all sides have towards the other participants/opponents, brainstorming ideas for restoration of the past and vision of the common future, negotiating the different interests with regard to the people's abilities and needs etc. it became apparant how useful this could be in a multicultural country like Namibia, much more appropriate than a majoritarian system of decision making.

We have seen the different possibilities of contextualization of mediation process, intervention and follow up, integration into existing traditional systems of resolving family, social, community or political problems that cannot be dealt with internally with the conflict participants.

Third party can take very different and even polarised roles, needs to continuously reflect on interactive process to elecit unconscious requests/ necessities/ wishes of conflict/problem owners. Too much method imposed on people and process can be overwhelming and can dissipate the original resources available to the constructively/openly discerting mind and perception.

What the interculturally working mediator needs is an unflinching willingness to cherish his/her assumption of competence in the clients or counterparts.

Contextualization of the role in society participants have, the training of conflict resolution they undertake and the exchange over attitudes, behaviors and methods they get into while in the seminar setting, all contributed to a widening, focusing and changing of their perspective on social, cultural and political concepts and structures.

It made sense to use these insights for an enlarged view on the intricate workings of the various parts of government and single ministries, administrations or NGOs. It also helped in understanding the effects of possible cooperative activities in dealing with conflict and development problems of society or economy.

For the immediate conflict and violence area they preferred my triangular model of acute, curative and preventive aspects of intervention into conflict settings and working with the related parties. Additionally this is to be set in the context of the structural level of the decision making process within a micro-, meso- and macro-political or -social hierarchy.

To relate this model to everyday operative procedures of military and develop an ethical dimension independent of the legal framework (Code of Conduct, Mandate) they had to adhere to, we used it as a reference matrix for the Generals' experience while on UN missions. It also was supposed to serve as a help in taking quick operative decisions in the line of (preventing) combat.

A common practice of most military personnel (in and out of action) is connecting with and paying for the sexual services of local women while on UN Missions. Everybody in the group could relate to this scenario and we then further combined this model with the micro-, meso- and macro-level of society. The hierarchical levels they could easily refer to in the military structure.

When on peace mission military tend to increase the amount of prostitution in the area they are stationed in. Taking a single soldier as an example they developed and considered different options of helping the particular woman he was dealing with towards not having to sell her sexual services.

1. Starting option was paying more than the normal amount, next was paying the required amount but not using the services, this being a very direct and short-lived intervention on the micro-level.

2. Widening the spatial frame, they included the family, children and relatives of the woman and developed standard questions about the acute deficits in their situation, with or without paying or using the services. In direct relation to this they checked their own range of possible support to alleviate the worst suffering thirst,

hunger, shelter, security, etc. the actual implementation of one or more of the possible relief actions they able to do was then checked against the legal mandate within the UN line of command. This meant including the legal and political macro-level of decision-making between the UN and the local countries leaders/key-actors. In their own range of actions we are still on the local microlevel. Proceeding to the meso-level meant attempting a deficit and support analysis for the whole village or wider local area and finding further-reaching causes for the particular destitute situation.

On a spatial level this included a much wider range of people and local systems of administration, support and infrastructure, in the time dimension it meant promoting interventions to secure a longer term provision of necessary water, foods and seeds to ensure a next harvest and with it the beginning of local ability of self support. They would have to identify and connect with local leaders and heads of families, which in a war situation could be mainly women. In a moral dimension it meant presenting themselves as trustworthy people thereby contravening the image of male military brutality. If put into practice, it also meant using their own support systems to help a locals regain working order. In working out the details of an exemplary intervention they had to think in at least two different systems: their own well known and the local unknown culture.

This process of working with several unknowns could be made easier by introducing a third element in the equation and a second in their range of competences—their own cultural background. Using it meant consciously relating their own cultural knowledge and references to the local situation and supporting the locals into whatever their operative procedures would have to be. So the necessary attitude was described as one of solid knowledge of the importance of cultural elements combined with a respectful reticence and a speedy implementation of operational steps to secure survival. This competent use of the military infrastructure they saw as a necessary package, which also included securing villages and water catchment or agricultural areas for the re-implementation of civilian rule.

These findings correspond to results in a European context, where international training groups in the Military Leadership Academy of the German Army develop similar scenarios in cooperation with civil society and civilian agencies.

The Project still has to be evaluated, Namibian and German participants cooperate on different levels, the two Namibian Universities have integrated elements of CR and Mediation into their curricula, emphasis is put on traditional consensus processes in land disputes, and NGOs and government use it increasingly, though not as part of normal procedures. The interest of people throughout the country is growing due to further experiences with these methods when trained mediators assist in finding constructive solutions.

References

HAYNES, J. M. & CHARLESWORTH, S. (1994) *The Fundamentals of Family Mediation,* New York, The Federation Press.

KELMAN, H. C. (2009) Interactive problem solving: Informal mediation by the scholar-practitioner. *Zeitschrift für Konfliktmanagement,* 3/2009, 74-79.

KLEIN, N. (2007) *The Shock Doctrine: The Rise and Fall of Capitalism,* New York, Metropolitan Books/Henry Holt.

MAYER, C.-H. (2005) *Mauern aus Glas. Südafrikanische Narrationen zu Differenz, Konflikt und Identität,* Münster, Waxmann.

MAYER, C.-H. & BONESS, C. (2004) Interkulturelle Mediation und Konfliktbearbeitung. Bausteine deutsch-afrikanischer Wirklichkeiten, Münster, Waxmann.

MAYER, C.-H. (2005) *Trainingshandbuch Interkulturelle Mediation und Konfliktlösung. Didaktische Materialien zum Kompetenzerwerb,* Münster, Waxmann.

NATHAN, L. (2004) Mediation and the African Union's Panel of the Wise. IN FIELD, S. (Ed.) *Peace in Africa: Towards a Collaborative Security Regime.* (63-80), Johannesburg, Institute for Global Dialogue.

LEWIS, S. (2005) *Race Against Time,* Toronto, House of Anansi Press.

MICKLEY, A. (2009) Mediation als Interventionsansatz. *Spekt. der Mediation,* 1/2009, 17-20.

MICKLEY, A. (2007) Mediation als Friedensmission und Krisenprävention. Konfliktbearbeitung, Kompetenzaufbau und Versöhnung in Namibia. *Zeitschrift für Konfliktmanagement,* 2/2007, 36-38.

TROTTA TUOMI, M. (2004) Human dignity in the learning environment. *Institute for Educational Research at the University of Jyväskylä, Report 10.*

WINTERSTEINER, W. (1999) Die Pädagogik des Anderen. Bausteine für eine Friedenspädagogik in der Postmoderne, Münster, Agenda-Verlag.

About the Contributors

Nadja Alexander is Professor of Law designate at City University Hong Kong and Adjunct Professor at Murdoch University in Australia. She has won international recognition for her innovative teaching and contributions to the mediation field. Professor Alexander is currently on sabbatical at the Mandela Institute in South Africa working on projects around mediation, human rights and restorative justice.

Claudio Baraldi is professor of Sociology of cultural and communicative processes at the University of Modena and Reggio Emilia (Department of Language and Cultural Studies), Italy. He holds a PhD in Sociology and social research at the University of Trento (Italy). His research includes works on cultural presuppositions and interaction in educational systems, promotion of children's social participation, intercultural communication, interlinguistic and intercultural mediation in institutional settings, conflict management, and the development of techniques of dialogue. He has published over 100 papers in national and international journals and books, and several books on the above topics.

Viola Barbieri holds a Doctorate in Anthropology and History from Modena and Reggio Emilia University, Italy. Her main research areas are Interlinguistic and Intercultural Mediation with specialisation in healthcare settings. Since several years she holds seminars at Universities and training courses for Public Administrations. Her main areas of expertise include Intercultural Communication and Mediation.

Mark Davidheiser is a socio-cultural anthropologist specializing in Africa and in human conflict and peacebuilding. He is Assistant Professor of Conflict Resolution and Anthropology at Nova Southeastern University, and he is Director of the Africa Peace and Conflict Network. Several Africana, peace/conflict, and anthropology journals call on his expertise. Davidheiser's background in conflict resolution includes researcher, practitioner, and trainer experience. He was Academic Director of the International Institute for Mediation and Conflict Resolution's 2006 seminar in Prague.

Federico Farini, PhD. holds a research grant at the Department of Language and Culture Sciences (Modena and Reggio Emilia University). He specializes in Conversation Analysis and Applied Conversation Analysis. He has done work on sequence organization and participation rights in student-teacher interaction and doctor-patient interaction. Presently, his research focus is on the relationships between interactional practices and social norms, involving the distribution and rights to knowledge.

Samuel Togolai Kussaga is the Principle Education Officer for Secondary School Education and Vocational Training at the Minstry of Education and

Culture in Dar-Es-Salaam, Tanzania. He holds a Diploma in Education from the Teacher's College in Dar-Es-Salaam, a Certificate in Education and Environment from Tokio, Japan and a Diploma in Management in Sports from the International Olympic Organization, as well as a Certificate in Mediation from Germany. For many years, he worked as a teacher, a mediator and a facilitator. His main areas of expertise include conflict mediation, coordination of sports and educational administration.

Creativity, culture and collaboration are themes that run through **Michelle LeBaron**'s work. She is an internationally renowned scholar/practitioner, currently serving as a professor of law and Director of Dispute Resolution at UBC. Michelle has done seminal work in many areas of conflict resolution including intercultural, international, family and commercial. Her books include Bridging Cultural Conflicts: A New Approach for a Changing World and Conflict Across Cultures: A Unique Experience of Bridging Differences, the product of collaboration among five authors from four continents. Her current research explores the arts and contemplative practices as vital resources for transforming cross-cultural conflicts.

Angela Mickley is Professor for Peace Education, Conflict Resolution/ Mediation and Ecology at Potsdam University of Applied Sciences, Dept. of Social Studies. She acquired a Master of Arts and a Doctorate in History and Political Sciences from the Free University of Berlin. In the Institute of Irish Studies at Queen's University Belfast she researched Catholic Constitutional independence movements and participated in the nonviolent N.I. Peace Movement for several years. Her research and concept designs focus on intervention in escalated and political conflicts, elicitive processes, reconciliation and security.

Stella Ting-Toomey holds a Doctorate in Speech Communication and is a Professor of Human Communication Studies at California State University, Fullerton, USA. Her teaching passions include intercultural communication theory, intercultural communication training, and intercultural conflict management. Her research interests have focused on testing and fine-tuning the conflict face-negotiation theory and the cultural/ethnic identity negotiation theory. Stella's most recent books include: *Understanding Intercultural Communication* (with Leeva C. Chung; Oxford University Press) and *The Sage Handbook of Conflict Communication* (co-edited with John G. Oetzel; Sage Publications). As a trainer, consultant, and certified mediator, she has designed and conducted a variety of intercultural conflict competence workshops for corporations, universities, and non-profit institutes around the world.

About the Editors

Christian Martin Boness is Teacher and Senior Lecturer at the Department of Education at the University of Göttingen, Germany. He holds Master degrees in Theology and Political Sciences and a Doctorate in Intercultural Didactics and Education. His main research areas are Intercultural Communication and Mediation with specialisation in East African countries. Since several years he holds seminars at Universities in European and African countries and is a consultant at the Institute for Intercultural Practice and Conflict Management in Göttingen, Germany.

Dominic Busch is Junior Professor in Intercultural Communication at European University Viadrina in Frankfurt (Oder), Germany. His research interests concentrate on academic and everyday concepts of culture and its assumed impact on social interaction, as well as intercultural mediation, research on intercultural training and border research.

Claude-Hélène Mayer holds a Masters and Doctorate in Cultural Anthropology from the University of Göttingen, Germany, and a Doctorate in Management from Rhodes University, Grahamstown, South Africa. Her research areas are cross-cultural conflict management and mediation, identity, value and health research in organizations. She was a Post Doctoral Fellow at the Department of Management at Rhodes University in South Africa and is currently Professor of Intercultural Business Communication at the University of Applied Studies in Hamburg, Germany.

Studien zur interkulturellen Mediation

Herausgegeben von Hartmut Schröder und Dominic Busch

Band 1 Dominic Busch: Interkulturelle Mediation. Eine theoretische Grundlegung triadischer Konfliktbearbeitung in interkulturell bedingten Kontexten. 2005. 2., korrigierte Auflage. 2007.

Band 2 Dominic Busch / Hartmut Schröder (Hrsg.): Perspektiven interkultureller Mediation. Grundlagentexte zur kommunikationswissenschaftlichen Analyse triadischer Verständigung. 2005.

Band 3 Dominic Busch (Hrsg.): Interkulturelle Mediation in der Grenzregion. Sprach- und kulturwissenschaftliche Analysen triadischer Interaktionsformen im interkulturellen Kontakt. 2006.

Band 4 Anna Baranova: Wirtschaftsmediation als alternative Methode der Konfliktlösung. Möglichkeiten und Problemstellen der Wirtschaftsmediation in der Praxis. 2009.

Band 5 Dominic Busch / Claude-Hélène Mayer / Christian Martin Boness (eds.): International and Regional Perspectives on Cross-Cultural Mediation. 2010.

www.peterlang.de